Dr. John Bull

Also from Westphalia Press
westphaliapress.org

The Idea of the Digital University

Masonic Tombstones and Masonic Secrets

Treasures of London

The History of Photography

L'Enfant and the Freemasons

Baronial Bedrooms

Making Trouble for Muslims

Material History and Ritual Objects

Paddle Your Own Canoe

Opportunity and Horatio Alger

Careers in the Face of Challenge

Bookplates of the Kings

Collecting American Presidential Autographs

Freemasonry in Old Buffalo

Original Cables from the Pearl Harbor Attack

Social Satire and the Modern Novel

The Essence of Harvard

The Genius of Freemasonry

A Definitive Commentary on Bookplates

James Martineau and Rebuilding Theology

No Bird Lacks Feathers

Earthworms, Horses, and Living Things

The Man Who Killed President Garfield

Anti-Masonry and the Murder of Morgan

Understanding Art

Homeopathy

Ancient Masonic Mysteries

Collecting Old Books

Masonic Secret Signs and Passwords

The Thomas Starr King Dispute

Earl Warren's Masonic Lodge

Lariats and Lassos

Mr. Garfield of Ohio

The Wisdom of Thomas Starr King

The French Foreign Legion

War in Syria

Naturism Comes to the United States

New Sources on Women and Freemasonry

Designing, Adapting, Strategizing in Online Education

Gunboat and Gun-runner

Meeting Minutes of Naval Lodge No. 4 F.A.A.M

Dr. John Bull

by Leigh Henry

with a new introduction by
Matthew Brewer

WESTPHALIA PRESS
An imprint of Policy Studies Organization

Dr. John Bull

All Rights Reserved © 2013 by Policy Studies Organization

Westphalia Press
An imprint of Policy Studies Organization
1527 New Hampshire Ave., NW
Washington, D.C. 20036
dgutierrezs@ipsonet.org

ISBN-13: 978-1935907459
ISBN-10: 193590745X

Cover design by Taillefer Long at Illuminated Stories:
www.illuminatedstories.com

Updated material and comments on this edition
can be found at the Westphalia Press website:
www.westphaliapress.org

JOHN BULL:
ENGLAND'S INTERNATIONAL PLAYER

INTRODUCTION TO THE NEW EDITION

The task of documenting the entire life of a towering historic figure is no small one. It becomes even more daunting when the subject lived almost half a millennium ago, but it is precisely this task that Leigh Henry takes upon himself. Bull is a familiar figure in both the historic mythology of his native land and that of the wider discipline of music, being held in the same regard as his celebrated contemporaries William Byrd and Orlando Gibbons. Bull moved in the company of Queens and Dukes, and his fortunes rose and fell with their royal favor. His vicissitudinous personal life saw him balancing the demands of noble society with his own torrid temperament, and his legendary exploits run the gamut from Marlowesque continental espionage to Byronian flights of passion, such that, following his flight to Flanders to escape charges of adultery, George Abbot commented, "The man hath more music than honesty and is as famous for marring of virginities as he is for fingering of organs and virginals." Obvious wordplay aside, to attract the attention and scorn of the Archbishop of Canterbury was no mean feat. Yet from this life of constant adventure and intrigue sprang some of the most brilliant music of his time, so much so that it would mark itself indelibly upon the consciousness of his native England.

To most, this legendary status would be cause for consternation. The bulk of the account would be devoted to rooting out embellishment and exaggeration to find the true character of the subject, but Henry revels in the mythos of Dr. Bull. Henry assails the dusty accumulation of facts and boldly asserts that the myth is the man, albeit magnified. To this end, Henry employs a wide assortment of reputable anecdotes in his attempt to portray the flesh and blood of John Bull, rather than the fossilized skeleton of raw data.

More recent scholarship has cast doubt on some of the details that Henry presents as accepted fact, such as the exact place and year of Bull's birth[1] and occasional spotty biographical evidence sometimes leads Henry to deduce from the general conditions of Bull's time to the specific peculiarities of Bull's character, but the narrative is richer for it. Henry's vivid depictions of Elizabethan England provide exactly the liveliness and color that he strives for and leave the reader with a fuller understanding of both the man and the world he inhabited; a world fraught with adventure and excitement.

The world Henry describes is in the middle of a thrilling period of transition and contrast. The Age of Exploration brings new into direct contact with the old, the Enlightenment topples outmoded ideas, and the Renaissance is slowly evolving into the Baroque. The people who inhabit this world are equally indicative of this sea change. Caught between worlds, Henry notes "Poetry and piracy frequently went hand-in-hand. The reckless adventurers of Elizabeth's day were also polished gallants and courtiers,"[2] and, to Henry, no one is more emblematic of this dichotomy than John Bull.

Against the backdrop of continuous court intrigue and such dramatic events as the defeat of the Spanish Armada, Fawkes' famous gunpowder plot, and his own flight from England, Bull established an immortal musical reputation that not only captured the spirit of his own volatile time, but also presaged the innovations of the great masters of the Baroque such as Johann Sebastian Bach. This dichotomy finds further expression within John Bull's music. Famous for his virtuosity, Bull's compositions for organ remain some of the most challenging works in the repertoire, and, despite adhering closely to the strictures of counterpoint, show an extraordinary amount of innovation and continually pushed the very limits of contemporary musical theory. Rigidly organized yet characterized by fireworks of pianistic virtuosity, persistent chromaticism, and highly exotic mixed meters, his works remain as a testament to the skill, passion, and genius of an extraordinary man in an extraordinary time.

NOTES

1. Dart, Thurston. "Search for the Real John Bull." New York Times, sec. 2, p. 1, November 01, 1959.
2. P. 17

Dr. JOHN BULL

Dr. JOHN BULL

Dr. JOHN BULL
1562-1628

By Leigh Henry

FIRST PUBLISHED IN 1937

TO
MARGARET GLYN
who first discerned the man behind
his music.

CONTENTS

CHAPTER		PAGE
	INTRODUCTION	7
I.	PORTALS OF ADVENTURE	21
II.	CLOSE CONFINES	39
III.	CROSSROADS OF DESTINY	61
IV.	"GOD SAVE THE QUEEN"	83
V.	STRANGE PROGRESSION	101
VI.	A TURN OF SPEECH	125
VII.	INGENIOUS DESIGN	151
VIII.	WANDERJAHR	171
IX.	PASSING PAGEANT	193
X.	APOLLO AND THE MERMAID	211
XI.	MOSTE SWEETE AND FAYRE	237
XII.	CLOSING CADENCE	257
	BIBLIOGRAPHY	281
	APPENDIX A	285
	APPENDIX B	290
	APPENDIX C	291
	APPENDIX D	298
	APPENDIX E	300

INTRODUCTION

THIS is not a study of an Old Master. It is an attempt to tell the story of a man young in his day.

It traces, through historical document, legend, anecdote and tradition, the life of one whose character, as well as the name given to him in baptism, entitles him to be known as the true John Bull of England.

That name typifies the Englishman the world over; but the figure popularly associated with it scarcely does justice to the qualities of the English nation. It has the solid traits; but it lacks the imagination, humour and subtlety characteristic of England's best and finest types throughout history. It has solid strength; but it is incapable of the quick adaptability of thought which has made the true Englishman able to deal so agilely with incalculable and startling emergencies throughout the country's annals. It is anything but adequately representative of the manifold genius which has built the material and spiritual greatness of the British Empire.

The popularly-known figure of John Bull is a comparatively late creation, which came into being about the time of the Napoleonic wars, when many political pamphlets were published using the name as a pseudonym for the authors. The figure as depicted shows by its dress that it is identified with this period.

The nickname, John Bull, was known much earlier, as applied to the Englishman, being used in German writings

INTRODUCTION

of the seventeenth century under the form " Johannes Bull." There is no doubt but that the figure of John Bull the musician, the subject of the present book, was famous throughout Europe in his day, on the evidence of writers of his own day and the succeeding century, such as Wood. This actual John Bull was of entirely different type from the popular figure now known. Mentally and physically his life was one of keen, nervous activity. He had the strength and pertinacity of his popular namesake; but in him this was enhanced by creative gifts, by sensitivity, humour and vivid imagination. He was obstinate, but impulsive; his strength was of the supple kind.

In physical appearance, as preserved for posterity by contemporary portraits, he was wholly different from the popular figure. He was dark, spare-featured and oval-faced, with intense black eyes. He wore the small moustache and imperial of his period, that of Drake, Raleigh, and the heroes of the Spanish Armada—probably the most characteristically English period in history.

He was not a stolid farmer, but a musician. It may be startling to realize this to-day, and also to consider that his vocation made his fellow-countrymen of his own age proud to have him recognized as the national type abroad. In the sixteenth century, the great Elizabethan Era, however, England stood foremost in music. The whole populace was interested in the art and proud of its leading native representatives, who were accorded a place in popular respect and affection beside the martial leaders and statemen of the day. Music played a part in the people's work and pleasure alike. It was a major factor in the Shakespearean drama. It was typically English in character at the time. It had direct links with English folk-song and dance, which Bull did more than any to develop. It was characterized

INTRODUCTION

by more initiative than that shown in any other country at the time. It shared the spirit of adventure and discovery which was building the foundations of a world empire. It was a vital element in the creation of Merry England.

The life of the original John Bull is not simply a musical biography. Its vicissitudes extended to many wider fields of activity. Its central figure mingled with the leading personalities of the period, here and abroad. It is a story of adventure and achievements, actual and spiritual, some of which have left indelible marks on our national history. It was bound up with momentous events, giving it much more than individual significance. It was inspired by the most vital forces of Bull's own age, and, seen in all its contemporary relationships, it was an epitome of its period.

To realize the personality and significance of this original John Bull, it is necessary to visualize the age which was his background. Beyond the events chronicled in dry historical documents, the material and spiritual influences of his time have to be considered, if we are to understand, not only his actions as revealed in records, but their motives also. Only so can we realize how much of the spirit of his age was incorporated into his music and why the man and his work are so nationally as well as artistically significant. Many incidents of his life, seen only as records of fact, baldly chronicled, have little apparent significance. It is only when these are related to other circumstances that they assume their true importance.

This book does not attempt to provide any addition to the solely studious literature concerning John Bull. There are many bibliographical and biographical records of him; none gives any full picture of the man or his work, though Margaret Glyn has shown a remarkable comprehension of his character and the late Sir Hubert Parry treated him

INTRODUCTION

sympathetically. What has been attempted here is to reconstruct Bull's life, not only from the historical records directly concerning him, but also from such contemporary literature of all kinds as illuminates the conditions of his period, its incidents and their motives, including all traditional stories and legends and even anecdotes relating to him.

It is true that such records include many with touches of seeming hyperbole, as related by Wood and others. It cannot be emphasized too strongly, however, that even legends cannot evolve without some foundation. However fanciful, exaggerated or fictitious the anecdotal circumstances, these inevitably are suggested at first by the actual characteristics of the personalities around which such narratives centre. They illustrate their most generally known traits with some reasonable degree of accuracy. In this sense, therefore, if open to scepticism in fact, they are usually psychologically credible. It would be difficult to find anecdotes of Rabelais' prudery, Shakespeare's illiteracy, Henry the Eighth's misogamy, Mary Stuart's chastity, or John Knox' frivolity. Yet anecdote filled the records of their times. Stories of such kind as those suggested, if conceived, would die at birth, owing to outraging the popular sense of probability by contradicting the characteristics of such personages as established in the facts of their lives. We require our historical documentation; we need bibliographical records and researches; but if we end there, we shall often lose a conception of human personalities in a mass of dry data. Further interpretation is required. The often fanciful observations and passing comments of writers such as Fuller, Pepys, Moryson and their like, illuminate an identity and give it a human significance which vitalizes the historical records of the personality in question, even where such annotations are exaggerated

INTRODUCTION

or superficial and where there is a strong element of fancy or fiction in them. The anecdote builds itself around personalities sufficiently pronounced and familiar to catch the popular imagination. Myth and legend may invest popular heroes with preposterous powers and even godhead; but the traits of the wonder-workers and deities so created remain essentially their original human ones, magnified.

I have been actuated, in writing on Bull, by considerations other than those which go to make up the writing of an historical biography. Bull's work is marked by strong traits of initiative, imagination, national feeling and personal temperament. No biographical notice which I know makes any attempt to explain these or to link the character of the man to his music. Much of the neglect with which Bull has been treated, in spite of his having been acknowledgedly the first composer and performer of his age, is due to the fact that, with the exception of Margaret Glyn, those dealing with him have done so pedantically, adhering to data only and neglecting all else. The human figure of the man is one which demands more human treatment.

As a musician myself, I am aware of the qualities which make up the appeal of the great masters to musicians. I am also aware, however, that at least two-thirds of the popular appeal which they make has been achieved by their being presented as picturesque figures. By such presentation, their identities have been invested with popular human interest, even if much on which this is based is purely imaginary or traditional without support in historic documentary fact. As Jean Cocteau has said, there is a folk-lore of to-day, as of yesterday, which many antiquarians forget; and each of the striking figures in history enters into such folk-lore in his own day, according to the concept

INTRODUCTION

of his identity impressed on the popular mind of his period. Such impress cannot be neglected when one comes to attempting the human picture of any historical personage.

Hence I have included all anecdotes which come from reputable sources and which bear the marks of some original authenticity, by comparison with the known, recorded facts of Bull's life and character. In this I follow authorities such as Wood, whose tales of Bull have been cited by Margaret Glyn, Barclay Squire and other leading historians and musicologists of our own time, as well as by Dr. Burney, Dr. Pepusch, Dr. Ward and other famous writers of the past, who have had the good sense to realize that these provide sidelights on his character, as popularly known, which dry data do not reflect.

The stories of Bull at Hereford were related to me by the late Sir Herbert Brewer, during some of the musical gatherings of Three Choirs' Festival weeks, which maintain the spirit of the old Western cathedrals' musical life. That kindly and informed musician had them, I understand, from Dr. C. Lee Williams, to whom they were told by Samuel Wesley, both predecessors of Sir Herbert Brewer at Gloucester Cathedral.

To Mr. Anthony Cummings I am indebted for the story of Bull's duel, from old papers in his possession.

The references to Bull in Holland, Philips, etc., were related by the late Julius Röntgen, one of the most informed of Dutch musicians concerning the period of Bull, for whose work he had a remarkable fondness, regarding the English composer as almost Netherlandish by adoption.

The remark cited in the final chapter as made by Bull is further based on information, not only from Röntgen, but also from Mrs. Jan Sweers, to whom, as to Dr. Percy C.

INTRODUCTION

Hull, Bull's present successor at Hereford, I wish to express my thanks for their help in searching records, etc.

I would not have musical history or biographical study degenerate into anecdotage. In each instance, I have based my present narrative on all possible historical data available. If it differs here from other biographical studies or records, then it does so only because, while I am a musician, I am not interested solely in music. I have delved into the data of the life about Bull, in the endeavour to arrive at some better understanding of the man and his life. I am convinced that, in so doing, I have done better than to attempt a dry, technical study. It will be obvious that I would not have been attracted to Bull, especially in view of the scant insight into his life and work provided by the usual kinds of records, unless I had had some particularly close and informed musical acquaintance with the works which are his greatest claim to historic fame and his most lasting appeal to human beings. I am not, however, interested in any art which I cannot link with life; nor do I believe that any art which stands too far apart from such relationship can ever survive in the long run, save in the archæological libraries of museums.

I have the authority of precedents in musical writing throughout the history of the art. Bach, Haendel, Haydn, Mozart, Beethoven, Liszt, Chopin and Wagner; all these have been impressed on the public mind as much by personal story as by their music. The eye of the public, reading such histories and narratives, has mentally prepared the public ear to hear their work from a sympathetic and human angle. Without such preparation, they might still remain known only to the most exclusive few, if they did not lie on dusty shelves, as have so many others of prime worth, who have lacked their human chroniclers.

INTRODUCTION

Germany, France, Italy, and even Russia, have each in turn produced such records of their great musicians, compounded of scientific historical fact and interpretive, imaginative fancy. Absurd as are the pictures of little Haendel sitting in a hay-loft, playing a spinet inexplicably hoisted there, or Haydn, crossing the North Sea in a thunderstorm, as in old oleographs, yet able to stand nobly on the deck, with unwetted music-paper, writing " The Creation," it is from such concepts, behind which lie definite shades of feeling towards the figures and work of such composers, that the universal acceptance of them as world personalities has arisen for the greater public. Such things irritate the musician; they have irritated me; but the determinative factor is the quality of idea which goes into such anecdotes. There will be stupid ones, as there will be stupid technology; but given imaginative vision or original fancy, as with Fuller, Pepys, Boswell and many of their kind, then something creative, worthy of the creative minds with which they deal, will result. It is, indeed, a moot point whether Johnson would exist for the public to-day, in a general way, had Boswell not written his famous Life.

There has been a growing gentility about our national attitude to music for some decades. After a prim age when musicians, actors and all kinds of artists were regarded as " rogues and vagabonds " conventionally as well as legally, the realization that quite respectable people could be artists came as a revelation and a shock. Ever since there has been a sedulous effort to underline how respectable our music is, and the growth of recent musical institutions with a wider public than the concert audiences of former times has tended to emphasize this attitude of mingled stuffy pedantry, prunes-and-prisms and heavy priestcraft. It is not in the musical biographies or the programme

INTRODUCTION

books that future history will find the human identities of our composers, past or present. We have erred in our over-concerned gentility with regard to our musicians. We have denied them the nimbus of human sentiment and appeal which would have come from the recording of their foibles, eccentricities, weaknesses and lovable traits. In most of our respectable books on music they appear as the churchwardens of our chapel of art. There is not an inspired priest of the temple among them, much less a Dionysian.

We have to discard the prevalent ideas of the musician and his life when we consider Bull. He was no vapouring immaculate, such as nineteenth-century romanticism fabricated. He was far from the prevalent sleek, well-mannered and mediocre conventionality of broadcasting bureaucracy. He was no cheap publicity-touting musical demagogue.

His age was one when things as dissimilar as poetry and piracy frequently went hand-in-hand. The reckless adventurers of Elizabeth's day were also polished gallants and courtiers. In between burning ships and cities, raiding ports and slitting throats, they wrote flaming love-poems and exquisite pastorals alike for recreation and took pride in their ability to take up a sheet of music after dinner and sing their parts at sight in a round or madrigal.

A musical talent was no hothouse growth in Elizabethan days. It had not degenerated into the sycophancy of the salon or the smug inanity of Suburbia. The musician mingled with statesmen, courtiers and soldiers on level terms. He took his part equally in the active life of the times, when stirringly courageous exploits, dark conspiracies and courtly intrigues jostled each other as matters of everyday occurrence.

As I have entered into all the records of Bull's life and compared them with coincident circumstances, certain con-

INTRODUCTION

victions have grown on me. It has become clear that, while Add. MSS., Brit. Mus., etc., contain no record of such things, his very presence on such and such an occasion, in such and such a place, made it impossible for him not to have been in touch with such and such events and personages. I have been struck by the many striking, bizarre and picturesque glimpses which even the most dry records reveal; but I have not been contented to leave these as bald records, as most of the musicologists have done, without attempting to relate them to Bull's work and life as a whole, or to the nature of his music.

In short, on a skeleton of fact, most of which is extremely explicit and which has clear implications, I have tried to build the human flesh and blood of a great figure of a great epoch. How far I have succeeded, I cannot estimate, and I am truly humble, in view of the deep feeling which the music of Bull and the character of the man as I discern it after some eighteen years of study, have inspired in me.

The work has brought its own rich reward. Little by little the dry facts, generally so tritely set forth, without consideration of their personal implications or historic significance, have gradually shaped themselves into a definite portrait, sharply thrown up against a background of events which forms a colourful panorama of a glorious period.

The man who thus emerges is a fascinating creature, as attractive for his foibles as for his qualities. In an age of outstanding personalities, his remains distinctive and invested with strong human appeal.

Bull's life and his work were singularly one. His music has all the impulsiveness, whimsicality, humour and sensitivity, as well as the imagination and strength, which the events of his career reveal. It shows him to have been poet and patriot as much as do the chronicles of his acts and

INTRODUCTION

experiences. In a country still not ashamed of Shakespeare and still imbued with a love of the native soil, such traits alone would entitle John Bull to something of the regard which his infinitely wider range of character should evoke to an unusual degree.

I can only hope that I have caught some of the glamour which he possesses for me, in such way as to convey it to others. I can only trust that, through such human picture as I have been able to glimpse, I may have done something to illuminate both the man and his music, from the human viewpoint which has been so sadly neglected in his case.

All said, every considerable authority, imaginative or pedantic, agrees on the outstanding originality of Bull, the extraordinary imagination and initiative in his work, and the high place which he deserves in our musical history. Yet still his work—long virtually suppressed, as I believe, for political ends, and further retarded by its technical difficulty and the lack of erudition to translate it which existed for long—remains little known and less performed. Though I believe that John Bull composed the British National Anthem, " God Save the King," for which readers are referred to the Appendix to this volume, his importance for me exists on much broader foundations, on which I view him as one of the most significant and representative of our national composers as well as one of our most interesting and characteristic national figures.

John Bull epitomized one of the greatest periods in our history, the Elizabethan Era, in his creative gifts and his personal character. He stood strongly for the rights of our native English speech in our centres of learning. He imbued our music for the first time with a consciousness of the folk-idiom which is its strongest national trait. He foresaw, two centuries ahead of his time, the possibilities of

INTRODUCTION

that keyboard music which has constituted the backbone of our most intimate, domestic musical development, and he visioned also the colour of the orchestra of subsequent times. In all these things he was representative of England, not only in his own age, but for all time. He had imagination, initiative, daring, and a keen sensitivity that often hid behind formal masks.

As a figure Bull has dual immortality. He was the most famous musician of his day, in a country pre-eminent in his art: he was also the herald of a new era of music in which he remained without equal until the advent of Johann Sebastian Bach. The one was the commencement, the other the culmination. In the procession of our national musical genius, in spite of all lapse of time, all difficulties of changed expression, he is still one of our most arrestingly and characteristically national minds in music. His figure stands, after the passage of centuries, as man and musician, a type and a symbol, not only of his own period, but of the most fascinating features of both English music and the English character for all posterity. He remains as much to-day what he was in his own age, when the land he loved led in the art to which he was devoted—John Bull of England.

LEIGH HENRY.

LONDON, *March*, 1937.

Portals of Adventure

CHAPTER I

PORTALS OF ADVENTURE

JOHN BULL was the child of a new era. He was born into a world which was assuming startlingly transformed dimensions. It was an age of alluring adventure and glamorous enterprise. The earlier Atlantic horizon had been transcended: unknown continents had appeared beyond it. The strangest miracles dreamed of by the Middle Ages had become trivial compared with the actual events of the times. After centuries of enthrallment to superstition, tradition and convention, the mind of Europe had awakened to rationalism and innovation.

Bull entered upon life at an auspicious moment, when unprecedented circumstances opened up a new freedom to vital impulses and initiative in all fields, and gave a fresh stimulus to every kind of intrepidity and originality. He was fortunate in his birthplace. It provided an environment particularly favourable to the development of the traits which gave such typically national character to his genius. John Bull was a West Countryman.

The history of Elizabethan England is largely the story of the West Country. There were born and bred most of the great leaders of action in the struggle for sea-power which would give the victor the key to dominion and expansion in the New World. As a consequence, patriotic feeling developed there in an emphatic way, more fervidly than in any previous national emergency, since circumstances uniquely identified the interests of the country with those of a local kind. The West Country, also, had become inevitably a focal point in the new order of England itself. It was the most concentrated meeting-place of the race-currents which had animated the successive phases of England's civilization—Kelt, Roman, Saxon, Dane and Norman—which the urge of the new epoch now swept for the first time into the broader stream of unified British nationality. It epitomized the new nation of Tudor vision.

John Bull came of reputable and established yeoman stock, the seed of the later English squirearchy. On the evidence of his contemporaries and of historical chroniclers such as Anthony à Wood he was descended from a well-known local family, the Bulls of Peglinch, or Peylinch, in the parish of Wellow, Somersetshire. The known date of his birth was 1562, and he appears to have been the third son of John Bull of Peglinch, though the destruction of the parish register precludes conclusive documentary evidence of this.

The facts of Bull's life show intimate associations with the West Country, maintained throughout his career. These far exceeded those of ordinary acquaintanceship and indicated closer ties. From his earliest days he was well known there, visiting familiar circles in the West frequently, throughout the long period in which he held Royal appointments in London. His early call to the position of organist at Hereford Cathedral was extremely significant, since it was an established custom in the Western dioceses to select the holders of such offices from among the musically talented of local families. We know, also, that Bull was well known and highly thought of in Hereford before he was chosen for his Cathedral post there.

Our knowledge of Bull's boyhood days is limited, but

at least we are aware of the atmosphere in which he grew up. On first thought the life of a yeoman family, however imbued with local culture, seems remote from the main trends of a patriotic and political resurgence. The new development of maritime enterprise, however, relied, as did military recruiting, upon the yeoman population. There was as yet no clear distinction between Army and Navy. Drake's warships were manned by soldiers drafted for sea service, so far as their fighting force went, more than by trained naval men as we now know them. Such drafted soldiery formed the nucleus of what later developed into the British marines. The high estimation in which the rurally recruited soldiery were held in Tudor days is further illustrated by the fact that the Yeomen of the Guard were custodians of the Tower of London and part of the Royal Household Troops.

The marine expansion of the Elizabethan Era was therefore quite intimately connected with rural life. In the Western counties this was pronouncedly the case, to a degree which affected even the local folklore. Somersetshire, with a third of its boundaries lying along the Bristol Channel, was as permeated with the mood of the moment as its famous sea-dog neighbour, Devon. Even inland, the folksongs of Somerset centre remarkably upon sea topics, and are frequently identical, in words and melodies, with airs known to us as sea-shanties. This maritime relationship is also evident in such forms as the hornpipe, popularly regarded as a typical mariners' dance. Originally, however, it was a pastoral one, deriving its name from the pipe-horn, or cornemuse, which accompanied it at rustic revels. It developed first in regions of the West, such as Cornwall, close to the sea, as is shown by Chaucer's reference to " horn-pypes of Cornewaile " ; but it only assumed a maritime character when the levies of the Elizabethan fleets transported it from hamlet and village to entertain forecastles and speed work aboard.

Thus the nature of the boy Bull's early surroundings tended not only to imprint on his mind the impressions of the English countryside, but also to imbue him with the spirit of patriotism engendered by the local concentration on maritime activity.

The yeoman life of his childhood was something vastly different from the entirely bucolic one of previous generations. Yeomen were attaining a new status in the changing social order. They had purchased land at easy rates after the sequestrations of the English Reformation under Henry VIII. The ancient powers of the local barons and abbots had been suppressed through the new Tudor consolidation of monarchy. From such acquisition of land a new squirearchy was emerging which, together with the new merchant plutocracy of the cities, was assuming minor aristocracy by marriage with the nobility and, by the powers vested in it as local Justices of the Peace, the deputies of the central government.

In the new commercial expansion, younger sons of manor houses took not only to scholastic and artistic pursuits, but also to trade, manufacture and military service or marine adventure overseas. The developments of Tudor architecture show the growth of affluence and the increase of culture among this rising middle class, whose deepest interests concentrated, naturally, on the activities of English exploration and conquest abroad, on which the new prosperity depended. The Western countryside of Bull's boyhood thus was animated by the strongest national impulses of the moment.

Above all, such surroundings played a vital part in the

development of his personal genius. They made him familiar with English folk-life and folk-lore, in his most impressionable years, in a fashion unknown to his urban contemporaries. The Peglinch homestead was one of substance, as we know from the records of the visitation of Laud in 1623. It was a centre for social gatherings, when the village notabilities and worthies met to join in rounds and sing the old songs of the district. The boy's mind absorbed such lilts, while his imagination fed upon the legends and fables recounted by the local tale-tellers and gossips.

The Bull home also lay close to the routes taken by the adventurers returned from the New World, when journeying to and from Bristol City and Plymouth Hoe. Such travellers were welcome guests in all West Country houses. They brought tidings of how matters fared with English arms and enterprise overseas and tales of wonder and excitement to entertain their hosts on quiet country evenings. They carried the glamour of strange, fabulous regions into the placid country homestead, with their bronzed, weather-beaten features, their travel-stained garments, their booty of exotic treasures and souvenirs. Fantastic in the glow and flicker of the blazing logs in the wide inglenook fireplace, they were figures fascinating to the little John Bull, curled up in his shadowy corner, listening enthralledly, his curiously intense, large dark eyes wide as he visioned the images of their narratives in the smoke-clouds of the Indian weed curling up from their long-stemmed clay pipes.

From such early impressions derived that marked love of folk-melody and delight in its thematic use and development in creative art-forms which so strongly and humanly characterizes a great deal of Bull's music. The influences

DR. JOHN BULL

of his childhood clearly affected his inspiration throughout his life, and they sprang in the most spontaneous way from the soil of England and the spirit bred by it.

Lacking such contact, Bull might have become the victim of his own extraordinary skill, a mere artificer, instead of being a great artist. His genius might have degenerated into a facile talent displaying itself in shallow depths, or have drifted into some stagnant backwater of musical intellectualism. His early associations filled his spirit with the breath of popular life and enabled it to ride the broad tide of the times.

Bull was still a child when he first emerged on the stage of history. At the age of ten he was chosen for enrolment among the Children of Queen Elizabeth's Chapel Royal. Such early distinction would have excited even a London boy, used to the proximity of royalty; but it meant much more to the provincial youngster. It was an event which transformed his entire world. It transported him suddenly from the familiar calm of the countryside to the strange crowds and clamour of the capital and the awe-inspiring pomp and ceremony of the Court. The vivid contrast was bewildering at first to his child-mind, making him feel himself a figure in a fairy tale, moving in a realm of marvels.

The journey to London would be a trivial matter to-day, accomplished in comfort in a few hours. In Elizabethan times it meant days of exhausting travel, with such variable and dubious accommodation or hospitality as could be secured at night, since parts of even the Queen's highway held dangers after dark, when lurking robbers lay in wait for belated travellers. For the boy Bull, however, it was an expedition of strange delight and wonder. Every stage of the journey brought him into novel surroundings. Each turn of the road held the possibility of some fresh surprise, some enchanting vista or curious spectacle. He was not only bound for London town, with its aura of magic and majesty: he was travelling the route of the heroes of the day, the daring adventurers to the New World and the Spanish Main. He had the eager excitement of encountering some of their number from time to time on his way. Here it was a solitary rider mounting over the crest of a hill ahead in all the bravery of his accoutrements, his sharp silhouette against the skyline picked out with glints of sunlight reflected from his steel helm, his cuirass and sword hilt; there, a gallant troop in multi-coloured raiment, trotting along gaily to the rollicking strains of a lusty sea-shanty; or again, in a wayside tavern, a group of homeward-faring voyagers revelling over their beakers and tankards and exchanging stirring or hilarious memories of miraculous escapades. The glamour of such meetings made him forget the ache of his young bones, jolted and jarred by the jogging horse which carried him, seated uncomfortably on the hard saddle before the family servant in whose charge he had been placed. There was little trouble or tedium in a journey which entranced him continuously by its ever-changing kaleidoscope of fascinating shapes and colours, its vivid images and strange impressions.

That early experience did much to arouse in Bull the keen sense of the picturesque and the susceptibility to local colour which made his music, taken as a whole, a brilliant panorama of his period. The alert observation evoked by that first long journey persisted as he travelled through life, giving an unusually sensitive and graphic quality to his musical depiction of people and places.

Arrival in London was a stirring climax to the excitement of such travel. The teeming life of the capital astonished him after the quietude of rural surroundings. The scene changed continuously and breath-takingly. The shops in the arcades over the covered bridges, their stalls heaped with a medley of silks, velvets, laces, tapestries, jewels and trinkets, seemed to him like a vision of the treasure-trove of Hy-Brazil or El Dorado, which he had heard described by sea-wanderers visiting his home. Below, in the broad river, the cargo ships which had brought them lay at anchor, a forest of tall, slow-swaying masts and riggings, through which floated gay gilded barges with bright-hued canopies, while here and there loomed up the towering, many-windowed poop of a majestic double-decked war galleon, bright with tiers of polished brass cannon, painted figurehead, fluttering ensign and bunting, and billowing, vividly emblazoned sails.

The streets of London were not paved with gold, as country gossips had told him; but they paraded a wonderful pageant before him all the way to the Palace. The great markets were more crowded and clamorous than any country fair young Bull could remember. There was an endless variety in the variegated throngs of pedestrians along each thoroughfare. Pedlars and flower-girls sang their street cries. Porters, serving-wenches, journeymen and artisans and apprentices of various crafts, each in their distinctive garb or livery, jostled each other in a maze of motley. Grave merchants in fur-trimmed gowns, attended by soberly attired clerks, ambled on their palfreys through the concourse, at the head of trains of pack-horses laden with the rich fabrics of India and Cathay. Every now and then the crowd parted, making way for a wagon filled with farm produce, the scent of which made the boy momentarily homesick; for a company of marching halberdiers; or for the ponderous, ornately-gilded coach of some grandee, rumbling heavily behind its proud team of richly-harnessed horses, with all the pomp of footmen and outriders. There were even more exciting moments, when the mob was cleft asunder, with shouts, exclamations, curses and laughter, by the clattering carriole of a gay blade recklessly urging the prancing steed drawing it, or by a swift-flashing cavalcade of courtiers dashing by with fluttering plumes and mantles.

At the Palace young Bull's excitement deepened into awe. After bidding farewell to the servant who had brought him and watching the last familiar form fade from his strange new world with as stiff a lip as possible, he found himself in the charge of an imposing figure, a Yeoman of the Chapel in his crimson and black livery. This individual appeared important enough to be the noble General of all the Queen's armies, but he proved genial in spite of his awe-inspiring aspect. With some kindly remarks, he conducted the youngster to the rooms of the Master of the Children, William Hunnis, where the boy's name was entered in the Chapel Register and he was instructed in the rules and regulations. This done, he was escorted by his magnificent custodian to the quarters of the Children and left to make the acquaintanceship of his future companions. He felt shy among these uniformed boys in his country garb, even though it was the one specially reserved for ceremonial occasions. Their dress made them part of a united community, in which he was doubly a stranger. He carried his discomfort as well as possible, answering and asking questions politely, though with a touch of shy stiffness which amused the others, and parrying the sallies on his name to which he was to grow accustomed, and in which he later was to take a whimsical delight. His initiation, indeed, was much after the fashion of any new boy's reception at any boarding school. There was, perhaps, less horseplay than was prevalent at most schools of the time, since the Master of the Chapel was of a remarkably gentle nature, which influenced all under him. After such preliminaries young Bull found himself free to prepare his quarters and to take stock of his new surroundings.

At first the Court atmosphere investing the Chapel made these seem strangely formal and cold to him. The other boys also knew the routine, and this made him feel even more an interloper. This feeling faded quickly, however, as common interests in the work and play of the Chapel familiarized his companions. The donning of his own livery also helped him greatly to feel part of the community. Strange though it was, he felt less singular among the others when he first took his place at the table in hall clad in his crimson doublet piped with black, with his black trunks and hose and carrying his black cloth cap.

Nevertheless, he had his inevitable moods of loneliness. Apart from the novelty of life at the Chapel, the atmosphere of the metropolis even then was complex and bewildering to a provincial boy. Less intelligent youngsters, accustomed to attention in simpler communities, might have resented the feeling of oblivion produced by the alien activities and distractions with which the boy Bull found himself surrounded. Regarding unconscious indifference as hostile ostracism, they might have shrunk into self-conscious isolation, sentimentally clinging to the habits of their old environment, exalting and exaggerating its moods and manners and obstinately refusing to recognize the advantages of their new home. Young Bull, notwithstanding the innate independence which showed itself all his life, was too sensitive to swagger foolishly, and too alert to ignore the variety and interest of the novel London scene.

The organization of the Chapel Royal tended to make him feel at home more quickly than he would have done at many other institutions. The Children of the Chapel were limited to eight in number, selected for their especial musical talents. The membership of the Chapel, although housed in the Palace, formed a distinct community among the other personnel of the Court. It had its own officials, holding office under the Deanne of the Chappell—the Chappell Organiste and Maister, or Master, of Songe; the Maister of the Childrene; and the Maister of the Gramer Schole. The full organization comprised twenty-four Chaplenes and Clerkes, the latter known as the Gentlemen of the Chappell; the eight selected Children, who sang in the Chappell Choir; and two Yeomen, or Pistoleres of the Vestry and Chappell.

The Children were housed and boarded in the Palace, where room was also set apart for their general tuition and musical practices. They were provided with special Court liveries once yearly and the linen and blankets for their quarters. Young Bull must have felt cramped after his free country life; but he was not badly cared for according to the habits of the times. The contemporary regulations specify that "Thes Childrene eate in the hall daylye at the Chappelle boarde, nexte to the Yeomane of Vestry; takinge amongste them for lyverye daylye for brekefaste and all nighte two loves, the messe of greate meate, ij galons ale and for winter seasons iij candles wicke, iij talshuds and lyttere to the pallets."

The Children were encouraged, not only in musical education and general study, but also in games and pastimes and in the manlier arts of single-stick and fencing, in which the Gentlemen deputed instructed them, and there are records of personal visits of the sovereign to bestow the "rewardes untoe the scholares for their prowesse in the sportes." It was therefore no cloistered confine to which young Bull went, however limited it may have seemed after the free fields of his Somersetshire village home. There was nothing of the nincompoop in his character, and he took his part manfully in the lusty sports, learning there the agility and athletic skill which was to serve him well in later life, with as much zest as he addressed himself to his musical studies. His life at the Chapel, indeed, was happy enough. He became popular early with his companions and remained equally so among his colleagues there all his life.

As he grew accustomed to his new home, his surroundings became inspiring to him. His place in the Court Chapel gave the young provincial constant, if casual, contact with the motivating powers of national activity, in a way impossible in a village environment. The Children having their quarters in the Palace, most of the famous figures of the day were familiar to them. The Queen herself attended the Chapel where they sang, and her presence fired their juvenile imagination; for Elizabeth was not only sovereign, but symbol of England's patriotic spirit, to her people. Bull's proximity to such personages, many even then invested with almost legendary glamour, made tangible the West Country lad's dreams. They also awakened him to current reality in a way impossible for him before. Many military and maritime leaders were from his own native region; their eminence at Court stirred his ambition and fanned his pride in their common folk-background. This led to no false insularity. Comparing the scope of their achievement with the local ideas of his home, the need of wider aims and experience to render folk-traits nationally important and effectual could not fail to become clear to him, as he matured.

Such interests and realizations did not alienate young Bull from the folk-influences of his earlier life. The seed had been sown strongly in a mind musically and imaginatively precocious for his years. The Children of the Chapel Royal were selected with extraordinary care and considerable musical aptitude was demanded before any boy could obtain admission to their very limited number. Such talent would imply natural qualities of intelligence and sensitivity in even the least quick, and the juvenile Bull was remarkable, even among his select fellows. We know that he evoked the immediate interest of " a moste excellent teacher," William Blitheman, Organiste and Maister of Songe to the Chapel, who, " perceiving that he had a natural genie to the faculty, spared neither time nor labour to advance it to the utmost."

To receive such attention was a real honour to the boy's gifts, for Blitheman was not only an extraordinary teacher " whose passing Skill in Musicke's Art " was renowned, but a composer of acknowledgedly high repute and one of the most esteemed, if not actually the most eminent, among the performers of the day,

" Whom all took greate delighte to heare
Him on the Organs playe,"

as a contemporary versifier informs us.

Child though he was, the bent of young Bull's mind was already set before he came to the Chapel Royal in London. His precocious talents had made him as sensitive to the song as to the speech of the folk-life in which he had been bred, at a very early age. His imagination had fed upon rural folk-lore and the stirring exploits of West Countrymen which were the daily topics of his yeoman home. Such impressions were enhanced, not obliterated, by his London environment, where he encountered West Country adventurers as public heroes in the centre of national life. The spirit nourished by his early contact with the soil gave him an immediate sympathy for the popular moods of the time, which he could never have acquired in a metropolitan study, since the major part of England was still rural. It endowed him with a permanent spontaneity of feeling which the care and understanding of Blitheman encouraged and thus preserved him from dry pedantry and superficial polish. It gave him that keen and profound interest in everyday life which enabled him later to participate so vitally in the liberation of music from the ecclesiastical dominion of centuries and to develop it in rich secular forms which reflected the rationalism of the new era. It taught him how to revitalize the art by the infusion of popular melody and the creative development of the dance-forms of the people. It made him, as man and musician, an outstanding type of the Merry England of Elizabethan days, with its yeoman strength revelling in a new freedom of thought and action.

Bull the boy remained remarkably persistent in Bull the man, through the vicissitudes of his life and in his music. Both showed the whimsicality, joviality and prankishness which was so characteristic of his nature and was of kindred origin to the humorous folk-songs, rollicking sea-shanties and capricious pixie-tales of the West Country folk-lore which Bull knew so well. For the preservation of such qualities posterity owes much to William Blitheman. Kindly, gentle and sensitively sympathetic,

" A friend to all, a foe to none,
Whom rich and poore did love,"

he did everything in his power to prevent anything from marring the boy's natural spontaniety, working ardently to inform his pupil of the best thought of the times and to perfect him in the highest accomplishments of the day. The regard of the two musicians for each other, as all records show, greatly exceeded the ordinary relationships of master and pupil. There was the closest affinity of thought between them, Bull recognizedly

" His master's veine
Expressing in eache kinde."

The older man's affection, indeed, was so deep that he could not endure their separation long. Barely three years after Bull had left the Chapel to become organist at Hereford Cathedral, he was nominated to the honourable position of Gentleman of the Chapel, through Blitheman's interest, and returned to London, where henceforth he resided permanently. There he was regarded as Blitheman's natural deputy and right-hand man, and on the death of his master, by the elder musician's expressed wish, he succeeded him as Organist of the Chapel.

Blitheman seems prophetically to have discerned that neither as man nor musician could Bull be subservient to merely formal authorities, although he could not foresee his beloved pupil's ultimate end in exile, rebellious against slights and the servility demanded of him. Turbulent, whimsical, susceptible and curious, Bull fretted always against empty convention and dogma. His traits were born of the creative urge of the times. They remained permanently rooted in the West Country awakened to the dawn of a new era, when it eagerly scanned fresh horizons for strange territories to explore. That they did not run to seed was due to Blitheman's devoted care. The sheen of sails on West Country vessels putting out for unknown waters illumined the boy Bull's earliest imagination. His mind followed the track of the West Country sea captains and adventurers who won England the sovereignty of the seas. The Chapel Royal, however, equipped Bull to emulate their achievements in other realms. Under Blitheman's guidance he launched his genius and learned to navigate it through life, weathering the storms of fate.

He embarked early: he was barely twenty when he departed for Hereford. However tranquil his immediate destination, he had commenced no placid voyaging. When the doors of Hereford Cathedral opened to John Bull, he passed in through the portals of adventure.

Close Confines

CHAPTER II

CLOSE CONFINES

HEREFORD is no great distance from the region where Bull had passed his childhood; only a part of Gloucester county separates it from Somerset; but it lay off the main routes of Elizabethan enterprise. The Queen's highways from London town to Bristol city and Plymouth Hoe ran farther south, for voyagers to the Spanish Main. The Wye flows placidly through the calm cathedral town. It continues so for miles on its course to the broad Severn estuary, leading to the open sea. No Bristol Channel or Atlantic surge washes Hereford. It was the embarkation point for Bull's adventures in the wider world; but only as some quiet inlying haven, sheltered from the stressful tides of the times.

No matter how tranquil or obscure the port, however, it is exciting and wonderful to the inexperienced seafarer who arrives there to set forth on his first voyage. Bull entered Hereford with high anticipations.

His work there showed his enthusiasm. He was indefatigable in preparing the mental outfit for his life's journey. No apprentice seaman ever devoted more loving care or painstaking craft to fashioning and embellishing his coffer than did the young musician to perfecting the technique which was to carry his creative genius.

Nevertheless, he was too young to be satisfied with study only. The first ardent urge to musical work might have burnt out his inspiration rapidly, had there been no other fuel to feed it but abstract dreams. Conditions at Hereford, however, gave him chances for activities more in keeping with his age and robust nature. He arrived at a happy moment in his life, on December 24th, 1582. His youth made him congenial and sympathetic to the youngsters of the Cathedral choir. They found him less alien and forbidding than an older man would have been. He was not dulled by routine. He did not hold aloof with the solemn habits and mannerisms of accustomed authority. His unaffected enthusiasm gave momentum to their own energies, while his natural sensitivity and waywardness made him understand and tolerate their foibles and caprices, especially when he remembered Blitheman's patience in his own case.

The Cathedral College was similar enough in its organization to that of the Chapel Royal to make him feel at home quickly. Barely out of his own student days, he was able to share the interests of his choristers. There was slight difference between the College life and that which he had known as an elder scholar at the Chapel Royal. He was now lodged with officials, instead of with other youths; but he had no youthful friends among his colleagues, excepting young Thomas Warrock, his assistant, who was granted a room "nexte to that of John Bull." Apart from his organ, the main interest of his Cathedral work centred upon his choirboys, and he was their most popular superior.

Bull's success with the youngsters led to his being appointed Master of the Choristers, in addition to his office as Organist, soon after his arrival; but the boys found him anything but a sedate pedagogue. He had fared forth to famous places, but was no time-hardened veteran. They had the attitude to him of quayside lads towards a voyaged cadet, admiring yet familiar, where more mature dignity would have overawed them. Initiated into musical mysteries fascinating to youngsters whose natural gifts and inclinations already had devoted them to the art, Bull was nevertheless of their own West Country breed, near enough in years to them to have a boyish zest in exploration and experiment which made their work with him a joyous companionship.

His youth made him able to share in their sports as well as their studies. This further endeared him to boys living so near the famous sports-fields of the Cotswold Downs. From childhood Bull knew all the lusty country games, from hoodman-blind to barley-break. He had not forgotten the rules of bone-ace, span-counter and handy-dandy, yet he could teach them the latest pastimes, fresh from London. He could show them knots and splicings learned from Somersetshire sailors and help them to model miniature ships to sail on the river. He was as familiar with longstaff as with the art of fencing and could instruct them in archery and tennis. He took cherry-pitch as seriously as skittles or bowls. On holidays he could be seen, earth-stained and muddy, leading eager young naturalists through bushes and brambles or returning with fishing parties, his grey hose soaked with wading in the Wye. He joined their game of base in shirt and trunks, his ruff crumpled and his sober black doublet flung on the grass, or, running against the wind, helped to fly the grotesque kites which he had learned to make from mariners returned from Chappon and Cathay.

With his arrival the boys felt themselves part of a wider world, yet one to which they were introduced on familiar terms. Bull spoke their Western speech. He had a similar background of folk-life, sharing their worship of provincially-born national heroes. Indeed, he was a hero himself to them, compared with the solemn Custos and Vicars. He had moved among the great figures of the day and had lived in the Palace of England's glorious Queen. Their practice-hours with him were as full of story as of song. After the anthems and hymns for the services, he taught them country folk-tunes, London street cries and sea-shanties. While playing, he described the places where such melodies were popular, the types and customs of the people who made them. As memories of scenes and stories came back to him, his playing slowed, until his hands slipped from the keys and lay clasped on his knees as he sat back, visioning great deeds and dreams. Clustering around, their dark jerkins silhouetted sharply against the white walls, the boys listened absorbedly, sprawling across the trestle-table where they did their copying, or leaning cross-armed on their music lecterns, seeing glowing images in the broad shaft of sunlight falling from the high window beside the virginals, illuminating his rapt face.

While such contact with his choristers preserved Bull's youthfulness, other factors matured his mind. The locality held fresh interests for him, different from those of his native county and London, yet enlarging his patriotic conceptions and developing broader national characteristics in his work. It brought him into direct touch with the blending of Keltic and Anglo-Saxon elements taking place for the first time in history under the policy of the Tudor monarchs, uniting England and Wales into the new British nationalism of the Elizabethan Era.

Hereford peculiarly favoured Bull's observation of this merging, as well as the liberal development of his musical ideas. In close proximity to Wales, the western cathedral towns had never lost the independent spirit of the old

British Church, which had never bowed completely to Rome or Canterbury. Linking Salisbury, Wells, Exeter, Bristol, Gloucester, Hereford and Worcester, this spirit had encouraged a local and distinctive development of ecclesiastical music, much freer and more imaginative than Bull would have encountered in other Church centres. Concentrated in the Wye and Severn valleys, this formed part of a general local culture, uniquely mingling English and Welsh traditions. Hereford, one of the most ancient British bishoprics, bordering on Breconshire and Radnorshire, in Wales, presented this racial fusion in a particularly concentrated form, and Bull's life there stimulated the growth of the manifold idiom which made his music so completely British.

The local culture was a happy influence for him in more intimate ways. The common cause uniting the Western cathedrals drew their organists and precentors together in an unusually strong fellowship. From this developed closer personal ties. There was a distinctive social life among the cathedral musicians and the local gentry connected with them by marriage. Fostered by visits from town to town, this linked their domestic lives.

Music was the chief recreation of Elizabethan family circles. Part singing was prevalent, especially in the west, where folk-custom had developed it highly much earlier. Such performance was limited, however, by the lack of printed music. Apart from traditional rounds and catches and ecclesiastical music hackneyed to those in cathedral circles and quite unsuitable for such secular meetings, even Bull's musical friends had little literature for such community singing. Their custom of writing short pieces for their own and each other's families did not greatly counteract this shortage. There was scarcely any published music,

DR. JOHN BULL

beyond William Damen's Psaltery of 1579, to which Bull, young though he was, had contributed an anthem, "Attende unto my Teares"; but this, again, was sacred music. Secular music was not available to any considerable extent until William Byrd published the first collection of madrigals, "Musica Transalpina," in 1588.

Instrumental performers were therefore greatly appreciated at such musical gatherings. Public concerts or recitals, as we know them to-day, did not exist. Public solo performances were almost entirely limited to church or cathedral organ playing, apart from a few royal or aristocratic functions. The virginals, forerunner of the spinet, was becoming a popular domestic instrument, however, being particularly adaptable for house music, small, legless and capable of being played when placed upon an ordinary table.

Bull, already noted for the brilliant gifts which were to make him known as "the father of keyboard music," was especially welcome and enjoyed such social performance. The delicacy of the virginals, the keys of which operated only a single tinkling wire to each note, allowed him to express his intimate moods better than did the organ, with its solemn associations. His whimsical improvisations added to the general gaiety of such occasions. He had a lively sense of rhythm, and his love of the folk-forms ignored by more pedantic musicians encouraged dancing, which he was always unaffectedly happy to accompany, in gigge, galliard, corante or pavan. Apart from his musical talents, his youthful grace and virile, dark-eyed good looks, with the charm of his courtly manners, made him popular. When serious moods led him to play variations on some amorous air, its tenderness and sentiment were reflected in the eyes of every demure maiden listening to him.

The home of Nathaniel Giles, organist of Worcester Cathedral, was Bull's favourite resort, whenever he could get away from Hereford. Giles, who was of a Worcester family, had been appointed the year after Bull's entry into office, and an immediate friendship had sprung up between them, maintained warmly all their lives. Giles was not only a highly-skilled musician, celebrated for his learned " Descant of thirtie-eighte Proportions of sundrie kindes " ; he was also a man of cultured and convivial tastes. At least one creditable poem by him survives, a generous tribute to a fellow-musician, written " in approbation " of Ravenscroft's " Briefe Discourse," in 1614. The Giles household was a centre of culture in touch with the best thought of the day. The host's wife was the daughter of a local magnate, John Stayner, and Bull met the chief personages of the district there. London visitors were frequent; for Giles enjoyed lively company. He was well known later in London resorts such as the Apollo Club, founded by Ben Jonson and others of the Court at the Devil Tavern in Fleet Street, and was Bull's future associate as a liveryman of the Merchant Taylors Company, famous for its festive functions. At his Worcester home, therefore, Bull was able to throw off the sedentary habits of Hereford College, give vent to his natural high spirits, and meet many who kept up his wider interests and who were to play a part in his future life.

An evening at Giles' house saw the commencement of one of Bull's most interesting and curious friendships. It was holiday time, near New Year, and the room was filled with many young people, as well as their elders. Bull, playing the virginals, became aware of a slight, sharp-featured, auburn-haired boy, huddled up in a corner, listening with unusual intentness. Speaking to him later, Bull learned that he was Welsh, the son of friends of Giles in Breconshire, and that he was studying music in London with Thomas Tallis, one of the most celebrated composers of the day. The lad was Elway Bevin, later to be organist of Bristol Cathedral, and famous as the author of one of the earliest British treatises on composition published, " A Briefe and Short Introduction of the Art of Musicke."

The boy was precociously advanced in his musical talent. Barely five years later, at the age of nineteen, he was to receive his cathedral appointment. His remarkable gifts interested Bull immediately, and a touching companionship between the young man of twenty-two and the boy verging on fifteen ensued. They had fanciful traits in common, shown by the young Welshman's virginals piece, " Bevin His Fancy," and the boy's poetic nature appealed to the sense of fantasy shown in the titles of many of Bull's works. The attraction was enhanced because Bevin, familiar with the Usk and Neath valleys famous in Arthurian legend and Mabinogion tales, was imbued with the Keltic folk-lore which was providing Bull with such fresh interest at the time, and knew many Cambrian melodies, which intrigued the Englishman's ears by their novel rhythm and cadence.

Beside the great log fire in the Giles hall then, and wandering the countryside during holidays the following summer, Bull listened while the bronze-haired youngster's eager words painted a new world of picturesque scenery and fantastic legendary figures. Young Bevin pictured for him the heights of Snowdon, where the clouds sleep; the Vale of Neath, where Gwynn-ap-Nudd rides nightly with his faery huntsmen; the Brecon lake, Llyn-y-Fan Fach, where dwells the water-nixie who married a mortal; and the submerged city of Cantre Gwaelod, the bells of which toll through the sough of the waves in Carmarthen Bay. He told of Owain-ap-Urien with his army of ravens; of Rhiannon with her magic singing birds; of Blodeuwedd, the maiden created of flowers; and of Morris the Wind, who juggles with golden autumn leaves, and after whom the Morris Dance, with its weather-cock spins and fluttering ribbon-sticks, was named. Bull learned to recognize what Wales had contributed to the imagery which Shakespeare was giving dramatic form in the Puck of " A Midsummer Night's Dream," the Ariel of " The Tempest," and the King Lear who reincarnated Lyr, the Sun God of the Kelts.

The boy's talk made Bull aware of the Anglo-Keltic nature of the new patriotism of his time, breeding fresh enthusiasm in him. He realized the mingled culture which had made Assur, the Welsh teacher of Alfred the Great, inspire the Common Law of England; had created English chivalry through the chronicles of King Arthur written by Nennius and Geoffrey of Monmouth, and had finally united England and Wales when the Welsh troops of the Lord Rhys and Ab Einion of Shrewsbury turned the scale on Bosworth Field and placed Henry VII, son of Owain-ap-Tudor, on the English throne.

Already disgusted with the imported Italianisms affected by many in London and a keen partisan of the movement for purified English inaugurated by Cheke and Ascham, his sympathies were stirred as he heard of Gryffydd Roberts, denied a printing-press in his native land, publishing the first Welsh primer in Milan; of whimsical Dr. Shon Dafydd Rhys browbeating Stationers' Hall into sponsoring the quaint Welsh Grammar which inspired Shakespeare's amusing Welsh scenes. He recognized a kindred spirit in William Myddleton, who wrote the Welsh version of the Psalms; Richard Davies, who produced the Welsh

DR. JOHN BULL

Book of Common Prayer; and Bishop Morgan, who suffered suspicion and derision for years before obtaining the support of Queen Elizabeth's favourite, Archbishop Whitgift, of Canterbury, in translating the Welsh Bible. These were fellow-champions in challenging the alien Latin over which he was later to gain so signal a victory.

Imaginatively and idealistically, this strangely assorted companionship exercised a powerful effect on Bull's mind. English to the core, he revelled in fresh discovery; he had in him the far-faring spirit which his Viking name suggests. The broad generosity of his nature found this as much reflected in Bevin's picture of the Elizabethan Welsh hero, Prys Gryffydd, "standing on the prow of his vessel, very splendid in his shining armour," as in his own image of Drake. Listening to the boy, his West Country enthusiasm expanded before the realization of the united Anglo-Keltic patriotism which was the essence of the Elizabethan Era. He felt no prejudice when he found his dream anticipated by a Welshman in Maurice Kyffin's "Blessednesse of Brytaine." Young though the boy was, the meeting with Bevin completed what his contact with the culture of the Wye and Severn valleys had commenced. It confirmed that greater ideal which was to make him not only the foremost English composer of his day, but the first great British musician in the widest national sense.

The association affected Bevin reciprocally. Bull's influence led him to the instrumental writing which made him one of the earliest British chamber-music composers, with his "Browninge," for concerted viols. The friendship started in Worcester continued in London. When Bull became organist of the Chapel Royal, responsible for nominations, Bevin was appointed a Gentleman Extraordinary. Their careers had much affinity. Both contributed memorably to British musical prestige, and both were to encounter disaster in the political intrigues of the times. Their association left two interesting records. In his "Welch Daunce" Bull was the first great composer to give classic form to a Kymric folk-type. Bevin, in an imaginative poem worthy of the age, written on hearing Queen Elizabeth playing the virginals, recalls, in the first two lines, an amusingly human incident in Bull's life:

> "Now Maiestie with Musicke fayre
> In regall State so well combynes,
> So grac'd is Songe, no juell rayre
> In Heauens diadem richer shines.
> Resteth Shee now 'mid Royall calme,
> In graciousnesse renew'dlie stronge;
> No discorde ill of Wars alarme
> Shall sullie now the lips of Songe.
> Bedeckt with Beautie yett more brighte
> Shee walks in Glorianas traine,
> Addinge, to fashion new delighte,
> A nobler and more regall straine.

> "Now Musicke by high Maiestie
> Is sett in queenlie fayre estate,
> Thatt, like the monthlie Moone shall Shee
> With eache dayes cadence wax more greate.
> Thus, Priestesse prowde, hir psalt'ry playes,
> To hymne sweete Peace to gratefull eares:
> No hostile tumulte now dismayes
> Or seales hir songe with threaten'd feares.
> In souereigne straines thus noblie dight
> Shall growe hir glorie thro the yeares,
> 'Till, scalinge Heauens empyrean height,
> Shee singes amid the chyminge spheres."

DR. JOHN BULL

In spite of such social interests and companionships, Bull's life at Hereford irked him after a time. He sought to escape this in composition; but his cathedral duties and surroundings distracted and irritated him. His exasperation, apparently, could not be controlled at times. There is an amusing glimpse of this in a quatrain ascribed to him by William Ellis, of Kidderminster, allegedly scrawled upon a window-pane in his room, in spleen against the Cathedral bells :

> " Soules nothinge haue to feare
> Of greater griefe in Hell
> Than hee who hath to heare
> This thrice accursed bell."

All trace of this has vanished; but a window-pane might be destroyed easily, and the College of Vicars of Bull's time was too jealous of its dignity to suffer the survival of anything suggesting derision or blasphemous levity.

Nevertheless, the incident seems probable. Bull was never very patient at any time, and at that period he was young and impetuous. Bell-ringing was inveterate in Tudor days, for church services, for chiming the hours and every kind of festive or funereal purpose. They were used to call people to work and to announce the time when it ceased. Some of these occasions must have been trying : for the funeral of Lady Isabel Berkeley " There was synging daily with all the bells contynually : that is to say, at St. Michael's xxxiij peles, at Trinitie xxxiij peles, at St. John's xxxiij, at Babyllake, because hit was so nigh, lvij peles and in the Mother Church xxx peles and every pele xij." Bells were also bequeathed with stipulations for their being rung for days together, about Christmas, Easter, or on the dates of the birth or death of their donors. On St. Hugh's Day, November 17th, the entire country resounded from morning to night with peals commemorating the anniversary of Queen Elizabeth's accession. Sovereigns and prelates had tried to curb the nuisance by public injunctions, but it persistently recurred, and nowhere more than in the West, where the famous foundries of Bristol, Gloucester and Worcester were, close to Hereford.

Bull's outburst, therefore, was understandable and quite in keeping with the times. Much of previous Church sanctity had suffered during the extreme phases of the Reformation, and doggerel inscribed on or written about church bells was a popular form of humour, born among the foundry workers and not confined to the pothouse, especially in the county of Somerset, where Bull was born.

At the best, however, musical interests such as Hereford afforded could not provide full scope for Bull's virile nature. Culturally interesting and emotionally congenial in many ways as the locality was to him, it was remote from the main centres and routes of Elizabethan thought and action. His spirit yearned for more spacious environment.

Whatever the fascination of the port, this nevertheless wanes if departure be delayed too long. The most weather-beaten mariner, grateful at first for safe haven, chafes if he has to lie at anchor indefinitely. To the West Country of Bull's childhood such figures of vagrant discontent were familiar. When the exuberance of landing passed and riotous celebration palled, the sea called them again. They grew weary of relating wonders and recalling adventures. The images of their sea dreams meant little to the land-bound around them. They longed for old companionships and new exploits. Words were not deeds.

DR. JOHN BULL

Withdrawn from wide waters, the spell of remembered sea spaces gradually enveloped their spirits, creating apparitions in the fumes of the strange weed in their long clay pipes. Drawn by its magic, they receded into infinite distances of broody silence.

Bull had encountered such sea wanderers in his boyhood. As his first enthusiasm settled down to the routine of Hereford Cathedral, he came to comprehend their mood and to share it with more sensitive intensity. Constrained maturity, with knowledge and remembrance to solace it, does not chafe with such impatience against delay as does youth, eager for the unknown of its imagination.

In such fretfulness Bull developed traces of idiosyncrasy. He had days of moodiness and grew absent-minded. Choristers had to be sent to summon him to services for which he was late, absorbed in composition or sunk into some fit of abstraction. He spent hours in the Chapter Library, poring over the old illustrated map of the world drawn by Richard de Haldingham in 1313, which, though fantastically inaccurate and out of date, fascinated him by its quaint vistas of distant regions and wide spaces.

There is an amusing story of his waywardness and eccentricity at that time. The Countess of Pembroke, patroness of Bevin and many musicians, poets and dramatists of the period, visiting Hereford, attended the Cathedral especially to hear Bull play, his fame as an organist being widespread already. The congregation was unusually brilliant, the local magnates being augmented by the lady's *cortège*. The Chapter dignitaries received the visitors ceremoniously, and vestrymen conducted them in state to the pews of the quality reserved for them. Then silence fell. The choristers were all in their places, but there was no sign of Bull.

For a while the calm dignity of the ancient architecture, bathed in sunlight from the arched windows, held the distinguished assembly quiet; but soon shuffling, coughs and low whispers showed that it was getting restive. Thomas Warrock, troubled, slipped from his place and went to seek his friend. He found him in his room, bent over his music-paper, copying, oblivious of the time. Aroused, Bull hastily scrambled into his gown, clapped on his cap awry and raced across the Close, reaching his organ just as the Countess, audibly voicing her opinion that "a musician shoulde keep more juste tyme," was rising to leave. The sound of the organ arrested her departure.

Entranced, she listened as Bull, at first covering his confusion by a grandiose display of virtuosity, gradually became absorbed in the evolving moods of his voluntary. Using as his theme the melody upon which he had been working when interrupted, he made magnificent amends for his tardy arrival. Spell-bound, his audience listened as the music, at first turbulent, grew tender and then, deepening in emotion, soared into the exaltation and triumph of what the world was to know as his prelude, "Aurora Lucis rutitat."

All through the service Bull excelled himself in brilliant touches of embellishment and richly-coloured harmonies, determined to obliterate the bad impression which he felt his negligence had created. His concluding extemporization transcended all. The Countess, greatly moved, requested that he should be presented to her; but when he arrived, still ink-smeared and dishevelled, his unexpectedly comical appearance caused her to burst into stifled laughter. Bull was startled and offended by her apparent rudeness, and when, controlling her mirth, she invited him to play at her reception that evening at the

Shire Hall, he excused himself curtly and stalked off with exaggerated dignity, further convulsing the lady and her friends.

When Bull reached the College, his indignation turned to consternation as Warrock made matters plain. Troubled at having appeared so absurd and boorish, he decided to write a short piece of music as a peace offering to the lady. It was very late when he finished, but, characteristically impatient, he would not wait until morning to deliver the music. All lights were out in the house where the Countess was staying when he arrived, excepting in one upper window, which was open. Obstinately refusing to return with his purpose unfulfilled, he flung up the packet through the casement and made off. The manuscript alighted in the Countess's bedchamber, where she was preparing to retire. She was touched by the tribute and intrigued by its quaint delivery. The interest aroused then showed itself on Bull's later arrival at Court, where she was influential as the sister of the royal favourite, Sir Philip Sidney, whom Queen Elizabeth called the "jewell of Owre crowne," and where, as Sir Thomas Browne wrote, few were so "fayre and learned and good as shee."

Bull's fame made Hereford proud of him. His company was sought. As tedium grew in the College, he found more frequent amusement outside. This increased his popularity among the laity; but it evoked censure in the Chapter. Bull's secular celebrity was not pleasing to the captious Custos, who desired his organist to remain a Cathedral subordinate. Many in the College were irritated by Bull's caprices and unconventionality. Some of the vicars were envious of his public fame, while the more austere took exception to his convivial habits.

There was mainly personal prejudice behind such

criticism. Bull's behaviour was not exceptional. It was a full-blooded age, and rationalism and the Reformation had modified lay conceptions of the sanctity of ecclesiastical institutions and officials. The trend of the times was already moving the country gentry towards the Cavalier reaction against Puritanism which developed early the next century. The position of musicians also was very different in Tudor society, where the understanding and practice of music was considered a necessary accomplishment of every gentleman, alongside gallantry and a good head for wine. The admonishment against adopting a musical career uttered by the father of the celebrated Victorian organist, Samuel Wesley, of Gloucester, "You must be content to be a gentleman only, such as you are born," would have astounded the Elizabethan Era by its priggish snobbery.

Bull lived according to the prevalent customs. He would never have been Queen Elizabeth's favourite musician, whatever his talent, had he been a nincompoop. His youth and vitality could not be constrained to the study only. His humour and high spirits required the recreation which inspired him with some of the liveliest and most genial creations in British music. He was representative of an age when scholarship had escaped from the seminaries and taken to the free ways of life. Bull, indeed, typified a generation which recognized genius—Shakespeare, Surrey, Bacon, Beaumont and Fletcher and his own later associate, Ben Jonson—in the Mermaid Tavern.

The growing strain between Bull and the Cathedral authorities was not unique. Successive organists there retired in conflict or were summarily dismissed because they offended the susceptibilities of the College. The foibles of the Custos and Vicars were probably as much

DR. JOHN BULL

to blame as anything: when any organization is continually on bad terms with successive officials, there is usually fault in it. Bull's immediate successor, Thomas Warrock, retained his position less than three years, resigning through a quarrel. Thomas Mason, who followed, also retired within three years. His successor, John Farrant, " resigned for alleged insolence," being " sconced for railinge and contumelious speeches to Mr. Custos in the hall at supper tyme." Matters reached a grand climax with the next organist, John Fidow, nicknamed " Laicus." He came to single-handed combat with the entire fraternity, the Act Book of Hereford College of Vicars containing the following entry:

"Februarie 22, 1594. Item ye said daye and place ye Custos and Vicars aforesaid and ye greater number of y^m concluded and agreed not to allow Jo. Fidow not to be ye Organiste, neither to paye him any wage, therefore neither to admitt him to come to there house and Comons. This Act was made a^{gt} him for y^t he gave out most slanderous words a^{gt} ye s^d Custos and company."

Only Hereford seems to have found these organists unendurable. Warrock went to the Chapel Royal later, leaving in 1630, his son being knighted and becoming a Secretary of State. Farrant proceeded from Hereford to Salisbury Cathedral. A month after Fidow's dismissal he became Master of the Choristers at Worcester Cathedral, shortly before Giles' successor, Nathanael Pattrick, died, continuing there under John Tomkins until actually summoned back to Hereford!

Bull could not conceal matters from Blitheman long. The elder musician, "haveinge such bent unto him, hee coulde in no wyse bate nor away with griefe " at his separation from his favourite pupil, was disturbed by the situation revealed in Bull's letters. As organist of the Chapel Royal, he had great influence with the Queen, who practised music with him. Elizabeth, sincerely loving the art and being shrewd in judging people, respected him as man and musician. Blitheman decided to recommend Bull's appointment to the next vacancy among the Gentlemen of the Chapel Royal.

It was time, as a story long prevalent in the locality tells us. A Christmas celebration in Bull's room had provoked a crisis. A number of Bull's musical friends were present, including Warrock, Elias Smith, organist of Gloucester Cathedral, Matthew Godwin of Exeter, and Giles, his special crony. The gathering was merry. There was the inevitable singing, mingled with noisier revelry. Hereford was always "a greate cyder countye," and musicians of an age when the Children of the Chapel Royal were rationed " ij galons ale " daily did not have light thirst.

Outrageous though such a meeting might be thought to-day, it was no great scandal then. Mr. Custos and his Vicars, if reports are true, were as good bibbers as trenchermen. That night, or rather early morning, however, the convivial din lasted too long and disturbed their repose. They determined to make the occasion one for settling various accounts with Bull. Breaking in on the merrymakers, the angry collegians, in their night attire, protested that matters had gone too far. Bull might have let things go at that and broken up his party had not the Custos thought fit to deliver a sanctimonious homily, probably to impress the visitors. This incensed Bull, always impatient with interference and petty tyranny. His humour could be sardonic at times, as his travesty Gigge on his own poignant piece, " My Greife," shows. In his annoyance, he vented it then, caustically informing the Custos that he would be happier to have the wind for his organ bellows which was being wasted in unctious rhetoric. This was too much for the pompous head of the College, who threatened his instant dismissal unless immediate apology was forthcoming.

It was a tense scene, and its climax was to provide a typically dramatic curtain for Bull's life at Hereford. Angry defiance was on his lips when the sound of galloping hoofs was heard entering the Close outside. It was Blitheman's messenger, bearing the royal appointment of Bull as Gentleman of the Chapel Royal. It placed the trump card in his hand, and he played it with characteristic humour and relish. Ironically, he congratulated the mortified Custos on his loyal perspicacity in carrying out the Royal will even before it was known, since the dispatch also commanded him to leave Hereford—but for the Court and the personal service of the Queen !

Confronted with such sign of Royal favour, there was nothing for the discomfited College functionaries to do but retire in as good order and with as much dignity as was possible. Bull's friends were exultant. As the door closed behind the Custos and Vicars they lifted him shoulder-high and the company, with brimming beakers raised, toasted him in chorus with the words which were to become famous :

> " The bull by Force
> In fielde doth Raigne,
> But Bull by Skill
> Good Will doth Gayne."

Crossroads of Destiny

CHAPTER III

CROSSROADS OF DESTINY

BULL left for London immediately after Yuletide. The Cheque Book of the Chapel Royal records his arrival:
"1585. Jo. Bull sworne the —— of Januarie in Mr Bodinghurst place. Childe there."

He was just in time to play his part in a great national drama. The curtain was rising on a series of episodes which were to have their climax in one of the most sensational scenes in the pageant of British history.

The man and the moment were strikingly related. The turn of fortune which brought Bull to the centre of national life meant more than immediate material advantage to him: it was to determine his spiritual future also. It coincided dramatically with a momentous spin of the wheel which was not only to crown England with victory then, but was to decide her historic fate. With his country, John Bull had arrived at the crossroads leading to disaster or high destiny.

From without and within danger threatened England. Rivalry in the New World had been breeding enmity with Spain for years past. Undeclared war had existed some time. English privateersmen—Drake, Howard and Frobisher—challenged Philip's galleons on the Spanish Main and raided his colonies in America. In Madrid, English exiles, headed by Sir Francis Englefield, found refuge and aid for plots to place Mary Stuart of Scotland on the English throne. In England itself, over a decade of murderous conspiracies against Elizabeth's life had been fomented and financed by Mendoza, the Spanish envoy at the English Court.

Every difficulty faced those of the Queen's ministers who sought to safeguard the country from both invasion and internal menace. No proper Navy existed. The sinister Mendoza was sheltered by diplomatic privilege. Even in royal circles courtiers such as the Earl of Stafford betrayed the Government's plans to Philip. Where actual treason was not active, pro-Spanish sympathies or timidity and procrastination had to be faced. Bodenham, on the Privy Council, worked for a pact with Spain. Sir Francis Walsingham, the Queen's Secretary of State, or Foreign Minister, was a devoted patriot; but his colleague, Lord Treasurer Burghley, who dreaded an open rupture with Spain, pursued a policy which made Walsingham declare " our half-doings doth breed dishonour and leaveth the disease uncured." Mary, fugitive from her own subjects in England, countenancing and abetting intrigue and treason, remained immune, through Elizabeth's refusal to condemn her, in spite of the Scottish queen's plots against her own life. This was not sentiment, as even those abroad knew. Walsingham, after interviewing the French king in Paris, wrote : " He telleth us that the Quene our Mistresse is too mercifull a princesse to shed the blood of so near a kinswoman ; but this is rather spoken *ironice*." Elizabeth's motive was political. Alive, Mary held off invasion. She was heiress to the throne if Elizabeth died, in which event Philip hoped to marry her and gain England without the cost of war. Mary dead, his only hope would be the country's conquest.

Happily, these difficulties did not discourage Walsingham or Sir Francis Drake, both ardent patriots singularly endowed to meet the national emergency. Drake, whom even the Spanish Admiral, Don Pedro de Valdez, acknowledged as " one of the greatest sailors that exist, both from his skill and his power of commanding," knew that, in spite of successful adventures in the far Atlantic or Pacific, England was unequipped to meet Spain's massed marine power nearer home. Improvised fleets of privateer gentry and ordinary seamen would not suffice for the coming crisis. Only a regular navy, with powerful armament and fresh discipline, could defend his country adequately against invasion. Walsingham, whom even the French Duc d'Anjou extolled to Elizabeth as " the most honest man possible and worthy of the favour of the greatest princess in the world," realized that Spanish guile must be fought with its own weapons. Having studied foreign political methods in exile abroad during the previous reign, he put his motto, " Knowledge is never too dear," into practice when appointed by Elizabeth. He devoted his private income to building up the Government's astounding unofficial espionage system, spread through every European country, by which he became known as " the smeller-out of plots."

At the time of Bull's arrival in London recent events favoured both Walsingham and Drake, after long frustration. Walsingham had gained the support of the Queen's favourite, the Earl of Leicester, for active measures against Spain. His discovery of Throckmorton's plot to assassinate Elizabeth had established Mendoza's complicity, and the Spaniard who had so long troubled England from within had been ordered to leave by the Privy Council. Drake, long refused the Privy Council's permission to fit out his fleet, had gained over Lord Howard of Effingham, Lord High Admiral, and set sail, no longer a simple privateersman, but the holder of a royal commission, in charge of a national expedition.

News of these happenings had reached Bull at Hereford; but he was too remote there to realize their significance. Plots such as those of Norfolk, Somerville and others were of frequent occurrence. Drake's departure thrilled him, but he did not see how imminent it made war. He regarded it only as another American expedition. He could remember the glorious time in 1580, when Drake returned, a simple adventurer, laden with the spoils of the Spanish Main and bearing records of his three years' circumnavigation of the globe. He recalled the national enthusiasm in which he had shared as a boy at the Chapel Royal, when Queen Elizabeth, with true Tudor sense of drama, had proceeded to Deptford to greet Drake personally, dining with him aboard and honouring him in the most spectacular fashion by knighting him on the deck of his ship, *The Golden Hind*. Spain had protested then, terming Drake a pirate; but the matter had ended there. It did not appear likely to him that his hero's latest expedition would have more serious consequences. The journey to London brought him into contact with travellers at inns and taverns, and gossip and rumours for the first time made him feel that events were moving unusually. It was not until he arrived at Court, after conversation with Blitheman and contact with the currents working there, that he became aware of the dramatic aspect which the national situation was assuming.

If drama pervaded the time of his arrival, his own particular re-entry into Court life provided a touch of comedy. Elizabeth was interested in Blitheman's protégé, as his appointment had shown. She remembered Bull from his earlier days at the Chapel Royal, and " the good Queen had a particular tenderness for handsome fellows." She decided to give her new Gentleman of the Chapel a special private audience, which would gratify Blitheman and impress Bull. With a characteristic eye for stage effect, she did not forget to prepare the tableau and arrange the accessories. She obtained some of Bull's music from Blitheman, unknown to the composer, and set to work to practise it, to surprise her new musician on his reception.

With Bull, however, the unexpected and unusual frequently happened. The whimsical spirit which appeared often in his music also took an occasional hand in his everyday life. Like Puck with Titania, Bull's comic muse decided to play tricks with Gloriana and her new courtier. His future colleague, Phillips, has told the story amusingly:

" The queenes will beinge to knowe the sayd musicke, her Grace was at that tyme at the uirginalls : whereupon, hee, beinge in attendaunce, Maister Bull did come by stealthe to heare without, and by mischaunce did sprawle intoe the queenes Maiesties Presence, to the queenes greate disturbance. Shee demaundinge incontinent the wherefore of suche presumption, Maister Bull with greate skill sayd that wheresoever Maiesty and Musicke so well combyned, no man mighte abase himself too deeplie ; whereupon the queenes Maiesty was mollifyde and sayd that so rayre a Bull hath songe as sweete as Byrd. So by Gods will and greate fortune it came to pass that distresse was turned to mirthe."

The wit shown in this incident, typical of others throughout his life, stood him in good stead in the midst of the undercurrents of Court intrigue and the heightening tension of the national drama, which made even the formal Palace life exciting. The march of events was accelerating. Philip had responded to Drake's naval demonstration by laying an embargo on England. Leicester, overcoming Burghley's protests, had assumed the command of English troops in the Low Countries, aiding the Dutch in their insurrection against the Spanish viceroy, the Duke of Parma. Sidney accompanied him, to meet his romantic death at Zutphen. Though national enthusiasm ran high, anxiety tempered it in many quarters. Ministerial timidity and turpitude had delayed England's preparations; Elizabeth's obstinate parsimony had further curtailed them. The faint-hearted floundered in last efforts to placate Spain, vainly hoping to evade the inevitable. The more circumspect prepared, realizing that the course of events was accelerating towards an ominous crisis. Incertitude existed only regarding its imminence and outcome. War had become certain.

Bull's position was advantageous. The arts were cultivated in the circles around the Queen. Many of those foremost in the political and military councils of Elizabeth were devotees of poetry, music and the drama, such as the earls of Pembroke, Worcester and Surrey, Sidney, Sir Walter Raleigh and Sir Francis Bacon. The professional segregation of artists known later did not exist. Many leading literary men shared in the military experiences of Ben Jonson, Sidney and Spenser, in actual warfare.

The Queen's interest in music, together with the taste of the times, made musical performances a regular feature of Court life, in both ceremonies and entertainments. This gave the best musicians of the day an unusual social prestige. At Court, therefore, Bull mingled freely with many playing an important part in society and politics.

Such social intercourse made him personally acquainted

with Walsingham. The patronage and friendship of the Countess of Pembroke, sister of the statesman's son-in-law, Sidney, brought Bull into direct contact with the Secretary of State's family circle. Walsingham was interested in music. At his princely mansion at Barn Elms some of the most magnificent social functions of the time were held, in which music played an important part. Bull enjoyed the statesman's hospitality on some of such occasions. Within a few months of his return to Court he was a member of the royal retinue when Walsingham entertained the Queen at his home; for Elizabeth was then accompanied by " diuers noble lords and ladies, gentilmen of the Courte and fauored musicians."

Bull's contact with this family circle was made closer by mutual artistic interests. The Earl of Pembroke was one of the most ardent supporters of the new development of drama. He maintained his own company of stage players, and employed William Shakespeare to write and revise plays for his actors. The Company was honoured by the first theatrical " Royal Command " on record. It performed before the Queen at Court, after its famous successes at Canterbury.

That performance brought Bull into closer touch with the drama of the day. Elizabeth was so delighted with the repertory and its performance that she commanded the formation of her own Court company of actors immediately afterwards. Nathanael Giles, who had left Worcester Cathedral within the year after Bull's departure from Hereford, to succeed William Hunnis as Master of the Children of the Chapel Royal, was issued a Royal Warrant to " impress " boys for the Queen's Revels, or Children of the Revels of the Chapel, since the youngsters enrolled came under the Chapel organization. It was considered unfitting for the Children of the Chapel Royal proper, who sang in the religious services, to appear as actors on the stage, but the boy actors were lodged near them at the Palace.

With his friend as Master of the Children of the Revels, Bull had therefore an unusually intimate connectoin with the stage productions so interesting to the Pembroke family. The importance of music in the Elizabethan theatre, when Shakespeare and other great poets of the day wrote some of their finest lyrics to be sung in plays, increased the strength of this tie.

The attraction which the emerging drama held for Bull was not so remote from his active impulses as might at first appear. It was intimately related to the maritime associations and seafaring folk-lore which had influenced him from early childhood. To these it gave yet more vivid imagery, and the growing picturesqueness of his music at that time revealed its influence.

The poetry and drama of the Elizabethan Era was not produced by professional authors or segregated scholars. It was the work of men of action. The drama, as the literature of the day, was in its very essence born of the narratives of the seafarers of the time. Much of its best and most striking style was borrowed from straightforward maritime chroniclers such as Hakluyt and Purchas. No matter in what fantastic form they appear, the figures of Elizabethan drama were born in the realm of native thought. Marlowe created plays around stories of Eastern tyrants and German necromancers, " Tamburlaine " and " Dr. Faustus "; but both remain at heart Englishmen of the same type as Raleigh, Hawkins and Drake. This was recognized by Stowe at the time, who wrote that Drake was " as famous in Europe and America as Tamburlaine

was in Asia and Africa." Marlowe's Asiatic had the dream of every Elizabethan sea wanderer, to
" behold
As much more land, which never was descried,
Wherein are rocks of pearl that shine as bright
As all the lamps that beautify the sky."

It was the sea-mirage and the spell of waters which gave such undercurrent of magic to the moods and arresting moments of Shakespeare's " The Tempest," " Pericles," " The Merchant of Venice " and " Othello." The routes along which Dr. Faustus directed his familiar spirits was that of the thought of every adventurer of the day :

" I'll have them fly to India for gold,
Ransack the ocean for orient pearl,
And search all corners of the new round world
For pleasant fruits and princely delicates."

His friendly connections apart, the social life of the Court brought Bull, as all courtiers, into constant contact with the drama. Theatre-going was one of the most fashionable amusements of high society. The Gentlemen of the Inns of Court were already developing their reputation for " sweet and ayry Activities," and Queen Elizabeth often visited the gardens and great hall of the Temple with her favourites, to witness their plays, which " crowned their grand solemnities with admiration of all Spectators."

There were also numerous public playhouses, such as The Theatre and The Curtain, at Shoreditch ; The Paris Garden, The Swanne, The Rose and The Globe, at Southwark ; The Blackfriars and The Whitefriars ; The Fortune, Cripplegate, and The Red Bull, in St. John Street, Clerkenwell. The most popular citizens' theatre was that at Newington Butts. Aristocratic parties attended such theatres regularly, the habitual patrons being supplied with keys to the reserved private rooms or boxes round the back of the auditorium under the scaffolds, or gallery-tiers. There the ladies of quality, discreetly masked, enjoyed the spectacle and the audience while smoking the short clay pipes that were the latest feminine vogue.

At such places the audience provided as much entertainment as the performance for one with Bull's keen observation and interest in popular life. The medley assembly in the yard, or pit, illuminated by the flaring open cressets, was as picturesque as any play, and frequently provided as much comedy as any farce. The throng of artisans, apprentices, clerks and tradesmen passed their time playing cards, smoking, drinking ale and cracking jokes from group to group while they waited for the curtain to rise. They bandied backchat with the wits and gallants who enjoyed swaggering on hired stools or sprawling on the rushes either side of the platform, on the stage itself, where their pages filled and lit their pipes for them, in prominent view of the audience beneath the pair of massive branch-candelabra which provided light for the actors' performance. Pedlars passed here and there through the throng, selling delicacies and shouting their wares. The din was finally augmented by the musicians taking their places in the gallery over the stage box and commencing to tune their trumpets, hautboys, lutes, recorders and viols, capping the excitement of the scene.

It was a period which delighted in the fantastic and flamboyant, and Bull shared its moods. The three ceremonial flourishes of trumpets which announced the commencement of the show gave the moment a feeling of adventure. There was an eager delight in seeing the curtains suspended from the sloping thatched roof covering the stage draw apart. There was expectancy as to what would be revealed even though the stage contained only the traverses, or part-curtains, and the raised balcony for dual action in the background. The very simplicity stimulated the imagination and threw up the actors' costumes into magnificence and glamour. Such costumes were rich enough in many better-class theatres, though they had not yet reached the luxuriance of the " cloke of velvet, with a cape imbrothered with gold, pearles, and redd stones, and one roabe of cloth of gold," for which John Alleyn paid sixteen pounds in 1590, not to mention the " blacke velvet cloake, with sleves ymbrodered all with silver and golde, lyned with blacke satten stryped with golde," for which the same producer and his brother Edward expended the costly sum of twenty pounds and ten shillings the following year.

The symbolism of the stage was such as to appeal to Bull by the freedom which it gave his imagination. Its changes of scene were made quite simply, by the exhibition of a board on which was painted the name of the locality intended. Furniture was pushed on and pulled off through the traverses in full view of the audience. There were, however, fantastic characters, and occasionally elaborate constructions representing the mysterious or magical, with chairs lowered and raised on ropes to transport gods and goddesses to and from the celestial regions represented by the painted blue boards under the stage roof.

The whimsicality of Bull's own nature found reflection in the extemporaneous buffoonery of the clowns throughout the plays, in the songs and dances between the scenes, and in the gay gigge with which even the performance of a tragedy was rounded off, before the entire company knelt to offer up the customary prayer for the Queen with which each production ended. The spirit of the theatre, in its pageantry and gaiety, underlay much of his music at the time, its dances and its delightful song-variations. In particular, it inspired the fantastic and whimsical virginals piece which he entitled " The Buffins," the first musical picture of clowns, drawn with gleeful delight in their fussy nonsense and jerky gestures.

Such amusements, however, were only a congenial setting for the more intimate moods of his social connections. The contact with Walsingham influenced Bull's life profoundly. His quick wits made him keenly aware of the Court intrigues which the great Secretary had to face. Contact with the statesman's family revealed to him the sacrifices made by Walsingham to his unswerving ideals of loyalty and patriotism and the private altruism of his nature. Where the minister had impressed him, the man now attracted him. He glimpsed in him his own vision of national destiny. Gradually the Queen's Secretary came to share equally in the homage which he rendered Drake as a national hero.

Walsingham was attentive to the talented young musician. He was always on the watch for those who could serve his State aims, as much as for those who menaced them. He was an astute observer of men and motives, and he knew the sincerity of Bull's ardent patriotism. A young, intelligent man, with the advantage of Bull's proximity to the Queen and his position at Court, could be very useful to the indefatigable, far-scheming head of the secret service. The implacable Secretary of State required every possible recruit who could be trusted absolutely. Through his chief spy, Jernigan, the first whispers of a fresh conspiracy had reached him, and he was again hot on the track of treason. The end of the trail was to run the Babington plot to murder Elizabeth to earth and, in so doing, to place in his hands such damning proofs of Mary Stuart's complicity as to enable him to enforce his long reiterated contention that " Mary must die ! " Already he had premonitions of what was to be revealed, and these weighed heavily on his mind. He knew there could be no security from treason so long as Mary lived ; but he also knew that her death was likely to precipitate war. The onus of convicting the Scottish queen would fall upon him in any event, for, as he admitted, " The Queen will in no sorte neither by support or otherwise make herself a party. The burden of the charges will light upon me."

Such service naturally appealed to Bull. The great maritime adventurers had been his national ideal types since childhood. His profession had prevented him from sharing in their exploits for England. He had neither military nor naval training ; but the secret service of Walsingham provided a way in which a young patriot might fight equally courageously for England—in a battle of wits against her Spanish enemies and the traitors who threatened the country from within.

Bull's vocation favoured such dual activity, musical and political. The social position of musicians of standing and their favour at Court provided him with unique opportunities for obtaining information, while at the same time the innocuous nature of his occupation sheltered him from suspicion. However much poets, dramatists and musicians were accepted socially, however their artistic gifts were admired, they were the least likely to be taken seriously in politics and diplomacy if professionals in such arts, or certainly not so much so as would be those whose official positions, interests or political connections linked them directly with matters of statecraft.

Such activities on Bull's part were not extraordinary. They were inspired by the popular spirit of the youth of the day. For young English adventurers abroad the greatest gratification was in spoiling the Spaniards of their riches. For those detained at home, especially in Court circles, there was as keen a zest in spoiling Spanish intrigues and spying out sedition, or in acting as agents for the dangerous communications of Walsingham's counter-espionage system.

Naturally, neither Bull nor Walsingham allowed much evidence of such a relationship to survive. Nevertheless, in view of all the facts of Bull's life and the circumstantial evidence surrounding these, it is the only satisfactory explanation of the mass of confusedly contradictory and otherwise inexplicably mysterious data dryly recorded by musicologists and biographers, without any attempt to elucidate their significance or even to find some coherent human relationship between them. Such activities account for the payments made for Bull's services outside his salary; for the grants of land on his behalf, which would at any time have been inordinate remuneration for a musician's professional work. They explain why those rendering him kindnesses, no matter how obscure their professional status, received the highest honours his colleagues in the Queen's service could bestow. They provide a reason why Bull, just after petitioning the Queen for aid in his poverty, should have freedom and means to holiday miles from London in such style as to make him worth robbing. They show some cause for his otherwise eccentric precaution of travelling "incognito" abroad "for his health," yet at the same time "touring the great cities as a virtuoso." Whatever construction be put upon these things, even allowing for the deliberately cryptic phrases in which conspiracy conducted its hazardous correspondence at the time, there was surely more than empty metaphor intended when an exile in Madrid wrote to his supposed fellow-conspirator, Parry—actually Walsingham's spy—in 1587: "I doo hartilie praye you in that respecte paye heede not onlye in the mater for the w^{che} I haue heretofore alreadie moued you, but knowe that shee (Queen Elizabeth) hath a cunninge Organe wherebye to heare such as cometh in no wyse to comon eares : the w^{che} in rayre kinde doth soe ad to (her) sighte, that in anye aime shee hath the Bullseye at al tymes, whomsoever other hath the clout."

Exciting though such service must have been to him, Bull did not allow it to detract from his music. Apart from the fact that his professional work was the best possible cover for his political activities, he was essentially a musician, whose most individual expression was in his art. The growth of his musical prestige received academic recognition for the first time, then, in the form of a degree from Oxford, which is recorded in "Fasti Oxonienses":

"July 9, 1586. John Bull who had practised the fac. of Musick for 14 years was then admitted Bach. of Musick —This Person who had a most prodigious hand on the Organ was famous throughout the religious world for his Church Music."

Even through his music at that time, however, runs the trace of his other preoccupations. This confirms his connection with Walsingham in a curious manner, by a work bearing the statesman's name, which still remains one of Bull's greatest masterpieces.

Though the popular sentiment of the time centred around Drake, Walsingham had a subtler patriotic reputation among the thoughtful and informed, which recent events had enhanced. His name became a slogan for the more cognizant patriotic organizations. It acted as a password at their meetings. The Queen might be prayed for or toasted with covert implications so long as the Queen of Scots lived, according to whether those concerned meant Elizabeth or Mary. Walsingham's name, however, was synonymous with loyalty to the reigning sovereign and devotion to English independence.

Never safe from treachery among their own compatriots and in constant danger from Spanish assassins so long as Mendoza remained in England, the loyalists had to exercise great discretion, in spite of the patriotism of the greater part of the population. Even where no treason threatened, timorous or venal politicians sought to repress all too open demonstrations of anti-Spanish feeling, which might precipitate war. Subterfuge therefore was constantly necessary. " As I went to Walsingham " was a popular folk-song. It became a signal and rallying song employed by the anti-Spanish faction. It even created a catchword, " Sing Walsingham for England and the Queene."

Through such use the air became as politically significant as " The King Shall Enjoy His Own Again " among the Cavaliers under the commonwealth, or " Charlie is My Darling " among the Jacobites under the Hanovarians. Every Court patriot knew its political meaning. The Gentlemen of the Chapel Royal particularly found it easily familiar, being a melody. It is impossible, therefore, to think that Bull selected it accidentally as the theme of his greatest work. Byrd, of course, used the theme also ; but his high position among musicians and the privileges he received from the Queen showed that he was beyond suspicion, although a Catholic. There was a vast difference between the two musicians' treatment of the folk-theme. Byrd presented it as a brief series of variations on a melody pure and simple. He retained the folk-song title, " As I went to Walsingham." Bull entitled his work " Walsingham : Variations."

Bull made his work an architectonic masterpiece. Among all his often elaborate treatments of folk-melody none had such sustained thought, breadth of mood, profusion of decorative device or massive proportions of form. It was not only the outstanding keyboard composition of one " famous throughout the world for his music " in his own time and esteemed then " the first performer in the world " ; it towered above all other virginals music of his age, revealing the epic imagination and invention of " the father of keyboard music." In its epoch it was the legitimate ancestor of " Das Wohltempierte Klavier," conceived over a century later by Johann Sebastian Bach.

Bull clearly intended " Walsingham " as a memorial to the great statesman who typified Elizabethan nationalism. Its monumental character grew from his knowledge of the magnitude of the man as well as the politician. He did not entitle it " Sir Francis Walsinghams Variations " as a formal dedication to an eminent personage, as he did " Lord Hunsdens Galliard," " Lady Lucies Galliard " or " The Duke of Brunswicks Toye." As he turned to his music from contact with the great statesman and his work, Walsingham inspired him as a symbolic figure of patriotism.

With all the skill in musical portraiture which enabled him even to compose musical self-delineations, he wove in the intricacy of craft, the cunning network of sound upon which the music is woven, the blend of fastidiousness, energy and exaltation which Walsingham's traits suggested. He touched it with something of the intimacy which existed between them, yet kept the great secretary's general aloofness. In spite of such characterization, his mould gradually transcended that of any personally depictive study. He came to see that it was not an individual, but a type, that he was exalting. Surpassing in its conception any homage to an identity, " Walsingham " was consecrated to an ideal.

Self-realization came to him as he worked. He saw that this ideal was the spirit of freedom, with its rich creative growth of individuality and imagination, animating alike Elizabethan patriotism and his own art. For good or ill, he knew that it would prove the determinative force in his life and career. It was to cause the dramatic fluctuations of his fortunes. It was to inspire not only the boldly imaginative strokes of initiative which enhanced his music, but also the broad vision and independence which he was to show throughout the vicissitudes of his life. It was to identify his creative thought with the most potent impulses of his age, making his music an epitome of the spirit of a singularly fertile and fascinating epoch. It was to extend the scope of his aims and achievements, rendering him not only the greatest English composer of his period, but an outstanding figure in British music, of rich human interest and significance for all time.

The first rays of a bright dawn through the window reflected his exultance as he finally threw down his quill. His mood maintained when, missing his breakfast in order to copy the music clearly, he entered the royal apartments for the Queen's music practice. The whole Court seemed inspired. Excited bright faces passed him in the corridors. The great anteroom was crowded, and over the assembly the same joyously triumphant spirit reigned.

Waiting in attendance, he learned its cause. Drake,

hearing of Philip's preparations for an Armada against England, had sailed impudently into Cadiz Harbour and fired the vessels in their docks. Not only had the destruction of the galleons postponed the danger of invasion; the daring of the exploit heartened the nation to meet that emergency with confidence. Above all, England adored Drake for having the laugh on the Spaniards, " singeing the king of Spain's beard."

As Bull listened he became aware of a tumult outside. Looking out of the window, he saw a helmeted and cuirassed group gallop up before the Palace and rein in their steaming horses. One of them, a short, stocky figure, lifted his casque and mopped his forehead before swinging from the saddle. The sunlight caught the bright red gleam of his hair and beard. Bull's pulse beat more quickly as he recognized the figure, around which a mob of courtiers had already clustered, forgetting all etiquette in wild cheers. It was Drake, come hot-foot after his couriers to receive the Queen's reprimand for his outrageous crimes —and Elizabeth's gleeful thanks for his courageous example to the nation before the coming crisis.

" God Save The Queen "

CHAPTER IV

" GOD SAVE THE QUEEN "

JULY, 1588, brought the epic moment of Bull's life and Elizabethan England's history. That month the mighty Armada sailed from Spain. The news of its departure came as no surprise. Philip had long boasted of his intentions, flaunting his might before what he considered a weaker adversary. Walsingham's English spies, working in the very heart of Madrid and the Spanish ports, had kept England informed of every move in the Spanish preparations to an amazingly detailed degree. Howard of Effingham and Drake had made their preparations. Beacons had been built throughout the country to communicate the first sighting of the enemy fleet over the entire land. England waited.

There was great tension. Every Englishman sailing abroad had thought it his duty to collect every possible scrap of information. Such reports magnified themselves on their way home and were fantastically exaggerated by popular rumour on their arrival in England. The reports of Spanish might had the reverse effect on the English public mind of that anticipated by Philip. They did not cow: they hardened the national resolve into stern desperation. Not only every sword, musket and halberd, but every scythe, ploughshare, and even pitchfork, would be turned into a weapon before England suffered Spanish dominion.

Although Bull's office withheld him from participating in the actual coming conflict, the national emergency made its calls upon him. Neither Elizabeth nor her ministers were such poor State leaders as to allow tension to develop into public pessimism or panic. Every possible means was taken to infuse the populace with a spirit of confidence in ultimate victory. The Queen's Tudor nature had endowed her with the histrionic qualities to make the most of dramatic appeal. She rose to the occasion with magnificent gallantry. In the almost festive functions with which she heartened her Court, Bull was prominent, and Elizabeth's courage not only evoked his devout admiration, but spurred him on to writing some of his most striking music.

He had found it no easy task to comprehend the contradictory traits of his royal mistress. Elizabeth, passionate autocrat possessed by the belief in deputed Divine authority inherited from her father, was yet endowed with an ironic sense of humour which did not spare even herself. A woman called to govern in an age of new forces which seemed to demand the utmost masculine energy, she had a seemingly desperate position to maintain. The insularity of her country, though it secured its safety, placed England in isolation from the main groupings of European politics when she came to the throne. Philip of Spain, the most powerful monarch in Europe and the New World, was her antagonist. Though the French king dallied with the idea of an alliance, in a diplomatic correspondence which read like a personal flirtation with Elizabeth herself at times, no nation risked standing in with England until the needs of the Netherlands, rebelling against Spain, made Elizabeth their obvious and useful ally.

Within the Queen's own realm, not the least of her difficulties arose from her sex. Many felt that no woman should govern alone under such stressful conditions. Alliance after alliance was planned for her, which she only

"GOD SAVE THE QUEEN"

evaded by the utmost ingenuity, knowing her own disabilities. To juggle with such situations required her deepest political guile. Others feared any alliance for her. They recalled the bitter memories of what the marriage of her predecessor, Mary, with Philip of Spain had meant to the country. At the prospect of another union with any Catholic prince outcry arose, and some of her subjects even carried the matter of protest into print, exposing the " yawninge Gulph " which threatened the country with a sensationalism which modern journalism might envy. The patriots were determined never to be subjected to foreign dominion again merely because their sovereign was a woman.

So, against those who would have her married at all costs and those who were resolved to keep her single, Elizabeth added to her already heavy load of administrative labour and political vigilance the further burden of controlling her own innately feminine nature. She knew that, if possible foreign consorts were viewed with detestation, possible native ones were regarded with suspicion and jealous hatred. If ever the dictates of her heart inclined her towards some noble subject, she had to face immediate intrigue. She dare not flout her servants and subjects. The country stood still too close to mediæval times in many sentiments, in spite of all apparent changes, for a woman to dare to carry regal pretensions beyond a given degree of defiance.

Hence Elizabeth, half fanatic imbued with a fantastic idea of her own high destiny, half feminine egoist greedy for all possible forms of possession and gratification, gradually and deliberately developed a position of regal isolation with all the craft inherited from her father. This, actually allowing her the maximum private latitude, surrounded her publicly with something resembling a halo of divinity in her role as the Virgin Queen.

Yet beneath all Elizabeth, queen, autocrat, crafty politician, miser and something of a megalomaniac, remained a very susceptible woman. Beneath all she had a desire for the normal experience of love, marriage and motherhood, denied her by inborn physical disabilities. Thus her divinely regal pose of superhuman isolation was constantly shaken by her emotions. Her private life was storm-beaten by passion, torn between successive infatuations and the rigid dogma of royalty which her own convictions and the demands of her public position imposed on her. Blind in faith at times, she was rendered savagely cynical when external events or the falsity of her favourites betrayed her. Little by little—probably in an attempt to evade being too deeply involved in her emotions—she developed a frivolous attitude, to which her innate vanity contributed. She flirted outrageously and complicated her life with coincident affairs of the heart. She was avid for homage to herself as a woman and absorbed the most obvious and exaggerated flattery greedily. She developed an inordinate jealousy, tolerating no other woman within her own orbit and rounding brutally on such of her male courtiers as showed attachment to any other but herself. Consequently, while a supreme realist in practical affairs, she was surrounded in her personal life by an atmosphere of subterfuge and pretence. Try as she might, she could not conceal this from her keen intelligence at times, and so her mind became filled with suspicions and bitterness where she might have enjoyed the loyalty and sincere regard of the many among her subjects and immediate circle, who truly loved and revered her.

Gradually, as Bull became absorbed into Court life, his

sensitive nature enabled him to comprehend her. Each day he came into contact with the Queen. He saw Elizabeth the woman in all her pettiness, miserliness and jealousy, as well as in her sentiment, her humour, her penetrative human insight and her profound genius for managing situations. At first her careless caprices and exhibitions of her weaknesses, so far removed from his previously romantic conception of a queen, which his boyish days at the Chapel Royal had not diminished, shocked him. In the Queen's love of music, however, he found common ground on which to approach her. Elizabeth, appreciating his talent, was also not insensible to his vitality and charm. In the moods which her growing affection for him induced, he came to understand her complex traits better. He came to realize many of her problems. He learned to revere her when he discovered that, though certain aspects of her life were truly tragic, the bigness of her spirit, with its unquenchable humour, its broad vision and determination, precluded his pitying her.

The Queen made heavy demands upon him. His presence was required at entertainment after entertainment. His mornings passed in heavy rehearsal with his fellow-musicians of the Chapel Royal. Blitheman, aged and in poor health, was not equal to the strain of the situation. Most of his duties devolved upon Bull, his recognized deputy. Elizabeth demanded creative work as well as practical performance. On occasions this necessitated entirely extemporaneous work from Bull. One evening, when a mood of despondent reaction was apparent under the ostensible gaiety, she suddenly stopped the players in the music gallery with one of her typical outbursts of violent temper, upbraiding them for their " clownes mallincholy," and, rounding on a grave-faced courtier, bade him " change the manner of his Puritan sournesse " and partner her in dancing, Bull being obliged to substitute for the " clownes " at the virginals. The Queen was in an overbearing mood and nothing played satisfied her until at last Bull, desperate but catching her spirit, commenced to improvise, using a martial trumpet call as his theme. This caught the spirit of the moment, and the Queen, delighted, led the company in the Pavan, on which form Bull was basing his impromptu dance. There was something of the exaltation of the time in this stately measure, designed for dancing " by Kings, princes and grave seigneurs, with their grand mantles ; and by queens, princesses and ladies with their long trains." Elizabeth paced it with full majesty ; but when Bull turned the measure and followed with the usual Galliard on the same theme she bore not only the company, but the music, along on the momentum of her gaiety. It was as much as Bull could do to avoid being commanded to accompany not only all that evening, but on many subsequent ones. He returned to his rooms tired ; but the picture of the Queen imperiously riding down the dangerous moodiness of her Court and carrying all along with her so victoriously, in spite of her cares, persisted in his mind. He could not sleep until he had committed the image to paper in what remains for us as the " Trumpet Pavan and Galliard."

In spite of such gallant efforts, not only by the Queen but by most of the zealous patriots around her, anxiety sometimes overcame the bravest resolution. Walsingham's indomitable spirit quailed when he realized the terrible odds with which England was faced. There was desperation in his cry on the eve of the crisis : " Unless it shall please God in mercie and miraculously to preserue us, we cannot stande long." Bull could not avoid his own moments of despondency, when even his heroes faltered. The Court functions distracted him from pessimistic thoughts; but, back in the solitude of his room, the national peril overwhelmed him. His moving " Miserere " voiced his mood, and it had in it not only his own tribulation, but that of his people at the moment.

There was no essential weakness in such a prayerful hymn, any more than there was in the man, or in the daily services which were offered up all over the country. It sprang from a natural reaction; but the music of Bull then mostly reflects the national mood of defiance. Much of it was dance music. Precisely because of this, it showed Bull's sensitivity to the popular feeling about him. It was Elizabeth's mood; it was the mood which prompted Drake's almost impudent bravado in the famous game of bowls when the Armada was in sight at Plymouth. It gave Bull's inspiration a new turn. He no longer used the folk-tunes of rural life, of fields and streets, of popular sentiment of the gentler kind. There was a new dramatic feeling, even in the dances, and a new flamboyance. Bull, like England, was demonstrating, maybe inwardly with some trepidation, but outwardly with a magnificent and careless confidence.

There was more than musical interest in the record of the times which Bull's music then created. He found in the national crisis a new realism. The hour of war is as vividly painted as though in visual images. His " Alarme " expressed the national call to arms and the mood of excitement which it evoked. His " Battaile," so far as the instruments of the day allowed, was realism, echoing the clash and clamour of the martial scenes which obsessed the popular mind at the moment.

Such music was documentary. Even the figure of

Elizabeth herself was depicted in it. Bull felt the prevalent magnetism of her presence. At the moment there was almost a religious fervour in the public feeling for the Queen. The Age of Chivalry with its Mariolatry was not far past. Living men could remember Henry VIII riding to the tournaments of the Field of the Cloth of Gold. The new patriotism, confronting Spanish fanaticism, had developed its own traits of faith, making an emblem of the sovereign. Inviolate as the patriots would have the spirit and soil of their island remain, as the Virgin Queen—however euphemistically—Elizabeth had long been the living symbol of England. The crisis showed fresh qualities in her, histrionic but fervidly sincere. She had exchanged her vestal dignity for the martial splendour of an Amazon. Standing at his window the night that the Armada was sighted, Bull watched her depart, clad in armour that flashed under the torchlight, to ride through the massed ranks of her troops, inflaming their courage with her glamour and the power of her Tudor eloquence. At that moment she became for him England incarnate, and in its exaltation he painted her image in " Queen Elizabeth's Pavan and Galliard," with its initial majesty and its final brave gaiety.

Meanwhile, in the Channel, Drake's little " sea-hawks," having allowed the unwieldy Spanish galleons to proceed up Channel without joining battle with them, were harrying in their wake. The Armada presented a terrific spectacle as it hove in sight on July 19th. Into its 130 huge warships Philip had loaded an immense armament. There were 2,430 pieces of ordnance, 22,500 tons of gunpowder, 20,000 soldiers, 8,000 seamen and marines, and 2,000 volunteers from noble Spanish families. Against all this the most that Lord Howard of Effingham, Drake, Hawkins and Frobisher had been able to muster between them were

"GOD SAVE THE QUEEN"

180 small ships and about 18,000 sailors and marines. The odds seemed hopeless, but Drake had laid his plans. He knew that the spirit of his men far excelled that of his enemies. The Spanish vessels were manned with galley-slaves at the oars. His seamen were freemen, gentry and ordinary mariners united under his splendid discipline. In his famous phrase, "I must have the gentlemen hale and draw with the mariners," he had laid the foundation of the spirit of the future British Navy. The Spanish vessels also were too clumsy to deal with his sea-skirmishing tactics. As they sailed up the Channel, their commanders disconcerted by the holding back of the English, though their men exulted in it as a sign of fear, the agile "sea-hawks" followed. Here and there they commenced to dart, dealing swift havoc among their enemies and avoiding their heavy broadsides. The coming of night added to the horror of this guerilla warfare among the Spaniards, for then the English sea captains sent their fire-ships flaming into the midst of Philip's disordered fleet. The almost supernatural terror of Drake's name haunted the Spanish leaders. When at length a scattered general engagement ensued, on July 29th, Don Pedro de Valdez struck the ensign of his flagship simply on learning that his opponent was the dreaded "Sea-Devil." Drake, putting a prize crew aboard, sent him to Dartmouth, while he continued the work of scattering the demoralized enemy. Storm completed the ruin of Philip's proud fleet as the English sea captains returned in triumph to Plymouth and the dispatch riders raced in the track of the beacons leaping from hill to hill to acquaint the Queen in London of the glorious victory.

In the capital, Elizabeth had kept pace with events through messengers riding day and night from the West.

Before the actual decisive moment she knew that victory was in sight. With her innate dramatic sense, she anticipated nothing, but she made her preparations. When victory came, its celebration must be worthy of the national triumph.

All her Court musicians received their instructions. All the Chapter at St. Paul's prepared for the National Thanksgiving. Giles rehearsed the Children of the Chapel. Blitheman was still feeble, so Bull took his duties with the Gentlemen. At Westminster Abbey, the Chapel and St. Paul's the Queen designed to hold a series of impressive services. The Abbey had no regular organist at the time, and the organists of the Chapel Royal and St. George's frequently officiated at St. Paul's. For the Thanksgiving, Elizabeth determined to muster all her musical resources as they had never functioned publicly before.

· In the ordinary way Blitheman would have represented the Chapel Royal as Queen's Master in the celebrations. He was unwell, however, having been ailing some time, and Bull had been deputizing for him. When the moment came, therefore, he had to take his master's place. Elizabeth was not displeased at the opportunity provided for her favourite to figure in the great national event. Other musicians had special music in hand; but she commanded Bull to write a new anthem for the occasion.

At the height of such a moment Bull's wayward temperament asserted itself curiously. " The quenes Organiste woulde by no meanes be constrained to sett his hand to such worke, lest by the decree of God maters should goe against us." The exact cause of this capricious mood was never plain. Probably, in the general neurosis of the day, Bull felt that it might be tempting Providence if a triumph were assumed before it was assured. Again, he may simply have lacked the right inspiration and so have put matters off until it came. Even more probably he may have been in much the mood of Drake at Portsmouth, treating the whole matter as one which could bide its time, like the famous captain at his game of bowls.

If Elizabeth knew of his waywardness, she treated him leniently. Probably too many other matters were on her mind for her to give Bull much attention. She knew her man and had faith in his powers and, as Queen, relied upon being obeyed eventually, no matter how short Bull ran his time.

The actual eve of the Armada victory arrived without his having completed the work. The announcement of the event apparently took the Court by surprise, although it had been anticipated for days. "The Courte gathered in greate haste and confusion" and "the quene was delayed in hir coming," while "the musique being hindered in the copyinge thereof, must bee broughte by horse for the singinge."

The arrival of the moment spurred Bull at last by its urgency. He had been seeking to evolve something magnificent, with all the ingenuity of his powerful technique. Each result had disappointed him by its empty over-elaboration. In his last desperation, however, a simple strain came to him, which he recognized as stark and strong and truly fitting for the occasion. Suddenly filled with resolution, he sat down to commence his work.

With that air Bull became more than a great historical personage; he entered into the entire future history of his people. He was to hear his hymn catch the popular imagination for days to come, when the people rejoiced, "makinge greate clamour and singinge, with God Save Ovre Virgin Queene"; but, beyond the exaltation of that great moment of national exultation, his creation was to become reincarnate in the song of every successive generation of his race. His part in its conception was to become obscured, but his achievement was recognized in his own time. The importance of his contribution to the national cry of thanksgiving was recognized widely, even while he was the Organist of Elizabeth's Chapel. That recognition is recorded in passages such as that of the writer on a minor sea-fight in 1591, who wrote, " Bee it no mater so greate withal hir Maiesties organiste to hymne it, as hath bin made for the deliuerance by Gods grace from the greate Armada, yet doth it make braue showe and worthie of Songe."

In the political intrigues of his day he was to incur the displeasure of James I, with the resultant virtual suppression of all his works for some time. Yet his creations were to emerge again triumphantly, the delight of a future generation. Though his anthem survived and attained national glory, his part in its creation was to fade from the public mind. His work was to be ascribed successively to the Frenchman, Lully ; to his great compatriot, Purcell and his truly British successor, Thomas Arne, whose " Rule Britannia " was to stand close beside his hymn ; and finally to the Austrian, Haydn, who carried back so many British folk-melodies from England after his stay there, to give them genial new settings.

Bull's claim to the immortal tune was to stand, however ; it was recorded in his own work and was eventually to be vindicated. There were those in coming ages who would recognize and acknowledge his genius and affirm his right. The evidence of his own manuscripts, devotedly collected by Dr. Pepusch and catalogued by Dr. Ward two centuries later, were to establish him as the first composer of an air

"GOD SAVE THE QUEEN"

entitled "God Save the King," and on that evidence Richard Clark, a later member of the Chapel Royal, was to confute the impudent attempt of Henry Carey's son to usurp an authorship which his father had never claimed. The air so entitled only partially resembled that which he wrote for the Armada, and which later generations were to know as the British National Anthem; but his original was to be preserved in the folios also. Unearthed by Sir George Smart, the authoritative editor of Gibbons and other Elizabethan masters, and printed by him alongside the later versions by Purcell and Arne, it was conclusively to establish, not only his claim to the title, but also to the air of his country's national song.

Bull was no prophet, save in his vision of England's glory. He had no dream of these things as he sat down to write. He was immersed in the magnitude of his moment. It was a fight against time. He had delayed almost too long. Even with the original completed, dozens of parts had to be copied out for the singers. Giles and the members of the Chapel Royal were occupied "in greate travaill with the musicke al thatt nighte." Drake's messengers were tearing towards London, and the first red glow of beacons flaring up for victory was filling the room with lurid light before the music was completed.

Work was abandoned as the excited members of the Chapel saw the flames. Leaping to their feet, they gave themselves over to a frenzy of exultation. Laughing, shouting, singing, stamping, whirling each other round in a wild improvised dance, the scene showed how tense the national anxiety had been in them. Bull forgot his work for the moment. Rushing to the window he flung open the casement, and peered out eagerly. The clamour of hundreds of bells hurtled into the room, adding to the indescribable din. From the city the sounds of a pandemonium eddied and billowed. Giles caught him in a bear-like hug, and for a moment or two the friends lurched and leaped to and fro in a mad dance.

A knock at the door recalled them to themselves. A Queen's officer stood in the doorway. The Queen commanded the presence of her musicians at the Thanksgiving. His message delivered, the officer wheeled on his heels and clattered away. Bull, alive to the urgency of the matter, rushed back to the table and recommenced writing feverishly. The others, sobered, gathered round to their places and recommenced copying. Feverishly, sand was scattered over the wet ink as each page was finished; but the work was not yet complete.

With a sigh of relief, Bull at last flung down his quill. The final page was snatched up by Giles, who placed it between himself and Bull. Brushing his head wearily, Bull took up his quill again and the two friends copied hurriedly.

Choirboys brought them news as they worked, increasing the urgency, but disturbing them, as rumours spread. Public fancy grew wild as the fact of victory established itself in the popular mind. The boys' tidings grew more and more extravagant; but they dare not dispense with them as scouts. They knew that the Queen would be preparing to start her promised triumphal procession to the national Thanksgiving service. The thought pestered them as their quills scrawled, scratched and spluttered along the ruled paper feverishly. As the last copy was finished, a wildly excited youngster burst in, shouting that the Queen was already on her way. There was no time to run through the music, much less to rehearse it properly. A swift ride to St. Paul's alone could bring it in time for the service. The company snatched up their

"GOD SAVE THE QUEEN"

caps and, each with his part fluttering in his hand, dashed out for the waiting horses prepared by Giles' orders.

The ride was a wild gallop. The Queen was already well on her way. They must ride hard to overtake the royal procession, using every available byeway. Apart from the urgency of the race, the ride was breath-taking. The streets as they rode into them were packed with a riotously exultant multitude and blazing with torches, the pealing of bells from every London steeple capping the wild clamour. The press of the throng delayed them. They urged their way through, the mob parting for them with cheers and shouts as they cried " In the Queen's name ! "

St. Paul's was bathed in the crimson luminance reflected from the top of Barnard's Castle as they tore in from a side-street. They had barely arrived in time. Down Ludgate Hill, the royal procession could be seen advancing slowly through the frenziedly cheering crowds, its great gilded coaches illuminated by the flare of countless torches. Leaping from their smoking horses, they dashed in through the vestry door.

Bull's fellow-musicians protested as he appeared. Those not of the Chapel had been assembled some time. They resented the idea of having to sing music at sight, never seen before. Of the several organists participating many greeted Bull resentfully. After all their preparations, his laxity was likely to render the service a fiasco.

There was no time to argue. The royal procession was mounting the hill from Fleet Street. The Queen was almost at the door. Sullenly the singers took their places and Edmund Hooper, later to be Organist of Westminster Abbey, laid out the music for Bull. Nervously, the choristers gathered as close to him and each other as they could, but he spread them apart. He had commenced a few explanatory words when he was cut short. The clamour had paused outside the cathedral and as he turned to the keyboard, the great doors swung open. Framed against the blaze of a mass of torches and preceded by Yeomen of the Guard, Elizabeth stood in the great open portal. Behind her glittered the richly-clad figures of her Ministers and the Court, against a background of a sea of flame-lit faces and waving arms. Aware of the drama of the moment, the Queen held her pose a breath, then moved slowly forward into the Cathedral. As her feet crossed the threshold Bull's fingers touched the keys and the rich tones of the organ soared up through the building. Bull, inspired by the glory of the moment, was playing the prelude to his anthem.

The rich sonorities filled the cathedral as the Queen moved up the aisle to her place. The congregation already assembled bent in silence as she went by. The magnificence of the Court spread itself into the pews as she reached her seat. Opening up a diapason stop, Bull inclined his head. The voices of the choristers rang out above the throbbing pedal-note. For the first time in history they sang " God Save the Queen."

Strange Progression

CHAPTER V

STRANGE PROGRESSION

THE glory of the victory over the Armada was not only in the actual achievement, but also in its aftermath. The sinister shadow of Spanish menace, which had hung like an evil spell over England so long, had vanished with Philip's mighty fleet. Drake's " sea-hawks " returned, not only as heralds of naval triumph, but as harbingers of spiritual liberation.

The era which followed dawned luminously. The gloom of apprehension dissolved magically before the radiant consciousness of secure freedom. The land grew verdant with fresh impulse and aspiration in every field. It was a springtime of fabulous florescence. Imbued with perennial vitality, its multiple colour remains vivid now, undimmed by the dust of centuries. To Bull it brought a fresh lyric mood, that of Merry England, not merely jocund, but exquisite and at times ecstatic.

It was the hour of the musician. His art permeated every branch of national life. The prosperity which came with victory encouraged fresh independence and imagination in all industries. Music became the expression of the new spirit of labour. As the sea-shanty had regulated work at sea, so air, round and madrigal now accompanied the apprentice at his bench, women at spinning wheels, ploughmen driving their teams, reapers swinging their scythes and milkmaids at their pails. Singing resounded from workshop, foundry and field, as much as from tavern, fair or feast. It was a profuse blossoming of the new springtide of national hope.

Once again Bull's life ran parallel in curve of fortune to that of his country. The new phase of his career corresponded, in freshly expanding brilliance, to that of the national history. England was rapidly becoming acknowledged as the foremost musical country of Europe, now that she was free to spread her riches abroad. Her leading musicians were figures of national pride. They shared the fame of warriors and statesmen. In the new order of things, Bull found himself a hero.

The period brought him immediate honours; but his pride was tempered with pain. In 1590 Blitheman died and Bull was forthwith advanced to his place as organist of the Chapel Royal. The dead man had expressed his desire for such preferment to be given to his pupil as one of his last wishes. There is no doubt, however, that Bull would have received the appointment in any event. His talents justified it and the Queen favoured him. He had also been deputy for Blitheman for some time. Nevertheless, he felt that he had lost, not gained. He was still young enough to feel loneliness at the loss of his boyhood's guide and councillor. The gentle old man had been the closest human being in the world to him, more paternal than his own father. All that he knew and all that he hoped to do, had grown up in his mind tended by Blitheman's care. After he had returned from the funeral service at St. Nicholas Olave, he felt lost, chilledly alone. In his sadness of spirit he wandered into the old man's room. The familiar books and papers lay as he had left them. On the virginals he was touched to see one of his own pieces. Blitheman had held him in thought to the end. The music blurred before his eyes as he looked down at it. A queer little noise, almost seeming something outside himself, sounded in his throat, and for a moment the Queen's Gentleman was a small boy, wistful and bewildered, standing before a grave, quiet man with kindly eyes and a gentle voice, being welcomed to the Chapel, in an awe-inspiring palace in great, clamorous London Town. Then, suddenly, surprizingly, John Bull lurched forward and sank on to his knees, his head on his dead master's seat. For one of the few times in his life he wept uncontrollably.

It was growing dusk before his grief had properly abated. He had neglected his duties and must see if Giles had covered his absence. He took one long look at the room before leaving. The last rays of the sun touched it with a soft light. The presence of the dead man pervaded the place with tenderness. Bull's grief lost its bitterness as the moment gripped him. The gentleness of Blitheman entered into his heart. Forgetful that he was incurring still further reprimand, he seated himself at the virginals and commenced playing softly, as though Blitheman still sat in his high chair by the window. The love in his memory tempered the pathos of his air, giving it gentle beauty—the spirit of Blitheman spoke in it, still aiding his pupil's creation, as he played " John Bull's My Greife."

The new appointment received by Bull was extremely important. It placed him at the head of his profession. So far as musical precedence can be said to have existed, it was the leading post in the country. The Chapel Royal was the most exclusive of all the musical institutions. Its members were, to all intents and purposes, part of the royal household. Their quarters were in the royal palace, and the officials of the Chapel were officers of the court. The Dean, in Catholic times the Royal Confessor, was the Royal Chaplain under Anglican rule. Musicians in the highest cathedral offices throughout the country were honoured to relinquish these to become Gentlemen of the Chapel. Morley, who resigned St. Paul's in such fashion, is one celebrated example; Bull, who proceeded to the Chapel from Hereford Cathedral, is another. The position of Organist and Master of Song to the Chapel Royal made its holder virtually Prime Minister of music. He was the sovereign's advisor on all musical matters. He made the musical nominations to the Chapel. By virtue of his supervision over the entire musical membership of the Chapel, he governed the selection of candidates for inclusion among the Children of the Chapel. As superior to the Master of the Children, he was important in Court drama as well as music, since the Children of the Revels were also an auxiliary organization attached to the Chapel. On all royal and national occasions the Organist and Master of Song to the Chapel Royal was the official musician of the Court. Outside the Chapel itself his word carried great weight. He was consulted regarding appointments to cathedral posts of organist and master of choristers or precentor throughout the country. He could nominate Gentlemen or senior Children for such posts at his discretion, when so consulted, and the high status of the Chapel made institutions elsewhere anxious to have the services of those trained there. It was to this exceptional position as Organist and Master of Song to the Chapel Royal that Bull now succeeded. He was no longer simply " the Queen's favourite musician." He had become the Queen's Master of Musicke.

His appointment was extremely popular, not only with his colleagues, but with the general public also. At the Chapel and among musicians in touch with Court life, he had long been regarded as Blitheman's natural successor. The affinity between Bull and his master was patent to everyone who knew them. Their musical idiom was so closely related that Bull seemed to follow Blitheman by a kind of hereditary right. The elder musician's epitaph in the Church of St. Nicholas Olave, London, conveyed this impression:

> "Whose passing Skill in Musickes art
> A Scholar left behinde,
> *John Bull* by name his Masters veine
> Expressing in eache kinde."

In his own right, as a masterly performer, Bull had an astoundingly high reputation. Most of all, his patriotism was known. He was associated in the public mind with the events of the Armada and shared in the glory of Elizabeth. From the time of the victory he was a recognized national figure and his status was stressed by the public in giving him, whenever possible, the designation which linked his name with that of the Queen, the symbol of the nation.

The period of Bull's musical administration at the Chapel Royal was certainly illustrious. His work branched out into the other arts which glorified the Elizabethan Era. The Children of the Revels, who performed the court drama, came under his organization, being in charge of his Master of the Children. He collaborated with the great dramatist and first Poet Laurate, Ben Jonson, creator of the glamorous Court masques which inspired opera and ballet, and the spirit of the dance animated his music at the time. Celebrated composers such as Giles Farnaby, Ravenscroft and Benjamin Cosyn were his pupils. Some of the most distinguished musical figures of the time served under him. In addition to that "monument of erudition," Nathanael Giles, were his friends, Elway Bevin; William Byrd, himself "a verie maister of Musicke"; and Thomas Morley, the great madrigalist who, in 1590 " playeth upon the organ in poules (St. Paul's)," yet gave up that important post to become a Gentleman of the Chapel in 1592, being " sworne the 24th of July in Mr. Greene's roome."

Other public honours came swiftly and significantly to Bull after the Armada. Cambridge University led the way by conferring the degree of Doctor of Music upon him within a year of the Spanish defeat. He was young for such distinction, though his work for years had been precociously mature. The academic gesture, however, seems to have been made to his national prominence, which the previous Armada year had enhanced. Otherwise, Bull had not recently produced any masterpiece transcending works which he had written earlier and which, therefore, entitled him to the honour before then. He was academically and technically proficient to an unusual degree years before. Cambridge recognized him, not only for his musical genius, but for his patriotism and loyalty. The University had been the staunchest adherent to the new Tudor conception of nationalism and the national form of religion since the reformed faith had first reached England, in the days when Cranmer, Coverdale, Latimer, Cambridge students who had translated the Bible and written the English Prayer Book, had inaugurated the popular movement uniting faith with patriotism and loyalty.

He was still boyish enough to be elated at himself in his new academic robes, though he scarcely confessed this to himself. He felt vastly important the first day he gave a sitting to Childe for the portrait which was to preserve his features for posterity. He took immense care in selecting his best ceremonial ruff for the occasion, giving stringent instructions regarding its laundering. It was a delicate thing of intricate, fragile lace-work and reminded him of some of his own musical arabesques. He was no fop, but he always inclined to touches of drama, which made him essentially part of his time and found him ready for the striking incidents of his life. His sense of humour probably saved him from becoming theatrical. Elizabeth sensed this in him and knew a kindred spirit. This quality established a bond between them which informed and in some strange way subtilized their mutual interest in music.

He went to view the portrait when Childe had completed it. He experienced a queer feeling when he saw it in its frame, with the motto running round its sides so whimsically

The Bull by Force
In Fielde Doth Raigne
But Bull by Skill
Good Will Doth Gayne

Clear though the likeness was, there was a strangeness in the dark, deep-eyed young face, with its intense expression, that gazed out at him from the picture. Its robes and fur stole made it seem even more unfamiliar. It was like meeting someone with whom one had corresponded, yet not seen, or some friend who had held one's confidences, yet had an ambiguous reticence. Transcript of his physical features though it was, limned with all Childe's skill, it had something more, rather than less, of human feeling for him. In those moments Bull first dimly glimpsed himself as the historical figure which he was to become. The bizarre, slightly morbid device which he had instructed Childe to paint into the background—a skull-and-crossbones mounted on a looking-glass, in the true spirit of the age of Shakespeare's wistful clown's songs and the threnodies of Nash—was there to remind of mortality ; but the imaged personality painted before him was something which, like his work, would continue when his bones were dust. He was little more than a youth: his age stood in a corner of the portrait—An Aetatis Svae 27, 1889—but the spirit which looked out of the imaged eyes was ageless, undying through the ages.

Bull's elevation at the Chapel Royal did not bring him much profit. Elizabeth's notorious close-fistedness obsessed her, even in dealing with her favourites. She was generous enough in disposing of preferments when the salaries paid for such posts did not come from her own royal purse; but she allowed her own royal organist and favourite musician, a personality of national fame, to struggle with straightened means, even when dignified with the office of the Queen's Master of Musicke at her Court.

Bull was a younger son. He had no private means. His prestige had been achieved on merit from the start of his musical life in childhood. He was housed and boarded with the other members of the Chapel Royal, in the Palace; but even when he attained the position of Organist and Master of Songe, his salary was miserably inadequate. For his work he received the munificent sum of forty pounds per annum, about the value of two hundred yearly to-day. In spite of his royal position, financial worry haunted him for years. He might have claimed reward for services other than those rendered musically; but here he was of kindred type to Walsingham. Like a number of the devoted patriots of the day, risking all, he received nothing.

He was young, vital and high-spirited, with a taste for gaiety: yet, apart from Court functions, he had little means for amusement. Court life made demands on his very light purse. He had to consider apparel. His royal livery was provided for him, but the Queen's household budget was not extravagant. It had to last him a full year at least, and probably more. Even his musical expenses in the Chapel were subject to supervision, when he had to order books and ruled music-paper from Thomas Este, to whom Byrd had leased part of his printing monopoly.

He had a rich mind, but material wealth was remote. He bore with his situation patiently, but he felt it deeply. There were nights when he sat up late, puzzling how he would meet his small liabilities and procure things he needed. Retrench however much he might, he could not keep pace with the growing difficulties. His personality carried him through the social life of the Court and London; but there were many times when he viewed the magnificence of those around him wistfully, conscious of his own regally maintained shabbiness. Even in the Chapel circles his straightened means embarrassed him. His friend Giles came of a well-to-do Worcester family and had wealthy relations by marriage. He was generous and did his best to enliven Bull's life; but his hospitality could not be accepted unrequited. Bull had to invent excuses to avoid entertainment for which he was eager, but had no means.

Matters reached a head within a year of his eminent Chapel appointment. At the height of the prosperity following the victory over the Armada, in the midst of the brilliant Court of the illustrious Gloriana, Dr. John Bull, the Queen's Master of Musicke was obliged, on April 20th, 1591, to petition for a lease in reversion to the value of thirty pounds per annum " to relieve his greate povertie, which altogether hindereth his studies." In the face of this appeal, knowing Bull's proud nature and what it cost him to make it, the most that Gloriana could spare from her " realme so riche and rayre " was twenty marks.

There were other matters to complicate Bull's life at the

time. The destruction of the Armada had crippled Philip's power to invade England; but marine hostilities continued on the Spanish main. At times these attained considerable dimensions, as in the battle off the Azores, when Lord Thomas Howard attacked the Spanish Plate Fleet and his second-in-command, Sir Richard Grenville, attained undying fame by his heroic death on Drake's old Armada flagship, " The Revenge," fighting overwhelming odds.

At home, Mary Stuart had been executed, but England was not free from plots and sedition yet. When fears of invasion faded, with the defeat of the Armada, fresh political tendencies appeared. Catholics had troubled the Queen's ministers earlier; now the Government had to deal with the Puritan extremists of Protestantism, who were antagonistic to the Anglican Church and opposed to the royal prerogative. The Puritan movement was not yet powerful enough to constitute open danger; but it was working forward steadily and growing rapidly. By 1601 it was to have become powerful enough to attack the Queen openly in Parliament. By 1642 it was to challenge royalty by the Civil War and to dominate the country with the execution of Charles I in 1649.

Already discontent with the royal encroachment on the liberties of the House of Commons and the rights of the people had been voiced energetically in Parliament by Peter Wentworth in 1586, and though that intrepid member went to prison in the Tower, his words exerted wide influence, growing yearly towards open revolt.

The foreign policy of Elizabeth had inevitably involved England in the internal intrigues and conflicts of France. In that country, the successive Valois kings, with their mother, Catharine de Medici, had brought conditions to chaos by their vacillating natures and diseased minds. The splendour of the French Court, with its artistic brilliance and polish, scarcely veiled the misery of the people and the unbridled vice and violence which made it, in Voltaire's image, "a bloody robe of silk and gold." With the assassination of the last Valois, Henry III, the maniac whom d'Aubigné described as "female-king or male-queen," the French crown passed to the Huguenot king of Navarre, who became Henry IV of France in 1589. His accession was challenged immediately by the Guise party, headed by Mayenne and the nobles of the Catholic League. Civil war broke out, complicated by claims of the dukes of Lorraine and Savoy, and Philip of Spain on behalf of his daughter, the Infanta Isabella. The Catholic League suffered disaster at the battle of Ivry in 1590, but the struggle was continued by Spanish invasion, under the Duke of Parma. Protestant England's sympathies were with the Huguenot king, and when Philip advanced his claim, Elizabeth decided to intervene. She dispatched 1,200 soldiers to Henry at Dieppe, with provisions and a promise of 4,000 more men.

In the winter of 1591, Henry's general, Turenne, visited England and obtained further English reinforcements of 7,000 men from Elizabeth. The Queen had the main sympathy of the country behind her; but French Catholic intrigue was busy and Puritan suspicion had been aroused by rumours that Henry IV to secure his throne was contemplating a conversion to Catholicism. This actually took place in 1593. Hence the English Government had to deal with war abroad and currents of political feeling at home. The latter were the more difficult inasmuch as Elizabeth's ministers wished to consolidate the power of the Crown before the Armada enthusiasm waned completely. The Queen therefore needed every possible trustworthy agent.

Walsingham had retired, disgusted by " unkinde dealinge," which rewarded his magnificent work miserably and he died, impoverished through having to pay the debts of his dead son-in-law, Sidney, in 1590. The work of his secret service, however, went on.

Bull's elevation to a more prominent position curtailed, but did not sever, his connection with that organization. Early in April, 1592, he suddenly left London for the West of England, leaving Giles to deputize in his work at the Chapel Royal. The reason given for his absence was that he was urgently called to a sick relation in Somerset. His geography must have been faulty, however, so far as the locality of his relative's residence went; for it was to Bristol, not Peglinch that he travelled. In that port he remained several days, staying, not with his friend Bevin, but with a Bristol resident named Palmer.

The Western seaports at the time were the main maritime centres of the country, with the exception of London and the ports of the Thames estuary. To them came most of the foreign commerce and the first tidings from many parts of the Continent and the New World. Bull found many things in Bristol to interest him.

He took a curiously round-about way to return to London. He rode north through Gloucestershire, passing through the cathedral city, since he visited Elias Smith there. He may have seized the chance to steal a brief holiday, for Elizabeth was exacting with her favourites. A few days along the Severn banks would appeal to him after the enclosed Court and Chapel atmosphere, though where he obtained means for such holidaying, at that time of the year and with his straightened means, is a mystery. In any event, he seems to have intended proceeding to Worcester, probably to visit old friends there, for he took the road to

Tewkesbury, which is on the way to Worcester if one follows the Severn, on leaving Gloucester.

Later that night, as William Phelps, a musician of Tewkesbury, was returning home, he came upon two dismounted men, bending over a recumbent figure by the roadside. At his approach they took to their horses and galloped away furiously. Phelps dismounted and went to assist the prostrate man. It was John Bull, bleeding and bruised and semi-conscious, his clothes torn and ransacked. Phelps conveyed him to his home and tended him until he was able to travel again some days later. He probably conveyed some messages for Bull also, for two days later two foreigners, a Spaniard named Goula, an agent of the Duke of Feria, Spanish Ambassador in France, and Dubois, an adherent of the French League leader, Rose, were arrested while attempting to leave Bristol by sea, Goula resisting and falling into the harbour, where he was drowned.

Meanwhile, Bull left for London, accompanied by Phelps. They proceeded to the Palace, where Bull had audience of the Queen. Of what passed between them nothing is known. Irritable and domineering though Elizabeth was, she apparently took her Master of Musicke's absence for granted, and rewarded the musician who had aided him in a remarkable manner. The Cheque Book of the Chapel Royal contains the following entry, for the 29th of May, 1592:

"William Phelps of Tewksbury, in the Countye of Gloster, trayned up in the noble science of musick, for his care (and) kindness to Mr. Bull, organiste in her sayd Majestes Chappell, was in gratification thereof admitted by our generall consent (*quantum in nobis est*) by corporall othe," this cryptic statement being supplemented by a note that the appointment as "Gentleman Extraordinary" was bestowed on Phelps because "He dyd show a moste rare kyndnes to Mr. Doctor Bull in his greate distresse, being robbed in those parts." The Tewkesbury musician, of no particular eminence in his profession, therefore received an honour prized by the most eminent musicians, for which a number waited many years, for his purely personal service to the organist of the Chapel. Still more notably, the general assembly of the Gentlemen of the Chapel Royal, who made heavy stipulations in the case of the admittance of a musician as eminent as Bevin, immediately and unanimously gave their approval to Phelps, without any stipulation whatsoever.

The whole affair remains one of the most curious among a number of mysterious events in Bull's life. Linked to his activities with Walsingham, however, it becomes a little clearer. Seen in such light, it appears that Bull's visit to the West was more than his own private business. The stay at Bristol and the journey through Gloucestershire become significant if the nature of the seaport and the fact that Walsingham had established agents all over the country are realized. His own earlier connection with the West made such a journey plausible, though it was scarcely the time of the year for country visits of a social kind. On all the evidence, Bull appears to have been carrying out royal orders. In Bristol he had secret information to receive or obtain, or observations to make, and his Gloucestershire tour was made to carry communications to royal agents there. What he had to communicate to Elizabeth on his return remains, naturally, unknown; but it was of sufficient importance for her to receive him immediately upon his return, while his rescuer was considered to have done a service worthy of the high honour bestowed by the Chapel, but obviously in conformity with the command of the Queen.

Such incidents tempered the humiliations of Bull's economic difficulties. They recompensed him for much that he suffered through his devotion. They made him aware of the honour in which he was held by his fellow-musicians and the public of his time. Above all, they showed him how high he stood in the affections and favour of the Queen whom he regarded, in spite of the faults which close contact with her revealed, as the greatest and most typically English figure of her age. Elizabeth, indeed, was quite emphatic in demonstrating her partiality for him, on at least one occasion waving aside legal forms with the most drastic autocracy in his favour. She could not conquer her avarice or parsimony, though, like most of such nature, she had moments of absurd extravagance, which may even have come from some desperate attempt to overcome her obsessions. In more personal ways, however, she never lost the power of doing charming and gracious acts or making generous gestures, especially if these could be invested with the drama which her histrionic temperament relished.

There were occasions, however, notwithstanding her regard for him, when Bull, like all of Elizabeth's favourites, incurred her displeasure. It was her difficulty that, while she possessed an egotistical and domineering nature, she nevertheless had the intelligence and sense to demand character in those about her. Hence clashes were inevitable, as shown in her relations with Drake, Walsingham, Burghley, Leicester, Raleigh and Essex. For Bull, with his natural waywardness, his position with regard to the Queen was precarious at times. He was fortunate in possessing his sense of humour, since Elizabeth was strongly endowed with the same quality, of a kind bearing close affinity to his own. This enabled Bull, at the start of his Court life, to turn his blundering entry to advantage, by use of his wits. There were moments less easy and some could be dangerous. Elizabeth was ruthless when disappointed or angered, as the tragic fate of Essex showed.

Röntgen, who was imbued with the spirit of the age of Jan Sweelinck, Bull's Dutch contemporary and friend, and who regarded Bull almost as a compatriot, owing to the profound effect of his work on the Netherlands, preserved one story of a time when the Queen's wrath made the position of her Master of Musicke hazardous. Bull, having a difference with one of the gentlemen of the Court, grew heated. The courtier adopted a supercilious attitude, which incensed the musician. From harsh words matters developed to blows and eventually weapons were drawn. In the fray Bull received a scratch before the Queen's guards arrived to intervene. Right or wrong, the matter was serious for him: the Queen took an extremely stern view of brawling in the palace and his crime exposed him to severe penalties. Elizabeth was determined that her Court should not degenerate into the state of that under the Valois in France, when "the evenings were filled with fêtes and balls; the mornings with duels and murderous encounters when, indeed, the duel was not anticipated by a treacherous assassination." That Bull's escapade was the result of a quick-tempered anger was not likely to save him. According to the ideas of the times, he had not transgressed against society, but only against an express order of the Queen. There was nothing extraordinary in a musician coming to sword-play; Bull's own friend, Ben Jonson, spent some time in prison later, having killed a fellow-dramatist, Christopher Marlowe, in a duel.

Brought before the Queen, Bull tried to excuse himself, but Elizabeth was in a very evil humour. Rounding on him, she told him that his business was to play music, not to play with words. Bull, always quick, seized the chance her words gave him. He asked her permission to excuse himself in music, since, if he played when he spoke, he might speak better if he played. Elizabeth, always ready to recognize a quick wit or a *bon mot*, assented. Bull, seating himself at the virginals gave her a musical character-study of his own waywardness and grotesquery, grimacing meanwhile, partly to cover the pain of his pricked wrist and partly to placate her by affording her amusement. The Queen was unable to control her laughter at his antics and at the whimsical music which the world was to know later as " Dr. Bull's Myselfe." Bull received his pardon.

It was probably then that Elizabeth made her sardonic remark, " Of all the bulls that live, this hath the greatest asses eares," though this is attributed to her at the time when she was annoyed by Bull's protracted absence abroad later, and jealous of the stories which reached her, telling of his flattering treatment at foreign courts. The story of this burlesque performance is reflected in a contemporary passage of a student of Saviola, the famous *maître d'armes* where, pleading for princes to be tolerant in " honorabell quarrells," he reminds them that not all can " purchase their lyves " by " clowneinge their nature in musicke," after the manner of "the queenes musician, as it is sayd." The reference to Bull seems clear, for no other capable of musical parody or self-caricature existed.

The shadow of such displeasure rarely fell upon him. Elizabeth had a genuinely warm personal regard for him. She also knew, with her own excellent musical talent, that he possessed the higher quality of genius and that his growing fame added a distinctive lustre to the brilliance of the Court which provided her own setting.

That lustre was increasing. In 1592 Oxford, somewhat tardily, followed the example of Cambridge and conferred the degree of Doctor of Music upon him. A high honour at any time, in Bull's case it was peculiarly significant. As so often in his life, mysterious under-currents ran beneath the surface appearances of the matter.

The record in " Fasti Oxonienses " reads curiously, as entered by Anthony à Wood :

" 1592 :   " *Incorporations*

" John Bull, Doct. of Musicke of the said Univ. of Cambridge, and one of the Gentlemen of her Maj. chappel, was incorporated the same day, Jul. 7 This is the famous Person who was admitted Bach. of Musick of this University, *an* 1586, as I have told you under that year, and would have proceeded in the same place, had he not met with clownes and rigid Puritans there that could not endure Church musick."

The explanation given for the delay would have amused Bull, could he have read it. At the time he was absorbed in composing light-hearted, picturesque dances on popular forms. His work at the Chapel Royal naturally demanded that he should give some attention to ecclesiastical music ; but he was certainly not a typical Church musician then, or at any time in his life. The only time when he might reasonably have been regarded as an ecclesiastical musician was precisely that at which he had been admitted Bachelor of Music by the very university which the records allege to have withheld the higher degree from him a very few years later, because of prejudice against Church music. When Bull received his baccalaureate from Oxford, he was publicly known only as the ex-organist of Hereford Cathedral and a Gentleman of the Chapel Royal, though his extraordinary gifts as a virginalist were beginning to be recognized.

Between 1586 and 1592, the conditions of the musical world had changed considerably. The range of secular music had been greatly extended by the popular interest in the arts which awoke after the defeat of the Armada, when the country found itself free to follow peaceful pursuits. Its secular development had been markedly accelerated by the increase and spread of printed music, which had encouraged domestic performance on a higher level of culture. The growing popular interest in the theatre had also done much to stimulate secular song and dance. Bull, by his keen interest in popular life and by the rational and humane trend of his mind, had already developed musical traits which were making his mark in the new secular field, in which future generations were to recognize him as typical of his epoch.

Cambridge had honoured him the very year when he would have proceeded at Oxford, in the ordinary course of events. He was aware that this militated against him, owing to the strong rivalry existent between the two universities; but he was also conscious that such feeling went beyond any simple academic considerations. Nobody was in a position to know better than he that the antipathy between the two centres of learning at the time was mainly political. Cambridge was strongly loyalist. It reflected the influence of Archbishop Whitgift, previously Master of Trinity College there and now Primate of all England, and Queen Elizabeth's favourite prelate. Under his rule the Anglican Church had become more closely identified with the Crown than ever before.

DR. JOHN BULL

At Oxford, Anglicanism was strongly criticized. Cranmer, prime sponsor of the Anglican dogma of the royal prerogative, had been the chief influence at Cambridge before Whitgift. Most of his opponents had come from Oxford. Even before Puritanism had transformed its trend, Oxford had differed strongly from Cambridge. It had been closer to the Counter-Reformation of the Catholic Church, pioneered by John Colet, than to the Lutheranism which had so strongly influenced Cranmer, Coverdale, Latimer and Tyndale when students at Cambridge, to the extent that their meeting-place, the White Horse Inn, became known as "Little Germany," though it was the birthplace of the essentially English ideas which produced the Book of Common Prayer and the Tudor Bible. It was not until the next century that Oxford became the Royalist Cavalier stronghold. Catholic influences had persisted there until the early part of Elizabeth's reign, causing Walsingham to found a Protestant lectureship there for John Reynolds, to counteract them. The great Secretary's protégé had taken a course which his patron could not have anticipated. He had headed a Puritan movement strongly anti-regal, the seed of the Parliamentary protests against Elizabeth in 1601 and of the rebellion under Cromwell a few decades later.

Bull, therefore, knew that his position at Court and his enjoyment of royal favour made him antipathetic at Oxford. In such connection, also, he must at times have suspected that his political activities were sensed, if not known there, and as Puritanism was under strong surveillance at the time, this would tend to increase feeling against him.

His incorporation was therefore a singular tribute to his prestige. He could not help recognizing his triumph. In spite of opposition so pronounced that the university's chronicler makes special comment upon it in the records, the degree of Doctor of Music had actually been conferred by Oxford. The receipt of an additional degree, in view of his professional reputation, would not have been arresting, no matter how it redounded to his credit or testified to his scholarly attainments. What made it important for him—as it was to be in the light of historical retrospect—was that it should come just at that time and after such hindrance. It demonstrated to him the status which he had attained. Above all, it reinforced his resolution by the knowledge of the weight of public opinion behind him. It spurred him on to the fight which he was soon to wage for a native culture, from which he was to emerge so victoriously.

A Turn of Speech

CHAPTER VI

A TURN OF SPEECH

IN his greatest elation over his academic success, Bull had nevertheless never anticipated the effect which it had upon the general public. There was some reason for this, so far as cultured circles went. It was certainly an unusual distinction at that time to receive so high a degree from both Oxford and Cambridge, especially in view of his years. It was extremely high testimony to his talents and learning, in an age when both were highly appreciated. This, however, scarcely accounted for the wide-spread deference which was shown by the average public to his dual title, or for the consistence with which it was popularly applied to him. Others received musical doctorates in his time; but he remained almost exclusively alone in having his degree prefixed to his name by the public henceforth.

There was more than public respect in this; his designation was invested with a palpable popular admiration and affection. It featured him as a national figure, in a remarkable way. Academic distinction does not usually produce the reputation which creates national heroes. Scholarship seldom excites popular enthusiasm, least of all in the scholar's own lifetime. The masses are impressed by more sensational features. The study may produce the visions from which future civilizations arise, or the thoughts which create the mind of posterity; but it has not the dazzling glamour of courts, national assemblies, battlefields and other spectacular scenes of public life, for the public of its own day.

The artistic florescence of the period was now solidifying into a new civic pomp. The new culture had brought with it a growing sense of importance to the rising middle-class. They aspired to place their mark on the nation's buildings. Where the earlier aristocracy had erected their palaces, the great merchants now built, not only their magnificent mansions, but also centres of learning, in order that their endowments should preserve their names for posterity.

Such endowments were sometimes made during the lives of these magnates, sometimes by way of bequests in their wills. One of the most famous of the latter was that of Sir Thomas Gresham, an outstanding figure in the financial world of the Elizabethan Era. It was to prove a momentous factor, not only in Bull's life, but in the significance which he was to assume in British history.

Gresham was much more than an average talented business man. He was a notable thinker and personality in several fields, with highly cultivated tastes and a mind which worked along lines of originality and initiative. A leading figure of the Goldsmiths' Company, at the heart of England's expanding commercial enterprise in Lombard Street, he was also a merchant, a banker, the financial agent of Elizabeth's government abroad, especially in Antwerp, the money centre of Europe, and an economist. He led the fight against base coinage, being the first to formulate the principle that bad money drives good money out of circulation through the public's hoarding of the good money, overrated at a premium value and its use of the baser money, which is cheaper and underrated, or at a discount. Gresham's discovery of this acted strongly to put an end to the previous practice of many governments, whereby currency had been debased by a cheating method which reduced the amount of pure gold or silver in the coinage through adding more copper or other alloys. It became established under the name of " Gresham's Law."

Gresham belonged essentially to the era of new thought and reform. He established the Stock Exchange to regulate business transactions, and he was a keen supporter and patron of learning and the arts, being a student of astronomy and mathematics and a capable musical amateur. A man of pronounced views and dominating personality, he saw that a closer relationship between commercial thought and the higher branches of learning was necessary if England was to evolve a culture with conscious national mentality behind it. To this end he determined to provide London with a scholarly centre where such learning might be disseminated directly among her citizens. A widely travelled man, whose financial transactions and political activities took him constantly, abroad to the great Continental centres of commerce, he gave keen attention to institutions such as the Collège de France and the *università popolare*, or free academies, of Italy. He determined to model his London college along similar lines, bequeathing his own private mansion for such purpose.

Gresham's home was a princely estate on Broad Street, the grounds of which extended to Bishopsgate. It was famous for the magnificent functions which its owner held there, at which royalty was a frequent guest. In the heart of the city, within close touch with the municipal headquarters, the Guildhall, it would be a truly civic centre, perpetuating his name where his major lifework had been carried out.

A close friendship between himself and John Wilbye, one of the most celebrated musicians of his day, who lived nearly opposite Gresham in Broad Street, was a determinate factor in this decision. The two friends spent evenings together as frequently as Gresham could obtain leisure from his journeys and functions, and it was the great financier's delight to try out some new catch or madrigal written by his friend when " supper beinge ended, and musicke bookes, according to the custome, beinge broughte to the table," the gathering entertained itself with singing.

The terms of Gresham's munificent bequest became public on his death in 1579. It then became clear that music held a high place in the plan of organization which he had prepared for the college which was to bear his name. Lectureships in seven faculties were provided for, which the testator listed in the following order: Divinity (he being strongly religious); Astronomy (of which he was an earnest student); Music (honoured by the third place on the list); Geometry; Law; Physic and Rhetoric. For accommodation, the will directed that the seven professors appointed " Shall have the occupation of all my mansion, house, gardens and so forth, for them and every one of them, there to inhabit, study and daily to reade the severall lectures."

Such positions were alluring, even to the most eminent men in the various faculties. The salary for the music professorship transcended that paid by the Queen to her Organist at the Chapel Royal. The royal appointment was worth £40 per annum; that at Gresham College carried an annual salary of £50, equivalent, in worth at the time, to £250 to-day, a high remuneration as such matters were regarded then. There was great attraction in the prospect of dwelling in Gresham's splendid mansion and studying there and the duties were not onerous. The field was slightly limited, so far as candidature went, since it was stipulated that the lecturers, like Fellows of a university, must be bachelors and that they could not retain their positions if they married. There were a number of talented and celebrated young musicians who were eager for such a post, especially at a period when the Virgin Queen showed little interest in rising genius which was married and frowned on all attachments of the heart except those which centred on herself.

There was time enough for selection. The Mayor and Aldermen of the City of London, who were the public executors of Gresham's will, had nearly two decades to wait before its terms could be carried out. Gresham had expressedly stipulated that the College should not be founded until the demise of his widow, who should be left in enjoyment of his estate for her life. Lady Gresham did not die until 1596.

Meanwhile, the executors found themselves faced with difficulties in the provision of professors, in spite of the many eager for selection. For such an institution, which, by its nature, was a matter of civic pride, well-known personages of high academic prestige were desired. Invitations for candidature were extended to Oxford and Cambridge, but the two older centres of learning looked with suspicion upon an institution of such unusual character and with such relationship to mundane affairs. There was also some probable jealousy concerning their own prestige in the matter. In any event, whether through official channels or simply through the currents of local university prejudice, candidates were not forthcoming from Oxford or Cambridge, so far as persons of sufficient status were concerned. The executors decided to seek elsewhere.

The task of filling the music professorship was less academically circumscribed than that of appointing the holders of the posts in some of the other faculties. Music was a junior faculty in scholarly chronology. Nevertheless, the importance of Gresham's bequest rendered the position an eminent one and the status of the college and its connection with civic authority demanded that the holder should be eminent.

The obvious thing to do was to review those already in prominent musical positions, especially those of official kind. Thomas Tallis and William Blitheman were dead. William Byrd was not eligible, being married. There was no other figure in the musical world so eminent or publicly renowned as the Organist of the Chapel Royal, the Queen's Master of Musicke, a doctor of the two leading Universities of the country, the most famous performer and the most popular musical figure of his day. John Bull was the man for the post.

He had not lacked sponsors for his nomination. Every magnate in the city, interested in the growing movement for civic culture and anxious for the prestige of the new college, was eager to have the lustre of his name. Added to his intrinsic merits, he was the acknowledged favourite of the Queen, which ensured the royal interest in the city fathers' new centre of learning if he were installed.

Bull awaited the outcome of his nomination eagerly. He knew the importance of the position, not only so far as public prestige went, since Gresham's bequest had aroused wide popular attention, but also with regard to the potential influence which it would enable him to exercise. Thus far he had expressed himself as composer and performer; at Gresham College he would have the chance to put forward his ideas on the aims and æsthetics of music as a national art. He was not uninterested in the material advantages of the position also. The salary would relieve him of his constant worry and, added to his Chapel Royal stipend, provide him with the means for much that he had hitherto been obliged to forego. In the stately surroundings of the Gresham estate he would have the ease and atmosphere conducive to composition. In every way, it was a pleasing prospect.

He was therefore excited when he received a summons to the Guildhall. The Aldermen wished to confer with him concerning the appointment. Giles and Morley were delighted; they were convinced that this denoted his success. Bull, indeed, was touched by the general generous pleasure with which his news was received by all his colleagues. It was in a mood of high elation that he left for the Guildhall.

The City enhanced his mood as he traversed it. It always fascinated him after the Palace, with its ceremonious order. There was such unending variety in it. So many unexpected features were to be encountered, no matter how frequently he passed through it, or how familiar he thought himself to be with various localities. He felt a spirit of adventure in every excursion into it.

Even where it was well-known to him, its picturesqueness and busy life stirred him. Its scene was so strongly contrasted to the formal vistas to which the Palace accustomed him. The forces at work in it were, to him, as dramatic as any stage spectacle. He felt the solid power symbolized by the high, bare warehouses and spacious granaries, the variety of goods displayed in the big booths, and the even more mysterious wares filling the great cellars with their churchlike vaultings, which flanked the narrow, winding streets. He delighted in the streets themselves, each with its vivid, strong-featured identity. They were infused with the essence of the life of the people to which he always felt

DR. JOHN BULL

so strongly drawn. Passing through them, he renewed something of the unforgettable first childish delight which he had felt in the wonders of London as he was carried into its whirl from the country quiet of Somerset. The streets, as he came to each, unfolded the story of the everyday existence of England's capital. They symbolized the body and spirit of the new country of boundless commerce and enterprise which the Tudor vision had created. Here was Milk-street, with its dairymen's yards, its great buckets filled with creamy fluid, its wooden crates massed with the ovals of brown and white eggs. There was Bread-street, with its appetizing odour of baking borne out into the thoroughfare from scores of great ovens, the glow of which made the flour-whitened bakers fantastic. Others were strangely eerie and grotesque, half-ghost, half-clown, as their faces and forms showed at windows and doors, or emerged into the roadway, itself dusted with a grey-white powder, like phantom snow. Down Cheapside was Cornhill, nearby, where the great granaries vended the flour and the fodder for the horses of the noble and wealthy. All around Bishopsgate were the great, clamour-filled markets which supplied London's sustenance, a kaleidoscope of variegated hues, meats, vegetables and fruits. Threadneedle Street showed him the tailors' quarters, with cross-legged figures, plying swift needles among a medley of coloured cloths and fabrics, laces and gold thread. Almost within stone's throw of the new Gresham College itself were the streets of the goldsmiths and bankers, Throgmorton Street and Lombard Street, where armed guards conveyed the great bars of bullion, and the clerks of the Companies bore in and out heavy bags in which heaped coins jingled, among the heavily-barred buildings where the riches of East and West were stored.

A TURN OF SPEECH

The exuberance of life along his route had infused him by the time he turned into the courtyard of the Guildhall. The stately building, with its pointed steeple and pinnacled entrance, was a fitting scene for his entry into the life of civic culture. He tried to subdue his elation to a becoming dignity before making his business known to the solemn, pompous doorkeeper.

An even more imposing, liveried usher conducted him to the high-windowed Council Hall. He felt so gay that he had difficulty not to greet the massive figures of Gog and Magog in the great Entrance Hall as he went by them.

He was cordially received by the Mayor and Aldermen, seated in their robes and chains at the tables set round the Council Hall under the high-vaulted arches either side of the broad central aisle. He was informed that his nomination had met with general approval and that it was now their business to interrogate him formally and to read to him the conditions governing the tenure of the office for which he had been selected.

Bull listened quietly, replying to such questions as were put to him to the apparent satisfaction of the questioners. A clerk then commenced to read the terms of tenure as defined in Sir Thomas Gresham's will. He read sonorously, and the formal phrases carried no particular significance to Bull as he listened until the paragraph concerning the duties of the proposed music professor was reached. Then his mind became suddenly alert. He had remembered, from previous perusal of the published will, one clause which had disturbed him at the time. Then he had forgotten it until this moment.

The clerk's voice intoned unhaltingly:

" The solemn Musicke lecture to be read twice every weeke, in manner followinge, *viz*., the theorique part for one half houre, or thereabouts, and the practique, by consort of voice or instruments for the reste of the houre; whereof the first lecture to be in the Latine tongue and the seconde in the English."

The last phrase impinged sharply upon his mind, with a significance which his walk through the teeming English life of the City emphasized. Gresham had died before the Elizabethan Renascence had truly begun; but the tenour of his will showed that he had foreseen it. He was, however, a scholar of the old school; but surely he would not have maintained that clause had he died more recently?

The reader proceeded monotonously with his booming monologue. Bull's mind was filled with strife. So much depended upon his obtaining this post; yet should he sacrifice his ideals to gain it? By the time the reading was ended, his mind was made up. He had to stand for his principles. Now, or never, might he strike a blow for the patriotic conception of his native tongue for which Cheke and Ascham had laboured so devotedly and sacrificed so much. Now, if he could carry his point, his beloved native speech might receive its due in the teaching which formed the thought of the country. Where Chaucer had led in literature, Cranmer and Coverley in religion, he must follow. He would deal in none of the " inkhorn terms " satirized by Ascham. He remembered Cheke's words: " Our own tongue should be written clean and pure, unmixed and unmangled with the borrowing of other tongues; ever borrowing and never paying, she shall be fain to keep her home as bankrupt."

The Aldermen turned to Bull as the clerk resumed his seat. One or two smiled or nodded slightly; the manner of all was genial or urbane. It was a moment for polite gestures; the result was a foregone conclusion. Only the

A TURN OF SPEECH

final formality remained to be carried out. With dignified courtesy the Lord Mayor enquired whether everything was clear to Dr. Bull. With a significant emphasis probably only apparent to himself, Bull replied that it was. Again a slight ripple of urbane satisfaction passed over the assembly. The matter had gone quite satisfactorily, in spite of the whispers which had reached them that the new professor had the difficult whimsies of his artistic kind. The Mayor sat back with a sigh of satisfaction, rubbing his hands slowly together. He took it, he said, that Dr. Bull was prepared to accept office on the conditions stipulated. Everyone was assured that Bull's reply would be affirmative; some had already half-risen, prepared to reach for their caps and cloaks, since time was drawing on to the mid-day repast. Then, suddenly and unexpectedly, Bull loosed his shaft. All conditions were satisfactory—excepting one. He was unable to lecture in Latin.

The hitch in their plans was terribly disconcerting to the City Fathers. With expressions bordering on consternation, they turned back to him again, one or two who had partly risen resuming their seats heavily. It was incomprehensible. Dr. Bull had attended the Gramere Schole of the Chapel Royal, where Latin was taught regularly. He was a high graduate of the country's two leading universities. Surely he must be conversant with the classical tongue of all learned scholarship? The difficulty must be due to his diffidence; matters had gone so well, they must not be marred now. In every other way, Dr. Bull was obviously the right person for the post. His appointment had been so openly hinted at and rumoured, that it virtually amounted to his having been publicly announced as appointed. It would have an annoying public effect if such announcement were contradicted now. It had seemed so assured that he would be installed, that the worthy Aldermen had not troubled to seek possible substitutes. The delay involved in this would certainly bring public censure upon them. The will had already waited a decade and more to be carried into execution, during Lady Gresham's lifetime. The public was eager for its materialization now. A further delay would cause them to murmur. London was already proud of the prospect of having its own College; and the City Fathers hoped to gain glory themselves by the inauguration proceeding smoothly and impressively.

Their chagrin grew as various members of the Council advanced these matters to Dr. Bull. The matter became more embarrassing with every fresh sentence. If another had to be substituted for the Queen's Master of Musicke, that would also be deplorable for them. The Queen's Maiestie had been informed, unofficially, of the Council's choice and had intimated her gracious approval. It had been hoped that her Grace would make the inauguration illustrious by her august Presence. This, assuredly, would not be so if her own Royal Organist and favourite musician had to be passed over for another less eminent.

Bull listened, answering all arguments quietly and courteously, no matter how crotchety disappointment and vexation made the various Aldermen. He fenced with the question as adroitly as possible; he knew that it would be futile to advance his real reason. Latin was the conventionally established speech for all learning, and these worthy burghers, who would every one have laid down his life for England, were nevertheless too much the creatures of habit in thought and too subservient to accepted ideas, for him to plead openly that English should be used in his lecturing on patriotic grounds.

Nevertheless, some hint of an undercurrent in his thinking

must have come to the others. Some of their queries pressed him to say whether or no he had any other reason other than his alleged inability to lecture in Latin. Bull withheld his main thoughts; but, as the discussion continued, it was plain that one or two realized that the question was more significant than appeared on the surface. The movement for the purification of English from foreign mannerisms and its more extended use in various fields had not died with Cheke. Queen Elizabeth's own tutor, Ascham, though he had been hindered in obtaining a Fellowship at Cambridge because of his attacks on Latin, had not relinquished the fight all his life, and his ideals persisted and were supported by many. Little by little, with quick glances and raised eyebrows, pursed lips and slight headshakes, the general impression spread. Dr. Bull, true to his obstinate nature, was pursuing some plan to force the authorities of Gresham to set aside Latin and take the revolutionary step of introducing English into the " solemn lectures."

There were many who sympathized. Some of the Aldermen had made their way in the world from small beginnings, and had little, if any Latin, themselves. The classic speech had unpleasant Catholic associations for the more extreme Protestants. Others, however, mainly those with the least education, could not shake off the reverence for the classic tongue implanted by centuries of tradition and convention. Above all, it was difficult to see how they could act, as official executors of Gresham's will, in open contravention of one of its explicit clauses. Perplexity and indecision grew, augmented by these conflicting impulses. Eventually, it was decided to adjourn the meeting, meanwhile seeking some way to resolve the question.

The sense of elation, even in the face of what he felt to be a voluntary abnegation of a position which would have solved most of his material difficulties, had maintained itself in Bull during the discussion. He had the feeling of waging a good fight for an ideal. As he left the Guildhall it slipped from him suddenly and he felt drab and tired. He took the most direct route back to the Palace; he did not wish to encounter the vistas which had seemed to be so full of joy and vitality earlier.

It was a typical London November afternoon when he emerged. The morning sun had gone, and, early afternoon though it was, there was a thick mist rising from the river, and little more than twilight in the streets. The lanterns, which had already been ignited by the City watchmen, were blurred and dispersed through the dank obscurity, providing no real illumination. Eager though he was to reach his quarters, there was not a hackney-horse or conveyance to be seen, for hire. Halfway back, a drizzling rain commenced to fall. He was soaked in person, as well as damped in spirits, when he eventually reached the Palace.

Giles was waiting for him with Morley; both were eager for his report. They showed consternation at Bull's account of happenings at the Guildhall. Morley was a sensitive musician; but he was more scholar than fighter, though his pen was trenchant. Giles' patriotism was beyond question; but it was of obvious kind, which did not concern itself too much with subtleties. The Worcester musician had a good mind and a sensitivity which expressed itself in his music and his human relationships, as in his taste for literature and poetry. He was no bookworm, however; his convivial reputation testified to his social activity and robust enjoyment of mundane pleasures. His learning was tempered by a native West Country wit, which made him refuse to be drawn into any kind of controversy which might assume a religious or political aspect. His concern for Bull was therefore wholly without bias. He was simply troubled that anything should have arisen which might cost his friend the position which he would grace so well and which would relieve his mind of financial worry. With forthright commonsense, he endeavoured to persuade Bull to temporize, to reconsider his attitude and the whole question. It was useless. The growing gloom of his spirit made the Queen's Master obstinate, in one of his rare black moods.

Bull's abstraction and moodiness, continuing for several days, would have revealed to the Queen that something was wrong, in any event. Elizabeth, by the next morning, however, was already acquainted with the situation. She had instituted enquiries as to how matters had fared with her favourite, and was astounded to hear of what had transpired. She was perfectly aware that something more obscure lay behind Bull's behaviour. Among her many accomplishments, as poet, musician, dancer, horsewoman and shot, she was also a good linguist with a classical education, who visited Oxford and "delivered a Latin oration that astounded the dons." Bull's objection to lecturing in the classic tongue was therefore incomprehensible to her. She even doubted if he was as ignorant of it as he would pretend. She felt that the excuse which he had put forward concerning the Gresham will was a subterfuge. She determined to get at his real reason.

With typical Tudor finesse, she put the matter off until after the practice, that Bull's mood might be lightened by the influence of the music and by one of their discussions of common musical interest. Just as she was closing her music book, she rounded on him suddenly, asking him point-blank what game he was playing with Gresham College. Her tone stung Bull, evoking his eloquence to expound his ideals. The arts of poetry and music shared the same essence. English speech and song were related as are flower and scent; the sweetest of the one came alone from the other. Was not the language of Chaucer and Shakespeare pure enough, rich enough, noble enough to impart the highest learning in any English academy? Elizabeth was fired by his patriotic enthusiasm; but she was sufficiently a pedant and proud of her own classical proficiency to demur against everyday English superseding the speech of the immortal ancients.

Bull fired up again, using that astounding familiarity which frequently occurred in Elizabeth's discussions with her favourites. Did the Queen's Majesty desire to rule a vital kingdom of renewed vigour and youth or to vie with Persephone—who was, of course, an esteemed classical figure—in reigning over the dead? Were not the treasures of the New World more than the dry bones of the Old World's antiquity? How would the Queen's Grace's Majesty have her best subjects' brains keep in touch with the mass of her people, if the native tongue were not employed to convey the higher kinds of thought to them? Elizabeth was overwhelmed by the torrent of his vehemence; but she was still not wholly convinced. She sought refuge in pointing out that the matter was a legal, not an idealistic one. In law, the terms of Sir Thomas Gresham's will made a stipulation which could not be set aside for any personal reasons or theories. The law must be kept.

The word gave Bull his cue. Who had been the greatest law-breakers in the Queen's Majesty's kingdom, to the heinous extremes of treason, but the lovers of Latin, scheming for Mary Stuart? Who had aided them, with murderous plots against her Grace's own life for years together, but his most Catholic Majesty of Spain? What was the tongue that linked these enemies together, enabled them to feel a common identity, if it was not Latin? Aroused to one of his dramatic moods, he elaborated the picture. He presented the classic speech as a living danger in the realm, no matter how much a dead language it might be.

It had been a cunning move; it affected Elizabeth as nothing else could have done. She sat there, with something unearthly in her pointed, aristocratic features framed by her wide high-standing lace collar, against the dark tapestries, a touch of menace growing in her expression as Bull painted the dark hues of his theme. Only perplexity as to how to evade the Gresham clause prevented her immediate decision in his favour. She indicated this to Bull.

Again he found his cue. The Queen's Majesty was the law; it was for the sovereign to will and for the people to act as she willed. Elizabeth realized how she could gain the end which she now desired as strongly as he did, without assuming the open responsibility herself. Her eyes twinkled at her thoughts and a slow smile broke over her features as she caught Bull's answering glance. She said that what was possible should be done and dismissed him. He heard her call for ink, quills, paper and sand as he passed out. His smile to himself curiously resembled that of the Queen's Majesty.

Meanwhile, in the room behind him, Queen Elizabeth spread out the parchment on the table before her and selected a quill. With meticulous precision, yet in energetically flowing scrolls and curves, she wrote.

" Righte trustie and welbeloued Maister Lord Maier and Aldermen of our Citie of London, we greete you well . . ." From time to time she broke off, to straighten up and sit back in her high chair, regarding her script at arm's length. Finally she ended—" And this our lettre shalbe our Royall testimonie and your sufficient warrant and discharge in this behalfe. Giuen under our signet at our mannor of Greenewiche, the thirtieth daie of Nov. 1596."

If Bull pondered the Queen's possible course, he had not long to verify his conjectures. By noon the following day, a messenger arrived hastily from the Guildhall. The Mayor and Council prayed Dr. Bull attend their extraordinary meeting with all speed. The urgency of the message showed Bull that there was something unusual afoot. He was fortunately free for the afternoon. He mounted the horse that had been sent on the bridle for him and set out for the Guildhall forthwith.

He was again ushered into the Council Hall, where the assembled Aldermen sat much as on the day before. Now, however, there was little urbane courtesy, much less geniality. Several of the City Fathers regarded him with expressions ranging from mild vexation, through frowning annoyance, to sullen anger. Bull made no sign that he recognized anything different. He bowed and waited to hear what they had to say.

In spite of appearances, the Lord Mayor's opening words were ingratiating enough. The Council had summoned Dr. Bull to ask if he could suggest any way in which the contravention of the clause in the Gresham Bequest could be excused, were he appointed professor. Bull wondered what had happened. He had taken it for granted that the meeting of the day before had decided his fate adversely. It was obvious that the Council were not acting of their own volition.

He assured the assembly that he had no ideas on the subject whatsoever and asked their further views. None were forthcoming. Gloom and silence settled momentarily on the meeting. Bull broke it by expressing his regret that he had occasioned so much worry, suggesting that the best solution might be to veto his nomination. The Aldermen

A TURN OF SPEECH

glanced at each other uncomfortably; one or two seemed to suspect him of jesting or irony, by their suspicious looks. When, annoyed, he declared that he himself would withdraw, there was a startling change. The most ingratiating expressions appeared on all but two faces, and most honeyed tones answered him deprecatingly. Would the Queen's Maiestie, he was asked, permit him to withdraw? It dawned upon him that Elizabeth had already intervened.

Without revealing his ignorance of what the Queen had done he managed to elicit what had happened. Elizabeth had written a personal letter, recommending him for the Gresham post.

The Queen had been careful not to make her communication a command. She wished the Mayor and Aldermen, not herself, to be those who actually abrogated the clause of Gresham's will. The sovereign must not oppose her will to the law. The Council saw plainly the position into which they had been thrust; for, although her letter was not in form a command, in practical effect it amounted to one. They were in a dilemma. Either they must risk ignoring the Queen's recommendation, which popular feeling for Bull would support; or they must follow the royal wishes and so set the legal force of Gresham's will at defiance.

Bull sympathized with them; but it was also impossible for him now to withdraw, in view of the Queen's act. There were one or two of the men before him who clearly considered the Queen's intervention had been brought about by his connivance. Others equally plainly resented the Royal attempt to upset the legal clauses of a will. There was some heat in the discussion. At the end, however, Bull felt that he had convinced everyone that he had done nothing underhand and that he had been as ignorant of the Queen's intentions as they had been.

After this and that course had been considered, it was

Bull's original ground that was adopted as justification. He repeated it as his contribution to a solution. He assured them that, under no circumstance could he lecture in Latin. They took him seriously, though one or two eyes narrowed as he repeated the affirmation. It seemed the best way out. With as good grace as possible, the Mayor thanked him for his attendance, promised to notify him officially of his appointment, and had him ushered out to his waiting horse.

Although he knew that his appointment was now certain, Bull had still to wait for the official intimation. It did not arrive until March. He received the copy of the public ordinance of the executors of the Gresham bequest by messenger as he was proceeding to his study from the Chapel. He lit his churchwarden and settled down into his most comfortable chair to read it when he reached his room. He just glanced at the heads other than those musical. One paragraph contained the interest of the document for him. He commenced to read it with a slight smile:

"The solemn Musicke lecture, to be read twice every weeke, in manner followinge, *viz*., the theorique part for one half houre, or thereabouts, and the practique, by consort of voice or instrument for the reste of the houre; whereof the first lecture to be in the Latine tongue and the seconde in the English . . ."

(that part was familiar; he could recall the booming voice of the clerk reading it at the Guildhall). He read on:

"But because at this time Mr. Dr. Bull, who is recommended to the place by the Queenes Moste Excellent Maiestie, beinge not able to speake Latin, his lectures are permitted to be altogether in English, so long as hee shall continue in the place of musicke lecturer there."

His smile had grown broad as he laid the document down

on the table. He lay his head back against his chair, gazing musingly up at the rafter running across his room overhead. It was a simple, straight rafter, a broad oak beam, stained black in the Tudor fashion ; but he seemed to find the contemplation of it curiously humorous, laughing softly to himself.

A few moments later he turned round and reached from his seat to a small tiled shelf in his fireplace, pulling out a book. He laid it on his knees as he settled himself into his chair again. It was well-bound, with fine French tooling, gilt on brown calf. The cover was stamped with his name

IOHN. BVLL.
DOCTOR. OF.
MVSIQVE. ORGA
NISTE. AND. GENT
ELMAN. OF. HER. MAIES
TIES. MOSTE. HONORABLE
CHAPPELL

He opened the volume ; the cover fell back, showing the title page inside, " The Citharn School," by Anthony Holborne, 1597. Bull turned the first pages quickly ; they were English, in the rich type of the day. Then he placed a slip of paper between the leaves while he turned to refill his pipe from the tobacco-jar on the table. He lit it with a taper from the fire ; then he took up the volume again and commenced to read, softly murmuring the words under his eyes. The title of the second part of the volume, lying open, read :

Dispertissimi Viri Rogeri Aschami Angli.
Regiae olim Majestati a Latinis Epistolis,
familarium Epistolarum libri tres.
Londini, Pro Francisco Coldocko,
(Londini, Ex Officina Henriei Bynneman)
1581

DR. JOHN BULL

Meanwhile, work was proceeding on the alterations being made in Gresham's mansion, to accommodate the new College. Bull occasionally walked to Broad Street to watch their progress. It gave him a strange feeling of serenity and liberty to view the wide gardens where he would soon be free to sit and walk. He had not noticed before the enclosedness of his life, as he did then. Since his days at Hereford, he, the one-time West Country child, had moved in palaces and churches for the most part. Now he would live where his spirit might flower among fresh green.

The new appointment had added to Bull's prestige immensely, and his financial status seems to have been increased also. The Queen's State Papers at least contained one interesting entry, dated March 31st, 1597. This granted Robert Holland, cousin of Hugh Holland, the Welsh poet friend of Shakespeare and Bull whose verses on both became historic, a lease in reversion for fifty years " of messuages and lands in the counties of York, Surrey, Lancaster, Anglesey and Derby, at a rent of £10 8s. 4d. without fine, in consideration of the services of John Bull, organist of the Chapel." For so large an amount of land to be concerned shows that the Queen evaluated Bull at an extraordinarily high rate—one scarcely compatible solely with musical services.

The opening of the College was finally fixed for October, 1597. Bull was to deliver the Inaugural Musicke Lecture. He gave it deep thought, working on it daily for hours at a stretch, altering and amending, searching, not only his musical manuals, but also his favourite poets and playwrights for quotations to point his arguments.

He had not suspected how widely his attitude regarding the Gresham professorship had become known in the interim, or how generally its motive had been understood and sympathized with by the public. It added to the attraction of his first public lecture, where the people might not only see the famous figure of Dr. John Bull and hear his renowned playing, but could also hear him speak and openly declare his ideas on the national art in their native tongue, vindicated at last in the academic sphere through the celebrated musician's determined patriotism.

The streets around the College were crowded when he arrived. He was recognized and pointed out. As he turned into the College a loud cheer went up. In the lecture hall the auditorium was densely crowded as he took his place at the lectern to commence his address. In the foreground of his audience sat the Lord Mayor of London and his Aldermen, with an unusually large number of other noted personages.

Stirred by the manifestation of popular enthusiasm, he felt husky as he opened the pages of his lecture. He stood with both his hands pressed down on the lectern, gazing down at his discourse for an appreciable pause before he began to speak. Then, in a voice that sounded strangely remote to himself, but which penetrated with quiet intensity through the hall, he opened his discourse:

" Maister Lord Maier and moste worshipfull Aldermen of this Citie of London; moste noble lords and ladies and honored gentles, in the name of England and of England's moste glorious queene . . ."

The concourse hung on his words with a singular intentness as he proceeded. At the end, all tradition was broken by the shout that went up, even from the most solid and respectable burgesses. They crowded round him, seeking to grasp his hand, to speak one word of gratitude or homage. Bull was tremendously stirred. As he turned from his place by the lectern finally, he was accosted by a

DR. JOHN BULL

neat, soberly-clad citizen, who excused himself for intruding, but earnestly desired a word with Dr. Bull. It was Thomas Este, the celebrated printer, who specialized in musical work, holding a sub-lease on William Byrd's patent of monopoly. He very respectfully solicited a few moments' private talk. At its conclusion, Maister Este bade Dr. Bull farewell with cordiality and departed with satisfaction on his every feature. Under his arm he carried the leaves of the text from which the famous musician had delivered his discourse.

A few weeks later Dr. Bull received a packet by messenger at Gresham College. Opening it, he found that it contained a fairly thick bundle of printer's proof-pages. He looked at the first one, on top of the neatly packed pile and read

> The Oration of Maister Iohn Bull
> Doctor of Musicke and one of the
> Gentlemen of hir Maiesties Royall
> Chappell, as hee pronounced the
> same before diuers worshipfull
> persons the Aldermen and Commoners
> of the Citie of London, with a greate
> Multitude of other people the 6 daye
> of October, 1597. In the New erected
> Colledge of Sir Thomas Gresham. Made
> in the Commemoration of the sayd worthie
> Founder and the excellent Science of
> Musicke. Imprinted at London by Thomas Este.

It was more than a passing announcement. It was a record of honour for posterity. John Bull had struck a decisive blow for the lasting freedom and honour of his beloved English speech.

Ingenious Design

CHAPTER VII

INGENIOUS DESIGN

EARLY in 1601 Bull took another strange holiday. After the usual music practice he remained closeted with the Queen for a while. On emerging, he left the Palace immediately and took horse to the Guildhall. Arrived there, he scrawled a brief note on his tablets, which he sent in to the Clerk's office. The attendant returned quickly, and Bull was ushered in. His business did not take long. His physician had ordered him a rest and a change of air. The Queen had granted him leave of absence. He now notified the Guildhall authorities, as preliminary to seeing the Warden of Gresham College, putting forward the name of William Byrd's son, Thomas, who had been working with him, to carry on his work as lecturer during his absence. He was promised that the matter would be laid before the Aldermen forthwith. Their approval could be taken for granted, in view of the Queen's authorization.

Leaving the Guildhall, Bull rode back to his quarters at Gresham College. There he had a brief conference with the Warden, and then, going to his room, commenced to pack his coffers. This done after some time, he put on his cap and cloak again and left, telling the janitor that his baggage would be called for later. He then proceeded back to the Palace, pausing on his way to instruct a carrier in Eastcheap to call for his coffers. At the Palace he was closeted with Giles, whom he had nominated, with Thomas Morley, to deputize for him at the Chapel Royal, remaining some time. The remainder of the afternoon he spent in the City, making various purchases, meeting Giles for supper at the Mitre Tavern in Fleet Street. After bidding his friend good night, he returned to the College, where he spent some time writing in his study. It was late before he sealed and inscribed the final letter. With a sigh of relief, he took up his candle and went to bed.

The dawn found him already astir and dressing. The day was fresh and bright and he felt elated, in spite of his previous late night. Contrary to his frequent custom, however, he neither sang nor whistled. He was alert, but there was a touch of care and caution in his movements, and he sorted and checked his belongings before making them into a parcel, as though preparing for an expedition. He did not wait to breakfast in the College hall. Spreading out some cold viands which he had brought back from the Mitre the night before, he checked over the letters which he had written. Taking a small sheet of paper, filled with close writing, from his doublet, he read and reread it several times carefully as he ate. He was about to thrust it back into his pouch; but, on second thought, he glanced at it again, as if memorizing some detail, then struck his flint, lighted a taper and set light to the paper in a small salver. He watched it burn to a small, black-grey, shrivelled heap, stirred the ashes with his finger, opened his casement and scattered them on the air outside. Carefully wiping and replacing the salver, he took up his cap, cloak and bundle, and left the room.

An ostler was waiting with a horse in Broad Street. He spoke to him briefly, handing him money, then mounted and rode off, turning through Threadneedle Street into Bishopsgate and taking the direction of London Bridge.

The sun was gleaming on the Thames as he crossed the

INGENIOUS DESIGN

Bridge. It made an arabesque of shimmering, shifting patterns on the rippling water between the dark barges and the slowly-rocking masts of the vessels on the river, as a fresh breeze blew from the Upper Pool. His mood of elation grew. The stalls on the Bridge had not yet opened up, and the thoroughfare was empty as he rode into Southwark, excepting for the watchman by the bridge-head. Turning left, he set his horse at an easy gallop along the Kent Road.

The scent of the earth filled his nostrils as he reached Blackheath Hill, blown from the open common spaces. He snatched off his cap and threw up his head, exulting in the morning freshness. A troop of the Queen's guards passed him as he rode by Greenwich Park, taking their mounts for morning exercise on the Heath. The officer recognized him and saluted, with a slight expression of surprise. The trotting hoofs and clatter of accoutrements fitted Bull's mood of growing gaiety. He flourished his cap, with a cheery greeting, and rode on. On the crest of Shooter's Hill he turned, reining up his horse, and looked back over the wide panorama, Greenwich Palace in the foreground and the Thames shipping and London in the distance. Then, inclining right, he set off again at an easy trot along the Dover Road.

At Gresham College and the Chapel Royal, Bull's absence was noted with some surprise. He had intimated nothing, excepting to his deputies and the College authorities. Giles and Byrd stated what he had informed them, and little more thought was given to the matter. Dr. Bull was absent, " as it is said, for health," on indeterminate leave. His colleagues, students and choristers accepted the statement on its face value, as were to do many later historians, such as Dr. Ward and Dr. Burney. Sympathy was expressed ; but, if any felt curious at the suddenness of Bull's departure, such feeling soon evaporated.

The matter might have appeared more mysterious, had anyone been sufficiently interested to trace Bull's journey and the way in which he proceeded. The coffers sent ahead by post coach certainly had not been dispatched under his name, and, as Wood recorded later, in the "Fasti Oxonienses," "Dr. Bull took occasion to go *incognito*." There might be many simple reasons of quite normal kind for this; but had anyone linked his movements with the political ones of the moment in England, such an unusual precaution would have appeared somewhat interesting, if not extremely significant.

Once again, Bull's choice of a time for a holiday coincided peculiarly with certain political events. The Puritan movement against the establishment and authority of the Church of England had grown considerably, assuming a definitely political aspect through its opposition to the sovereign's jurisdiction in religious matters and to the royal prerogative. It was reinforced by a widespread popular discontent and resentment, aroused by the Crown's encroachments on the common rights of the nation and the freedom of its legislature. Above all, the Queen's right to grant patents of monopoly, in which Elizabeth traded scandalously, urged by her obsessing avarice, were a cause of great bitterness. This exploitation had led to the grossest abuses. The most necessary commodities, yarn, leather, oil, coal, iron, starch, lead, vinegar, saltpetre, skins and glass, had risen exorbitantly in price. The extortions of the patent holders were rendering domestic life wretched and hampering trade and commerce to a point of paralysis.

Open revolt had expressed itself in the Parliament of that year. The majority of the House of Commons supported determined attacks on such abuses. The Queen's supporters appealed in vain to the Speaker to rule against such attacks on the Queen's Highness. The coaches of Burghley and other Crown Ministers proceeded through the streets with great difficulty, surrounded and followed by angry crowds, shouting protests, insults and threats. It was a dangerous moment; but Elizabeth had the typical Tudor genius for dominating situations by dramatic strokes. Although herself the main cause of the trouble, she assumed the leadership of the reform party, tacitly casting blame on her Ministers, corrected the abuses and, with magnificent self-righteousness and dignity, thanked her Parliament for " their tender care of the publick weal," and their loyal aid in her task of governing.

This adroit manipulation of the situation had restored her hold upon popular affection, which had been badly shaken; but it had not solved her Government's problems, even within her own realms. Although there was no sign of open rebellion among Puritans or Catholics in England itself, Spain was still busy stirring up strife and aiding insurrection elsewhere in Elizabeth's domains. That very year the Irish broke into open rebellion, headed by the Earl of Tyrone, last of the Irish O'Neale princes, the Earl of Desmond, the Lord O'Donnell and Florence MacCarty. For the first time since the Armada, Spain sent a considerable fleet, directed, not towards England, but Ireland, and it was known that " They woulde land at Lymrick, beinge fortie five sayle, whereof seventeene were men of warre, whereof sixe were Gallions, the reste of one hundred, or one hundred and fiftie tunnes burthen and had in them six thousand souldiers." In " a letter ffrom the Queenes owne hand," Elizabeth wrote to the Lord Deputy, her viceroy in Ireland, in high tone :

" Since the braine-sicke humour of unaduysed assaulte hath seized on the heartes of our causeless foe, We doubt not but their gaine wilbe their baine and glorie their shame that ever they had the thought thereof,"

but her agitation showed in her writing in her own autograph and in the hurry which was indicated in her signature

" scribbling in hast
Your louinge Soueraigne E.R."

In spite of her assumption of disdain, she also thought it necessary to mobilize considerable reinforcements :

" We haue thought goode to sende ffrom hence some further forces for increase of Our Army there, to enable you the better to make head agaynst them, if they shall fortune to land,"

and the heavy operations carried out at the Siege of Kinsale, when the landed Spaniards combined with the Irish insurrectionaries to hold the town, showed that she had not overestimated the danger.

In facing it, therefore, it was imperative for her to know the temper of the Continent, as well as to trace all possible Spanish intrigue and to rally to her aid, if need be, the Protestant Powers, above all, those which she had rendered help earlier, such as the Dutch and Henry of Navarre, now Henry IV of France. That monarch was now well established on his throne, and his country was prospering under his astute Minister, Sully. He was the chief hope of Continental Protestantism, as opposed to Spain, although he had adopted the Catholic faith to secure his crown. He had shown that he was prepared to finance the Lutheran princes of Germany against the Emperor of Austria and the King of Spain, and Elizabeth, with her characteristic keen sense of bargaining, was quite prepared to accept

INGENIOUS DESIGN

from him a return for the military and financial assistance which she had given him earlier.

The French Huguenots, also, were in a strong position, and the Queen was uneasy regarding their relationship with her own restive Puritan subjects. They were scarcely in a position to intervene militantly; but, by their consolidation through the privileges of the Edict of Nantes granted to them by their old leader, Henry himself, they were prosperous and able to provide monetary support. In the Netherlands, where the Dutch under the Prince of Orange had cast off the Spanish yoke, was another Protestant Power which might support Puritan discontent, if appealed to on the score of religion. Beyond Holland, yet in close enough touch with England through their seaports, were the several Protestant States of Germany, recently unified and consolidated into the Evangelical League headed by Moritz, Landgrave of Hesse. It was vitally important for the Queen's Government to have reliable, first-hand information regarding happenings and the general state of political feeling in such countries, and all possible knowledge of any kind of liaison which might exist between them and the discontented factions in England.

For such observation someone absolutely reliable was required, with intelligence and a personality which could insinuate itself into court life abroad without suspicion. Few possessed such qualities to the extent that Bull did. He was not known politically. His reputation was sufficient to justify his soliciting the recognition of foreign rulers, yet not enough to cause him to be regarded as a possible royal confidant of Elizabeth. Outside England his figure was not familiar enough to occasion his being recognized personally where he wished otherwise. His profession, on its surface appearance, was remote from diplomacy, rendering him apparently innocuous, while at the same time presenting an easy way for him to enter influential circles abroad, on his artistic merits. Hence, *incognito*, as he left, or publicly recognized if he thought fit to declare himself, Bull was possessed of every attribute to render him useful in the Queen's service in foreign lands.

The voyage across the Channel interested and excited him. In spite of his affinity to the sea-wanderers of the times, it was the first time he had undertaken a sea voyage. He felt curiously as the white cliffs of Dover faded from view and he realized that he was severed from England. Not only were the places to which he was going unknown to him; they held unknown possibilities some of which might prove perilous.

The soberly-clad clerk or scholar who landed at Calais attracted no attention. Indeed, Bull felt not only queerly unknown, but strangely lost at first. English was his tongue, and he thought in it. Now he had to make his way with such knowledge of a foreign language as he had acquired at the Gramere Schole of the Chapel Royal and through his intercourse in Court circles. This was easier in Calais than elsewhere in France. The town had belonged to England for centuries, until lost in the previous reign of Mary. English was familiar in many taverns and hostelries there, since the friendly relations between Elizabeth and Henri Quatre made English visitors frequent, on their way to and from Paris or London.

Apparently Bull lingered awhile in Calais, or, at least, in the province of Artois; for the next trace of him was at St. Omer, where an amusing incident of his visit, typically whimsical, was recorded by Wood:

" At length, hearing of a famous musician belonging to a certain cathedral (St. Omers, as I have heard) he applied himself as a novice to him, to learn something of his faculty and to see and admire his works. This musician, after some discourse had passed between them, conducted Bull to a vestry or musick school joyning to the cathedral and shew'd him a lesson or song of 40 parts and then made a vaunting challenge to any person in the world to add one more part to them; supposing it to be so compleat and full, that it was impossible for any mortal man to correct, or add to it. Bull thereupon desiring the use of ink and rul'd paper (such as we call musick paper) prayed the musician to lock him up in the said school for two or three hours; which being done, not without great disdain by the musician, Bull in that time, or less, added 40 more parts to the said lesson or song. The musician thereupon being called in, he viewed it, tried it, and retry'd it. At length he burst out into a great ecstasy, and swore by the great God that he that added those 40 parts, must either be the Devil or Dr. John Bull, etc. Whereupon Bull making himself known, the musician fell down and ador'd him."

A Dutch variant on the story adds that Bull, with what appears a very typical touch, though denying that he was the devil, said that he had a devilish thirst, whereupon the organist conveyed him where refreshment might be obtained in a cellar. The two then celebrated their meeting, drinking each other's health and were found prone beside a cask the following morning.

It is clear that Bull was maintaining his incognito up to this time, and, as Wood's first sentence indicates, he had been in France some time before visiting St. Omer. It was necessary that his arrival should not be noted, if he was to proceed freely with his observations in and around Calais. His precaution also prevented word of his presence there being carried back to England to any whom he did not wish to know of it. Such communication would be probable, since Calais and Dieppe were the main ports of traffic between England and France at the time.

In Paris he resumed his own identity, being received there by King Henry IV. Elizabeth had entrusted him with messages to her French ally, which necessitated his appearance at Court. There his continued incognito was impossible, since the personnel of the English Court was familiar to many around the French King. The safest way was for him to appear in Paris as a visiting musical celebrity, recommended by his royal mistress, the English sovereign.

Bull found Henry IV attractive. He admired the French King's vitality and vision. He respected his determination to create a French navy worthy of his realm, which had already enforced the respect of the dreaded Barbary corsairs, who held all other Mediterranean Powers in contempt. King Henry shared his own interest in American colonization, financing Champlain's Canadian expeditions from his privy purse, when his Minister, Sully, opposed him. Under his rule a regular royal army was evolving, to defend the country and keep unruly nobles in check. From four regiments in the previous reign, this had grown to eleven highly drilled ones, backed by a mighty force of artillery. Internally, everything was being done to make France self-supporting. Backed by royal subsidies, factories were being erected all over the country, to produce crapes as fine as those of Bologna, gold thread equal to that of Milan, linen and porcelain to rival the Dutch, and tapestries, glass and crystal. The Tuileries and Tournelles were planted with mulberry trees, to encourage the cultivation of silkworms. From within, furthered by the genius for finance of Sully, the realms of Henry Quatre were being consoli-

INGENIOUS DESIGN

dated, augmented by the French-speaking territories recently acquired by treaty or conquest.

Paris at once delighted and disappointed Bull. Only there did he fully realize how English civilization had advanced under Elizabeth, not only intellectually, but in all human amenities. The French capital had features of magnificence difficult to match in London. The splendid new façade of the Hôtel de Ville designed by Androuet Doucerceau, had the grandeur of King Henry's era; the strength of the new Pont Neuf by the same architect spanned the capital's river with the sovereign's boldness and breadth of open outlook. The recently erected pavilions of the Tuileries and Fontainebleau were invested with the mingled grace and dignity of his personal charm, and the new home for old soldiers at the Hôpital de la Charité in the Rue de l'Ourcine evidenced his patrician care of his people. Nevertheless, Bull felt that these things masked less noble features. The solemn beauty of Notre Dame stirred him; but its looming immensity also awed and oppressed him, making him feel dwarfed. Looking out from the height of its balconies over the variegated network of the Paris panorama, with the Seine threaded through it like a silver ribbon, he felt exalted. The towers of St. Jacques, St. Germain des Prés and St. Geneviève, poised serenely against the firmament, accentuated this mood and the roofs of Montmartre reflected a quiet light; but the huddled buildings in the maze of narrow streets squatted like sinister dwarfs waiting the darkness to swarm into the green beauty of the royal gardens and tear down the calm pride of the stately edifices which they seemed to surround with latent malevolence.

The same mood affected him as he explored the city. In spite of the new order imposed by Henry's advanced thought and will, he felt an undercurrent of menace in Paris, which recalled to him the horror of savagery of which it had been capable in the massacre of St. Bartholomew's Eve, vividly related to him by Walsingham, who had been ambassador there at the time. The magnificence of the palaces and aristocratic mansions was arrogant, alongside the squalor of the quarters surrounding them. They stood in ill-repaired, muddy streets, lacking the pavements which had been laid down in London in 1533. At night the tortuous, narrow thoroughfares seemed to fall under a morbid spell; evil crept softly in their subdued echoes and lurked grimly in their shadows. They were dangerous in their lampless gloom compared to London, where street lanterns had been installed since 1415. Conveyances were scarce, and there were only 240 archers to police the city, half on duty by day, half by night. The only two theatres were forbidden to give performances excepting at 2 and 4.30 p.m., because the streets were unsafe after dark. Everywhere Bull felt, intangibly, potential threat. The city was symbolic of the State. Only the strength of King Henry's personality and prestige held the heterogeneous elements of his realm together. Minds like those of Sully in political economy and state-craft, of Malherbe in literature supported him in working for a new, though formal order; but the gaps in the social structure rendered the French State precarious. Probing among such conflicting elements, Bull had much to observe, gained much information.

The discrepancy between the contrasted features of the Parisian vista corresponded to that between the aristocracy and the people. The great, overbearing mansions and palaces, aloof above the dark, debased tenements and hovels of the muddy, twisted alleys, were no more detached from the surrounding scene than were the haughty French nobles in their cynical disregard of the miserable and squalid existence of the masses about them.

Henry IV might erect marvels of architecture to symbolize the new epoch of peace and order. The things which endeared him to the people were not these. He reached the hearts of the populace because he was aware of them and cared for them. He was aware of his feeling of paternity. " Now there is a father that cares for them and everything prospers," he had said, reviewing the agricultural reforms and improvements which he had introduced after reading the admirable books of Olivier de Serre, " Le Théâtre de l'agriculture " and " Ménage des champs." The people knew him as the King who sent courtiers packing from his ante-chambers, bluntly telling them to go about their business and attend to their estates. He was the martial leader who not only led his men to victory, but provided a home for old soldiers. He did not seek to drain the soil to fill his own maw; he remembered the mouths of the hungry and secured the " fowl in the pot " for every peasant's Sunday. He preferred the splendour of prosperous industry to the magnificence of courtly pomp. He considered it more important to build factories and to inaugurate public undertakings to provide work for the needy, than to embellish palaces in which his nobles could play.

However deep the love of the common populace might be for him, it still did not render his realm secure until this rift of blind indifference separating the nobility from the masses was bridged. The realm was not united until it was so spiritually as well as politically. So long as the cynical egotism of the aristocracy continued, they would never comprehend what his beneficence was doing to build the health of the body of the nation. Their proud conventions paralysed them. They were members of the body social, but they had become atrophied to the influence of the nation's nerve centres. They shrank away from the maladies of the tainted wretches that begged from them in the streets; but in them was the canker of a greater disease. They were themselves infected with a deeper malady. They scorned the starvedly stunted, yet could not grow with the times. They walked in fear of violence in the streets of their own capital by night; yet they nourished violence in their hearts and did violence to humanity by their cynical self-centredness every day. All the evil that stalked the nocturnal darkness of Paris did not come from the lower orders. Those on high cast many of the shadows that obscured the light. Pondering these things, Bull wondered if the King himself could avoid such sombre shades. As he bent to the common people, so he fell under the shadow of aristocratic resentment. Might he not find one day that it obscured even his powerful vision for ever? There was instinctive realization in his thoughts. Biron was already plotting; and, although his life would pay the penalty, the head of the French State was to fall within nine years to the assassin's knife. It was then that Bull wrote his " Salvator mundi."

At the French Court, however, he played the musician before all and, by all accounts, played superbly. There was not the same general love and knowledge of music among the French as in England, but Henry IV was extremely musical. It was said that this trait was a curious inheritance, due to his father, Thibaut of Navarre, having induced his wife to hold his hand and sing with him while giving birth to the son who was later to be King of France. In any event, Jeanne d'Albret, King Henry's mother, had a natural taste for music and encouraged it in her son. It was

INGENIOUS DESIGN

therefore natural that the French King took an especial interest in his musical guest from London. For the Court as a whole, his manifestly extraordinary technical powers apart, Bull's performances were a great attraction. He was invested with the exotic flair which surrounds foreign celebrities, even in the most sophisticated circles. He had regal favour and personal graces to recommend him, in an environment where both played important parts. In many cases his natural spontaneity came refreshingly to those jaded with the mad extravagances of the Valois Court and its successors around Henry of Navarre, immersed in complex political problems of every kind, their governing position yet scarcely stabilized. His nature relished the French admiration; his genius made him deserve it.

Nevertheless, there was the lighter side of French Court life. The King was susceptible to beauty, and the charms of those around the Palace were celebrated. Though Henry had ruthlessly suppressed the duelling which had drained the best blood of France during the Valois reigns, amorous intrigue and gallantry remained characteristic of the Parisian Court. The strain of the long strife through which France had barely passed had also encouraged an eager search for gaiety, much of which, however, was still nervous and hysterical. Among the more merry members of the French Court, therefore, Bull's prankishness, amusingly naive to the Parisian mind, made him welcome as much as his music and in some quarters created a real affection for him.

Henry IV was a composer of considerable talent himself, and Bull interested him greatly, both musically and otherwise. The genial French monarch, with his witty mind, found the whimsical Englishman a good companion and one with whom he could pursue his favourite recreation of music. The musician was ingenious in many ways.

One evening he came upon Bull at the virginals, amusing a group of courtiers by showing them that he could write a piece of music which could be played backwards or forwards and sound the same, as also when it was turned upside down. His interest in Bull's ingenuity grew when he came upon him working out an intricate geometrical music pattern. Bull's ingenuity in this way seemed to interest a number of illustrious people. Queen Elizabeth was always excited when she received such musical designs, and she spent much time in studying them with certain of her Ministers and officials, in the privacy of her royal apartments. It was remarkable how the musical culture of certain confidential courtiers developed about that time. They could spend hours poring over Bull's geometrical music designs, some rapidly arriving at a point of comprehension which enabled them to write explanatory notes on the patterns for the Queen. Surprised, Bull endeavoured to explain how amusing it was to preserve some of his musical ideas for his friends in a way which rendered the pieces pleasing to the eye, as well as to the ear. The King had a quick mathematical mind and a keen sense of design, in graphic art as in politics. He took up the sheet, examined it closely, and congratulated the composer on having accomplished something which " coulde conveye soe well to eye as toe eare," and begged the manuscript which Bull could not well refuse.

Some days later the King summoned his English guest to his closet. Arrived there, Bull found the King with Sully. On the table before them they had several sheets of music paper. Bull was at first amused to see that the King had been trying to copy his idea; but as he perused the sheets,

INGENIOUS DESIGN

his expression changed. For the design of King Henry read clearly in cypher, warning that this music should be treated circumspectly, "lest it shoulde come toe the hearinge of such as woulde esteem yt an excesse of musicke." Looking up from the sheet, Bull found the eyes of the King and his Minister fixed on him. Bull did not know what to say; but Henry relieved him by smiling and telling him that between friends an appreciation of art of such kind was no bad thing. Bull congratulated the royal craftsman, and the matter was left with a typically French avoidance of the obvious. Nevertheless, for the remainder of his stay at the French Court, Bull was less busy with his fancy than before.

In spite of the French Court's interests and attractions, Bull knew he must not linger indefinitely. He heard many things of interest from other lands. He wished to explore these, and, not unnaturally, his great success as a performer also impelled him to seek further musical conquests. His contact with French life had also renewed his interest in the various aspects of folk-idiom and their moving human traits. He absorbed quickly and had soon delighted the King by his tribute in the national dance-form of the day, the "French Currant," or Courante.

He timed his stay carefully. The stage was now set for his future action. He had carried out his first plans successfully, unobserved. Now the best cloak for his future designs was an ostentatious artistic publicity. This would free him to tour freely, without contriving further pretexts. The fame of his playing had spread widely through his success at the French Court. Invitations reached him from rulers throughout Europe, anxious to add to the lustre of artistic brilliance which every court deemed necessary after the Renascence, by having him appear under their patronage. He accepted or declined such invitations, according to how they fitted in with his plans, with all due form and ceremony.

His first objective was Germany. He announced it as the starting-point of an extensive tour. No suspicion was aroused, even though the German States were centres of political interest at the time. All potentates vied for the honour of a visit from the leading musician of the foremost musical country of Europe, whose desire for wider renown was comprehensible on purely artistic grounds. The Teutonic princes were eager for culture, even if pedantic in their attitude towards it. It was the obvious thing that, when Dr. John Bull went to Germany, " bereiste er das Festland als Klavier-virtuose."

Wanderjahr

CHAPTER VIII

WANDERJAHR

FROM Paris Bull proceeded to Brunswick. The Court of Heinrich Julius, Herzog von Braunschweig-Luneberg, was one of the first to which an artist would gravitate naturally. Both the duke and his consort were keen amateurs and patrons of the arts. The duchess had a taste and talent for music, and was a capable performer on the virginals. Her husband played the same instrument, together with the regalls and viola da gamba; but his main interest was in drama, in which he had made original essays as a playwright. He maintained his own company of stage actors and, with his friend, the Landgraf Moritz von Hesse, who had some talent as a poet, he gave the lead in establishing the earliest Hoftheater, or court theatres, for which the various kingdoms, principalities, duchies, margravates and counties of the German Empire later became famous.

It was a matter of curious coincidence that Bull's first step in his tour took him to the domains of the Duke of Brunswick, the closest associate of the Landgrave of Hesse, leader of the newly-formed German Evangelical League, whose territories directly adjoined his own. Such political matters, however, were not likely to concern a travelling artist. Had Bull proceeded directly to Hesse, it might have seemed more suspicious, since the Landgrave had visited Henry IV recently, in Paris, prior to announcing the formation of his league, and both were known to have mutual plans against the Habsburg Empire of Austria and the related kingdom of Spain. The Landgrave poet and the playwright Duke, having such close artistic interests in common, would naturally have frequent contact in a social way: but music, drama and artistic festivities were the features of their visits to each other. Bull's vocation therefore made his presence quite natural on such occasions.

A new kind of landscape unfolded itself before Bull as he journeyed into Germany. Approaching Brunswick-Wolfenbüttel, "a citie where the Duke of Brunswicke kepte his Courte," through "fruitfull hils of corne, not inclosed and groves and woods in a fruitfull and pleasant countrey," he emerged into a "plaine more pleasant then the former, havinge no inclosures . . . and full of villages." Everywhere he could feel the close sentiment of the people for the land. It was something quite different from England's folk-feeling, which led to expansion. Here it was consolidation; no matter how far any German expedition might go, it always gravitated back homewards and each Schloss, or castle, with its village nestling around its foot, lived, thought and spoke as a definite community or family.

Bull was welcomed at Brunswick-Wolfenbüttel with a typical German mixture of self-conscious formality and warm cordiality. He found life there congenial, and his stay was protracted. The ceremonial side of the Court had the ponderous pomp of the Germany of the time and much of its artistic activity was marred by the stereotyped artificiality, pedantry and pretension which characterized the Teutonic response to the Renascence and produced the paralysing influence of Opitz, whose "Buch von der deutschen Poeterei" confined the German Muse in literary formality so long. The duke's own plays were self-consciously long-winded and full of exaggerated melodrama.

In one case, his heroine, " Susanna," took thirty-two heavy sentences to make a farewell. Heinrich Julius, however, was an ardent patriot, imbued with German feeling. This reacted on his exotic pretensions. The spirit of German folklife persisted at the Brunswick Court, as at most German centres. The German aristocracy was still in close touch with the land, not remote from its estates, as was the French nobility in Paris. The heavy Teutonic pomp and solemnity of the duke's ceremonials differed little from that of the burghers of the trade guilds or the civic functions of the solid, wealthy Hansa merchant cities. The pedantic literary sway of Opitz could not suppress the vigour of the native German spirit entirely, which asserted itself in other writers—the tenderly melancholy Simon Dach of Königsberg, the vigorously masculine Paul Fleming, the lyric intensity of Andreas Gryphius and the epigrammatic brilliance of Friedrich von Logau.

A kindred folk-feeling dominated Duke Heinrich Julius' own plays, making them distinctive and interesting to Bull, in spite of their shortcomings. They made a definite breach with the prevalent conventions by blanding the burgher and peasant types, and the German dialect and idiom of current popular life into the scheme of flowery poetry and stilted rhetoric which characterized the pseudo-classic drama of the day. They therefore afforded glimpses of the folklife of Germany, expressed in homely phrases and everyday diction, even in the countryside Plattdeutsch, or patois, which appealed strongly to Bull, with his interest in the characteristics and conditions of all kinds of popular life.

Such drama had not only the appeal of indigenous interest and local colour for Bull; it was also infused with elements which made him feel unexpectedly at home in it. He realized in it yet further achievements of that English spirit which was his own strongest inspiration. The evolving drama of the moment in Germany owed much to England and showed the strength of the ties of common race existent between the two countries. Since the first visits of the Company of English Comedians in 1590, the civic and aristocratic theatres of Germany had been greatly influenced by the genius of the Elizabethan drama. The folk-feeling and spontaneous freedom of form of the English plays had encouraged the reaction against literary pedantry and the development of national types. The clowns so beloved of Bull had delighted the German audiences, and soon German playwrights, such as Jakob Ayrer, the contemporary of Hans Sachs at Nüremberg, had introduced their German equivalents into the German drama, German companies had been formed along English lines and plays introduced from England had been translated and adopted into the German theatre repertory. Shakespeare's works were so popular that they became henceforth a naturalized part of the development of German drama. In one known case, Shakespeare himself assisted the German dramatist, Andreas Gryphius, in the writing of his comedy, "Horribilicribrifax." As Bull realized these influences at work, his national faith received fresh stimulus. They vindicated his belief in the power of the English spirit to extend its dominion through the realm of thought as well as through material territories.

Pressed to extend his visit, Bull found compliance easy. His surroundings were happy and full of new interest. They provided a pleasing relief from the morbid feelings induced by Paris. The city of Wolfenbüttel and the surrounding countryside were permeated with folk-tradition, fascinating to him. The buildings along the streets and surrounding the Marktplatz had not the magnificence of the French capital, but they expressed a spiritual unity and had a definite national character. They were not show-places or formal edifices for public ceremony; they were the homes of a folk with a deeply ingrained national patriotism. The fine old 12th century Gothic Dom, or Cathedral, was not only a religious monument; it was the centre of the stern and simple faith of the locality. Its strength expressed the national spirit of that faith, which it sustained and did not overbear. The solid, towered fortifications of the city walls and the ducal Schloss exemplified the mundane aspect of that spirit. There was indomitable independence and dignity in their challenge; no stealthy menace crept in their shadow; they faced the world four-square, too stolid to threaten, but strong to defend. Within the walls, a common quiet homeliness united all classes and gave character to the architecture of the sturdy Rathaus, the full-fronted guild-houses with their many gables and big sun-dials on their walls and the square city-gate guard-houses. Lanterns lit the streets at night, fixed to walls and slung on the poles of the watch that patrolled the streets diligently. Singing came from homes and taverns. It echoed along Gasse and Marktplatz as merrymakers returned home, their feet ringing honestly and clearly on the rough, but solid cobbles. It was a world of smaller perspectives, but these had their own satisfying and comfortable quality. There was a simple domestic content in it all, self-contained and self-vindicating. It was the world of those scrupulously detailed, yet stark black-and-white etchings by Albrecht Dürer which illustrated Walsingham's Lutheran Bible, where every Scriptural figure was visioned as a German folk-type in the German landscape, in an art which had its source in the homely human intercourse and the practical woodcut craftsmanship of the German folk.

DR. JOHN BULL

In the ducal family circle such traits of German folklife persisted also. Formality and intellectual interests had not obliterated a certain homely simplicity. The ducal couple took an active part in the Hausmusik which was the favourite evening recreation, when the duke had no theatrical performance in hand. As in any burgher home, there was family group-singing, the preference being for old Lays and German folk-chorals. The dancing on such occasions was also simpler than at the French and English courts, for, as a contemporary play expressed it

" We Germans have no change in our dances ;
An alman and an up-spring, that is all."

These were the popular dances of the people and they remained the customary dances at the Brunswick Court. Bull felt their affinity with the dances of his native countryside, for they were peasant dances, born at rural festivals, where the up-spring, or Hüpfauf, was the traditional, round-dance conclusion of every merry-making. Bull found its boisterousness congenial to his high spirits. He soon learned to take his part in the revels in the ducal hall, causing merriment by his determination to excel in leaping when the jovial company took up the refrain immortalized by Ayrer in his " Dramen " :

" Ey, jtzt geht erst der hupffauff an ;
Ey, Herr, jtzt kummt erst der hupffauff ! "

His life at Brunswick-Wolfenbüttel inspired Bull with fresh musical ideas also. The form of the alman appealed to him. It expressed much of the character of the people whom he was observing and who were entertaining him in their midst with such warm-hearted cordiality. Duke Heinrich's typically German nature made it the most appropriate form for Bull to adopt in offering him a musical token of his regard. So another of the essentially human documents was added to the musical record of his time which Bull's work constituted, the " Almayn, the Duke of Brunswicks Toye " for virginalls, invested, not only with the local colour of the folk-form, but also with something of the intricate formality and yet genial gaiety of the German ruler. To the Duchess he rendered something more romantic, " The Dutches of Brunswickes Delighte."

The careless happiness of his stay gave Bull many such inspirations. The native dance-form enabled him to repay kindly hospitality by the compliment implicit in his use of it. Here, best of all, he could express his gratitude and appreciation in what was the natural musical language of his hosts. It also contributed in the most popular way to the Court entertainments, which were spirited and gay. The duke and his consort were both young, the playwright-prince being two years Bull's junior, and their circle consisted of high-spirited young people of taste and talent. In spite of his dignified titles, Dr. John Bull, the Queenes Maister of Musicke, Organist of the Chappell Royall and professor of Gresham College, was only thirty-nine years old, handsome, accomplished, witty and famous, on his first visit abroad to novel and fascinating scenes. The duration of his stay and the evidence of his music, indeed, hint that the charms of the Brunswick Court were not wholly of a general kind. The blonde beauties of the Brunswick Court were celebrated and the dark-eyed, polished, yet boyish foreigner, intriguingly unlike their conventional conception of the Englander, and much more volatile than the Teutonic nobles familiar to them, might well be attractive to blue Nordic eyes. If there were any such episode, Bull was commendably discreet and the young lady could keep a secret. The gentle gaiety and tender sentiment of the " Dallying Almain," however, confirms in feeling the suggestion of a romance which its title conveys.

Bull the master, as well as Bull the man, was evident during this time, however; the music conceived at the Brunswick Court was not all graces and gaiety. Though the happy spirit maintains, the " Fantasie Almain " is a work of considerable dimensions and expressive quality. It shows, once again, Bull's power of developing folktypes in the more elaborate art-forms. It is, in its way, a musical epitome of the German idiom of his day, expressed successively in its various most characteristic moods, with Bull's sensitive interpretive power. Its architectural build reflected the solidity of the German minds about him. In it, like Germany, he drew his new structure from the folk.

It could scarcely be otherwise. The landscape itself was bound up with folklore for the people, wherever he went, the tales taking their form from the shape and atmosphere of the countryside. In one place the moonlight on the broadflowing stream of the river at night peopled it in popular fancy with nixies, or Lorelei; in another, close to the Court, he was shown " by the way, a Hil called Brockesberg, famous with manie ridiculous fables of witches yeerely meetinges in that place." Yet, further afield, he was overjoyed to be taken to the " yeerely feat of a village called Millen, where a famous Jester Oulenspiegell (whom we call Owly-glasse) hath a monument erected: hee died in the yeere 1350 and the stone coveringe him is compassed with a grate, least it shoulde bee broken and carried away peecemeale by Passengers, which they say hath once alredy been done by the Germanes." Til Eulenspiegel was certainly a wit and prankster to whom Bull would pay ready homage.

After leaving Brunswick, Bull's travels assumed the nature of a regular virtuoso tour. He moved from German court to court, though, naturally, his visits were confined to those outside the range of Spanish or Austrian influence.

The free towns impressed him; they had that growth of folk-life which he, instinctively, knew to be the soundest thing for a nation. Lübeck, above all, held him spellbound. He felt its spell as he " came out of the woodes and saw two faire rising Hils and the third upon which Lübeck was seated." Architecture and nature combined to make it impressive. " On the top of this third Hil stood the faire Churche of Saint Mary, whence was a descent to all the gates of the Citie, whose situation offered oure eyes a faire prospect and promised greate magnificence in the buildinge."

The town fulfilled its promise. It was picturesque from the first glimpse. " The Citie is compassed with a double wall, one of bricke, and narrowe, the other of earthe and broad, fastned with thicke rowes of willowes. But on the North side and on the South-easte there were no walles, those partes beinge compassed with deepe ditches full of water." He spent much time exploring the lozenge-shaped city, for he found that it " Hath most sweete walkes without the walles." He also found there was much congenial in " the Citizens themselves, who are commended for civility."

The maritime activities of Lübeck held him fascinated. " On the South-easte side the water seemeth narrowe, but is so deepe as ships of a thousand tunne are brought up to the Citie to lie there all winter, beinge first unladed at Tremurren, the Port of the Citie lyinge upon the Baltick Sea."

" This Port, one mile distant from Lübeck " was the focus of his interest. Bull had been used to a sea-trade which brought back either the exotic rarities of the New World or the rich products of the Orient; Lübeck brought him into touch with a trade which bore traces of a strange yet magnificent barbarism. It was that of the Baltic, running to countries of the north, the Land of the Midnight Sun, the ice-bound fjiords, the immense steppes of Russia. It stirred him by recalling the "Tamburlaine" who had inspired Marlowe's play, or again by some subtle feeling for what was probably his own Viking derivation. It made real for him yet another enterprise of the England of his day and his dreams, that of the English Muscovy Company, whose cargoes of rich pelts, strangely-worked leathers and vividly-painted wooden articles he saw multiplied before him at Tremurren, together with the great loads of timber which came from the immense Slav forests. He recognized that here was another world, yet one which England was also exploring. He realized, with some breath-catching, as never before, the words of his contemporary, the chronicler Stowe, "The searchinge and unsatisfyed spirits of the English, to the greate glorie of our Nation, coulde not be contayned within the banckes of the Mediterranean or Levant seas but they passed far toward bothe the Articke and the Antarticke Poles." Hitherto his vision of English enterprise, notwithstanding its perils and pains, had been directed towards the rich Orient and the unknown wealth and marvels of the New World. Here, for the first time, and in a foreign land, he realized the spirit which could wrest from the frozen north and the trackless woods and vast steppes fresh spiritual victories and impress themselves upon a luridly magnificent barbarism the less easily touched because of its isolation from all other types of European civilization.

He conceived then a lasting regard for Lübeck, partly on the great maritime city's own merits, partly because of this mood of revelation. In later years, when engaged on some of his most epic conceptions and exiled from his native land, it was to Lübeck that he went to work out his ideas and from there they were dated, worked out on the splendid organ of "Saint Maries Cathedrall Church (vulgarly Unserfraw kirke)," where Buxtehude and Bach were to meet.

There were two other memorable times in his wander-year. The first was that of his visit to the Netherlands where he was to make one of his deepest friendships. Here, again, he revelled in fresh impressions and a new stimulus. Not only was the presence of the sea which so obsessed his imagination felt everywhere in Holland; he also encountered the medley traffic of the great rivers which were the arteries of Central Europe, bearing their imports and exports, on strange-shaped boats, down to the junction of the Rotte and Maas from the Rhine. He realized the spirit of the Dutch, whose fight for independence against Spanish tyranny had fired his enthusiasm for years, in a new, tangible way, as he saw the great dams and dykes with which they had wrested the very soil of their country from the vastness of the sea. The quiet, reticent sureness of the people appealed to him. They had the clarity of their canal-freshened landscape. There was a new, intimate picturesqueness in the Dutch scene, simple, yet vividly colourful. He delighted in the decorative patterning of the great windmill-arms rotating against the sky; the cities whose thoroughfares were waterways, wide canals on which floated the typical flat, squat-formed, blunt-prowed barges with their red-brown canvas covers; the many-gabled houses poised fantastically on their piles over the water; the great flat stretches of countryside by Haarlem, spread with their vivid masses of tulips. The mingled homeliness and hustle of the cities touched him; he spent hours on the Boompjes, the tree-lined quay of Rotterdam, watching merchandise being piled up under the leafy branches, or taking a childish delight in the painted red and yellow masses of oiled cheese in the weigh-houses. It was a country where the folk-spirit had transcended the forms of sovereignty retained by other countries and reigned supreme.

His stay in Holland imbued him with a close affection for the Netherlander mentality, which emerged strongly in his work when he found the sanctuary in the Low Countries where his life ended. No other foreign musician has ever come so close to the Netherlands spirit as Bull did; and no other from a foreign land had been so intimately adopted into its national art. That first visit, long before his closing years, produced proof of Bull's feeling for the folk of Holland, inspiring him with his " Duch Daunce " and the " Boerendans " which is imbued with the spirit of the Dutch peasantry.

It was at Amsterdam that Bull received his greatest gift from Holland, the friendship of Jan Pieterzoon Sweelinck. The Dutchman and the Englishman had a natural affinity of mind, immortalized in the fantasia which Bull wrote on a fugue by Sweelinck as a memorial when his Netherlander friend died. Both stood similarly high, with a curious resemblance in the popular affection which they evoked in the public regard of their respective countries. One is reminded of the record of Bull's Gresham address when one reads Tiedman's description of the public enthusiasm at Sweelinck's organ recitals : " There was a wonderful concourse every day ; everyone was proud to have known, seen, heard the man." Bull recognized his peer the first day that, attracted by report, he entered the old church to hear Sweelinck play. The building had an impressive simplicity, more touching than any sterner austerity. It was crowded ; but the congregation was motionless, unlike that of the New Church in the city, where the merchants gathered when bad weather prevented their meeting on the Bridge of the Dam, to " walke in two rankes by couples, one ranke goinge up, and another goinge downe, that there is no way to get out of the Churche except they slip out of the doores, when in one of these rankes, they pass by them." There was something uplifting to Bull in this stillness and silence. Where the sunlight entered, it fell in broad shafts, breaking up the broad stone flags, the walls and even the forms and faces of the people otherwise in shadow into angular patterns, reflecting the window-shapes with an unearthly effect. The dark habilments and dresses, mostly unornamented, merging into the shadow, with the stiff white linen head-dresses of the women lifting their faces out of the gloom with an effect of wings, added to this curiously ethereal impression.

Sweelinck's performance was masterly; but it was no mere virtuoso display. The Dutch musician had much of his race's solidarity and love of massive forms, with also the moods of child-like pleasure in naive detail. His mind, as the music revealed it, had, however, as has been said of him, a capacity for moving " over wide spaces with a grand sweep of the wings." It epitomized the spirit of the Dutch, indomitable in their struggle against the encroachments of nature and of man alike, capable of their wide-flung maritime enterprise. It was the music, truly of a land where " The Northerne winds of themselves ordinarily colde, doe here in a long course on all sides glide upon the German Sea, thereby gatheringe farre greater colde, and so rush intoe these plaine Provinces, no where stopped either by mountaines or woodes; there beinge no Mountaines, scarce any hils, no woodes, scarce any groves, to hide them from violent passage with their uttermoste force."

DR. JOHN BULL

Bull, listening and watching, realized that Sweelinck's hold upon his Dutch audiences was strong because he was himself their own symbol. His playing that day had the intensity and rugged strength, movingly blended with wistful tenderness, of his own striking Dutch features and those features were emblematic of his country. Through it ran the broad humanity of his feeling for his folk, which eventually inspired him to create from folk-lore the regular dance-sequences which became known as the Suite—the seed of the most important musical form of the future, the Symphony.

An immediate liking was felt by the two musicians for each other when Bull introduced himself after the performance. Both were precisely the same age. Each possessed the same type of musical outlook and an amazing similarity of technical skill. Both had known each other's work previous to the meeting and admired it. Bull was Sweelinck's guest for a while in Amsterdam then, and the two visited each other frequently in later years, when the English musician was in exile at Antwerp. It was to Sweelinck, indeed, that he owed that final sanctuary. Through the Dutch musician came the invitation to the Spanish Netherlands which secured Bull the interest, friendship and patronage of the Archduke Albrecht who was his later protector.

In Brussels Bull again found certain signs implicit in the popular life and the buildings about him. He recognized the affinity brought about by the Gallic-Walloon element in the Belgian population with the traits which he had noticed in some parts of Paris. In spite of the deep catholic feeling of the country, he had the conviction that the Spanish influence there could not endure, as he looked upon the Gothic beauty of the 15th century Hôtel de Ville, with its tall belfry crowned, in naive Flemish fashion, by the statue of St. Michael. There was the same complete remotesness from the Spanish feeling in the Gothic splendour of the Cathedral of St-Gudule and St-Michael dominating the city on the hillside. He little imagined then how closely familiar he was to become with its 13th century beauty when a royal organist later in the Archduke's capital. Most of all, however, his interest centred in the Grand' Place, surrounded with its magnificent old Flemish buildings, where he could observe the ordinary people on market and fair days and achieve personal contact with them and learn their ideas. There he was to gain much solace in times to come, maintaining his human sympathies when severed from kindred and friends, as in the great cathedral on the hill his spirit was to learn calm in the quiet aisles glorified by the rare light cast from its great pointed windows, with their richly-hued stained glass.

Sweelinck had been anxious for him to visit Brussels. Under the Archduke's rule, there had been a steady movement towards a better understanding between the two Netherlands. Although under the Habsburg Holy Empire, the ruler of the Spanish Netherlands had a sincere feeling for the people of his realm. His life among them convinced him that the rift of race brought about by religious differences was something which every effort should be made to overcome. So far as the Dutch were concerned, such aims had poor chance of success; Holland had suffered too much under the invasions and occupations of the Spaniards and the horrors of the Inquisition to risk any closer ties with the Spanish-ruled Low Country, once their independence had been achieved under William of Orange. They were the more suspicious at the time, because, though they were actually free, Spain refused to recognize their real independence, and every Dutchman knew that the risk of invasion always existed, on the pretext of dealing with rebels, so long as ambiguity regarding Spain's intentions remained.

Sweelinck, however, was an idealist as well as a patriot, and he had a sincere respect and regard for the Archduke's qualities. He felt that it was due to Bull that he should not return home without becoming acquainted with Brussels and obtaining the notice of so noted a patron of the arts as the Archduke. He had taken steps, through influential friends, to secure Bull's invitation.

That invitation, though so important for Bull later, brought about the swift termination of his travels abroad. His welcome in Brussels was brilliant. Bull's high place in the affections of Germans and Dutch made the Flemish people eager to greet him. The Archduke himself, a devoted patron of the arts was personally anxious to have him at his Court; for Bull's fame had become so widespread throughout Europe through his year of travel that "he became so admir'd, that he was counted to accept of any place or preferment suitable to his profession, either within the dominions of the emperor, king of France, or Spain."

Startling though it may seem, in view of Bull's antecedents, Spain appeared anxious to render him honour also. England's old enemy, Philip II, had died in 1598 and his son, Philip III, reigned in his place. He was a pious Catholic, but he had neither his father's strength nor cruelty. Although the decline of Spain under his father was continuing under his rule, Spain was still the main Catholic power and still at strife with the Protestants. It was, therefore, a difficult problem for Bull to solve when, through the enthusiastic praises of the Archduke, he received

WANDERJAHR

Philip's invitation to visit Madrid. That invitation guaranteed him safe-conduct; but Madrid was filled with England's old enemies, many still envenomed against the victory of the Armada. Bull's patriotic reputation was known there; and behind all lurked still the dark power of the Inquisition, which respected neither foreigners nor natives in its fanatical hatred of heresy. To refuse the royal invitation would be to put his host, the Archduke, in a very bad light, since it was to his recommendation that such gesture was due. To go to Spain was to take a precarious step. Bull, also, had been pursuing his mission during his travels; he was already too much within the orbit of Spanish influence to be entirely safe, even in the Archduke's domains. What information he had to convey could only be transmitted perilously and by elaborate subterfuges. He had found his idiosyncrasies useful. He still liked devising elaborate geometric patterns in which to transcribe his music. They were highly decorative in effect and he took a pride in exhibiting them. His fellow-musicians admired their ingenuity, while amateurs found then a quaint novelty and a habit which added to his reputation as a temperamental and whimsical character. They were obviously the charming and naive oddity of an erratic genius, and no doubt Queen Elizabeth perused as such any specimens which reached her.

News from home, filtering in through the Low Country ports, also disturbed him. Report had it that the Queen's health was far from good and, if anything were to happen to Elizabeth, Bull felt that he should be in London. He felt this because of his sincere regard for the Queen; and he felt it also as a patriot. If Elizabeth passed from the scheme of European politics, nobody could foretell what repercussions her death would have in other capitals and around the civilized world. There were many things with which he wished to make the Queen or her ministers acquainted, as results of his travels. Above all, he must not be out of England if any difficulties faced the country in the time ahead.

The possibility of renewed widespread conflict was also extremely dangerous for him. He was aware that all his doings could not have passed unobserved. The moment war loomed, no matter how much previous assurance had been given beforehand, the safety of anyone so identified with many big non-Catholic powers was dubious. If anything were known of his activities, then nothing could save him; probably the Inquisition would lay its hands on him and that body had unpalatable ways of removing those whom it suspected.

Bull had no open means of communicating his difficult situation to Elizabeth or her ministers; "but the tidings of these transactions coming to the English Court, Elizabeth commanded him home." It was a cunning move, though most commentators have seen in it nothing but an example of the Queen's jealousy. To this view colour was lent by the story that Elizabeth vented her vexation by saying that this, of all Bulls she knew, had the longest asses' ears; but that story has also been traced to another and earlier event in Bull's life, as legend goes. In any event, the command extricated Bull from his difficulties. It removed all possible suspicion from him by giving him the appearance of having incurred his sovereign's displeasure. It enabled him to excuse himself to King Philip on the score of obedience to his royal mistress.

He took immediate advantage of his opportunity. Within a few days he was again in England. For one under censure, he was received with remarkable urbanity. He resumed his duties forthwith at the Chapel Royal and Gresham College. Two years later, the Queen's will designated him one of the favoured loyal servants who were to receive special mourning for her funeral.

At the moment of his return, Bull envisaged no such melancholy event. There was at once elation and relief in his home-coming. His year had taught him much. Before, he had looked out from England at the great world; abroad, he had looked from the world at England. He had seen greater territories; but, in the human scheme of peoples, his comparisons had not decreased her magnitude. He had perceived his country's influence; the range of his travels had given him a fuller perspective of the extent of her spiritual power and significance.

He had worked for England; and, more, he had, though he little realized how much, contributed something to his country's lasting glory in his own work. His musical records of his travels were to provide future generations with a panorama of the world he had visited, full of colour and human interest. A few pieces, here a " French Currant," there a " Duch Daunce," or again, a " Germans Almayne "; yet in these he had recorded, more movingly than most literature, a vivid Elizabethan itinerary.

Now he faced towards his native land again. His travels had taken him through regions ravaged by the war which, for decades, had almost ceaselessly torn the Continent. He had lived among peoples with no barrier to defend them other than their own armed force and the dubious lines of a frontier marked on a map. As the cliffs of his country came in sight, he recalled the words of his friend Shakespeare, realizing as never before, the fortunate situation, spiritually and physically, of

DR. JOHN BULL

" This fortress built by Nature for herself
Against infection and the hand of war,
This happy breed of men, this little world,
This precious stone set in the silver sea,
This blessed plot, this earth, this realm, this England."

Passing Pageant

CHAPTER IX

PASSING PAGEANT

ON March 24th, 1603, Queen Elizabeth died. Anxiety had held the country in its grip for days before, from the moment it was realized that the great sovereign was seriously ill. The national mood grew heavy and full of apprehension as news of her critical condition filtered out from Richmond Palace to London and spread farther afield. The Queen had become identified in the public mind, not only with England's triumphant ascent among nations abroad, but also with the brilliance and prosperity of the period of peace subsequent to the defeat of the Armada. The thought of her passing seemed to many to mean almost the tangible loss of a part of the national heritage.

To Bull the possibility of the Queen's death was filled with a dual sadness. The patriot in him knew, with something of prophecy, that her end would also be that of a chapter of glory in England's story. The man stood, more deeply than he had ever imagined could be the case, before the imminent loss of a friend whose foibles had never outweighed the qualities of mind and sentiment which she had shown towards him. In much more than office, the Queen's Master of Musicke had come to realize how closely his own career and conditions of mind were bound up with the ideals so magnificently sustained by his sovereign.

In the Palace the atmosphere oppressed him. He felt

powerless before an event which, as time passed, he felt more and more as something fraught with disaster for his beloved country. He was strained and nerve-racked by surmise. Little or no news percolated out from the sick-room where the dying Queen lay. Her ministers were keeping a watchful eye on all reports. They knew that the situation demanded vigilance and that there were many waiting to take advantage of it. The Queen's death, if it ensued, must be kept secret until the last possible moment, that they might be able to control matters in the public interest in such way as to foil any attempts of opportunists to profit by it or cause any disturbance. In spite of this, rumour was busy every moment and stealthy intrigue could be glimpsed in covert gestures and expressions and in small groups in every corner of the Palace, conversing in undertones and breaking up or relapsing into silence as any outsider approached them. Bitterly, Bull recognized that the greatness of the Queen had never been more manifest than in the moment of her passing. She alone, by the magnetism of her personality and the power of her will, had held in cohesion these conflicting impulses of self-interest which were preparing to become active the moment she no longer existed to control and restrain them.

The tragic futility of his hanging about, waiting, unable to do anything to avert the ominous event which every moment made appear more inevitable, reduced him to a constricted mood of sullen gloom. Eventually, he could bear it no longer. Wherever he turned, the vista before him, its details of furniture, the figures waiting about were full of associations of the woman struggling with a dread power before which neither her own indomitable courage and wilfulness nor the deepest loyalty of her most devoted subject could avail her. As he tried to evade his perturbation by moving here and there, the entire Palace became intolerable to him. Whispering to Giles, who, like all the royal servants, was in anxious attendance, to summon him if anything transpired, he slipped out into the Palace grounds.

Outside, he had hoped that the air would revive his spirits after the crowded ante-chambers; but he found it heavy and oppressive. There was a damp latency in the March chill. Yet he had no energy to move quickly. The semi-paralysis of his mind affected his body. He wrapped his cloak about him and paced moodily to and fro by some shrubs beneath a clump of trees. He could not control his thoughts enough to pray coherently. He trudged aimlessly back and forth over a small stretch of pathway, his whole being filled with a mute appeal which, hopelessly, he dimly knew to be futile.

How long he lingered in this way he could never estimate. At the end of a turn, however, his steps brought him just beyond a corner of the Palace, and as he was about to wheel and retrace his steps, a slight stir at an upper window caught his eye. Somebody was opening a casement. Scarcely conscious of even idle curiosity, he paused. The figure of a woman appeared, peering out into the grounds below. Bull recognized Lady Scrope, a well-known figure in Court circles. A certain touch of furtiveness in her movements stirred the alertness developed by many of his activities. He drew back into the shadow of the bushes and watched. Leaning out, he saw her extend her hand, opening her fingers. There was a minute flash and on the ground some paces away a jewelled ring alighted with a tiny tinkle. Before he could step forward to investigate it further, a cloaked figure detached itself from the shade some distance away down the path and ran forward, crouching. As the stranger reached the spot where the ring had fallen, he bent and picked it up. When he straightened up, Bull glimpsed his features. It was Robert Carey, Lady Scrope's brother.

Stooping again, Carey dashed quickly back into the shadow from which he had emerged and, before Bull could collect himself, he heard the sound of galloping hoofs pounding away from the Palace, taking the course through the park that led northward to Kew. Realization flashed in on Bull. That route led to Scotland, where James VI, son of Mary Stuart, awaited news of the throne to which he was heir. With his breath suddenly caught in his throat, Bull spun round and ran back to the Palace. The groups were much as he had left them in the ante-hall. The doors leading to the Queen's apartments had not yet opened. He found Giles in a corner, talking softly with young Thomas Byrde. His hand trembling as he laid it on his friend's arm, Bull drew him aside. Giles noticed his agitation immediately, and his quick mind leapt to its cause. To his swift whispered query Bull could only trust himself to nod. Giles' grip on his arm tightened sympathetically, urging him towards the outer entrance to the ante-room. As they reached the door there was a sudden, rustling stir in the room behind them, then tense silence. Bull glanced back involuntarily. The door to the Queen's apartments had opened and a chamberlain stood facing the throng of courtiers, his hand raised. Bull knew what the announcement would be. He did not wish to hear it there. The massed forms of the courtiers craning forward either side of the way left open for the royal bedchamber attendants, their features acutely silhouetted against the light, looked like waiting carrion birds. He hurried out.

With nervous hurry, he urged Giles along until they were

outside the Palace, walking rapidly down the main drive. They had only gone a few paces when a great bell tolled suddenly, but sombrely. Bull halted, putting his hand over his eyes. He stood still so for a few seconds, wincing with each stroke of the bell. Then he glanced back. On the roof of the Palace the form of a helmeted, cuirassed soldier had appeared beside the flagstaff, hauling at its cords. Bull's arms fell limply to his sides. He stood there mutely, his features grown pale and drawn, as the Tudor standard, beneath which England had ascended to greater glory than ever before in history, fluttered down, to rise no more.

The next few days were a phantasmagoria to Bull. Three hours after Elizabeth's death the Privy Council had decided to proclaim the Scottish monarch as James I. From that moment there was ceaseless activity at the Palace, as to and from the royal residence and the Crown offices in London. It shocked Bull to see how soon the great Queen became a wraith, even to those who had been nearest to her and who owed her their fortunes. One thought dominated the Court. All were absorbed, almost hectically, in preparations to greet the new sovereign, sketching addresses, framing petitions, devising magnificent costumes, scheming every imaginable way to catch the royal eye or impress the royal ear. In all this petty scrambling for privilege, preference and profit, he felt the presage of a coming gloom, deeper than that which present emotion cast over his spirit. There was no echo of the chorus of praise and adulation which had risen about the dead Queen every day for years. Even the great poets of the Court maintained silence, probably busy in composing some panygeric on the awaited monarch. As Chettle wrote, in one of the few tributes that appeared, " England's Mourning Garment," even

Shakespeare, the one genius capable of creating the adequate memorial, seemed to have no urge to evoke

> "Deep from his honied Muse one sable teare
> To mourne her death that graced his desert
> And to his laies opened her royall eare."

He, himself, had to be concerned with apparel; but it was not festive, but funereal. With barely time to be fitted, he received notice from the Lord Chamberlain's office that his name was one of those listed for special mourning liveries for the Queen's burial. There was a rather wistful wry smile on his lips as he laid out the sombre garments of black cloth and sable velvet, ready to attire himself. He contrasted them with the well-worn crimson and black doublet which he was changing for them. Elizabeth, grudging the outlay on royal liveries to do her credit when alive, had bequeathed him, with her other favoured servants, new raiment to honour her when dead. He wondered how far her ironic humour had flavoured the bequest; for the cost, though from the royal exchequer, really came from the pocket of her successor, the miserly James, the moment she was dead.

At the funeral ceremony Bull's sombre mood lifted momentarily as he played the "Lux aeterna." Into the music passed something, not only of his prayer for the dead woman, but of his faith in her immortal fame. As the funeral oration was delivered, he glanced about him quietly, taking in the assembly. Many were obviously there for formal reasons; but he saw also those whom the occasion moved as much as it did himself. He noted, with the hypersensitivity of his mood, that some, such as Sir Walter Raleigh, seemed also touched by the strange foreboding which he himself felt. The congregation, in its mourning apparel, was strangely symbolic. The Court was bereft, not only of its main figure, the dead Queen, but of its brilliance and gaiety. Bull found in its sombre aspect the reflection of the shadow over his own heart.

The weeks that followed were filled with ever-increasing bustle of preparations to receive the new sovereign. On all sides could be seen excitement, and here and there, something of anxiety. The change of monarch meant changes in the Court. None quite knew who would be in favour when the Scots king arrived to assume the crown, or how the royal appointments might be shuffled. This feeling increased as new faces appeared at Court, the advance officials of James, bearing his messages and instructions. The outward aspects of London, however, suggested nothing but regal pomp and gaiety. The mercers and cloth-merchants were working day and night, for not only were new robes and costumes being clamoured for, there were also wide demands for material to decorate the houses of the nobles and the wealthy burgesses, with bunting to decorate the streets. Every tailor's needle flew; the goldsmiths hammered and smelted; the great, lumbering wagons of the wine-merchants carried their loads to the halls where ceremonial banquets were to be held, that the cellars might be replenished richly. The route to the Palace of Greenwich, where the new King was first to take up residence, bristled with scaffoldings, where seats for the better-class citizens were being erected.

The new King arrived early in May and was greeted with great pomp and ceremony. The magnificence of his surroundings only seemed to increase the peaked meanness of his features and the febrile lines of his weak-legged form. Bull, as the other officials of the Royal Household, was presented; but he was not commanded to be in attendance at Greenwich. Music was the first of the arts which had flourished so radiantly at Elizabeth's Court to recede from the royal orbit of James. The new King was also absorbed in making himself acquainted with the affairs of his new realm, especially its fiscal concerns, and had at first little time for more than the formal functions attendant on his arrival and inauguration of his Court.

The royal arrival at Greenwich ushered in a series of grand functions. Dour though James might be, his consort, Anne of Denmark, had a taste for gaiety of sorts. Through her influence, the King had already taken the Lord Chamberlain's players under his direct patronage, as the King's Players, giving licence to "these ovr seruants, Lavrence Fletcher, William Shakespeare, Richard Bvrbage, Avgvstine Phillippes, John Hemmings, Henrie Condell, William Sly, Robert Armyn, Richard Cowlye and the rest of their associates, freely to vse and exercise the arte and facvlty of playing comedies, tragedies, histories, enterlvdes, moralls, pastorals, stage-plaies, and svch other like, as thei haue already stvdied or hereafter shall vse or stvdie, as well for the recreation of ovr louing svbjects as for ovr solace and pleasvre, when we shall thinke good to see them, dvring ovr pleasvre." She even obtained her own company of Revels in 1609, the warrant stating:

"Whereas the Queene ovr dearest wife, hath for her pleasvre and recreation appointed her seruavntes Robert Daborne, William Shakespeare, Nathaniel Field and Edward Kirkham to provide and bring vpp a convenient nomber of children who shalbe called the Children of her Maiesties Reuelles . . . within the Blacke Fryers in ovr cittie of London and els where within ovr realme of England . . . and them to exercise in the qvalitie of playing, according to ovr royall pleasvre: prouided allwayes that noe playes, etc., shalbe by them presented, bvt svch playes, etc., as haue receiued the aprobacion and allowance of ovr Maister of the Rouelles for the tyme being."

In spite of such royal interest, it was soon apparent to Bull that the drama itself was changing with the times. The glory of the Elizabethan Era had faded with the Queen's passing; little by little, its luminance was eclipsed by the gloom and pedantry of James. The Tudor age had been one of mounting hope. With the Stuart King the glories of exploration, combat and conquest, the age of adventure and acquisition ended. James, nervous and cowardly by nature, as well as avaricious, sought peace at all costs, even that of national pride. He had his eyes fixed already, beyond the cessation of hostilities with Spain, on an alliance with the daughter of the mortal enemy of Elizabeth's sea-captains and colonists, through his son, Charles. In the place of daring and imaginative personalities, brilliant in thought and action, he surrounded himself with sycophants who would bow before his claims as divine instrument on earth. There was an end to the old spirit of enterprise and adventure. Unlike Elizabeth, James did not direct the vision of his people towards wider horizons; he turned the eyes of England in upon herself, making the centre of national interest his own regal state, so far as was humanly possible. With Laud and his like, he was preparing to suppress religious liberty by the Star Chamber, throwing people otherwise moderate over into the Puritans' ranks, to stand as defenders of the people's rights. Under his insane "king-craft," all had to centre round the infallible monarch; Church and State were but the instruments of his royal will. Little by little the old fire of patriotism and faith dwindled, settling down into a sullen glow of despondency and the growing shadow of pessimism.

The very arts which Bull loved showed this deadening influence. Gloom, cynicism, terror and nervous tension pervaded the drama, culminating in the horror-fraught tragedies of Webster and Ford. Shakespeare himself reflected the changed mood. The immediate outcome was "Macbeth." The essence of the times was distilled in plays such as Tournier's "Atheist's Tragedy." There was a new and often priggish, invariably pedantic moralizing in literature and poetry. Even those of genius, such as Donne and Herbert, were marked by a new harshness and dark sternness, the former frequently being cynically realistic. In music the King's taste for solemnity encouraged the pedantic and the importation of sombre forms, such as the Spanish Pavan, the more so since James desired to overcome the old antipathy to Spain. Bull, by his nature, could not play the sycophant, nor could he lose the image of his people in the effigy of kingship which was the most James could achieve with all that pedantic learning which caused him to be lampooned as "the wisest fool in Christendom."

Even apart from his Court position and his artistic vocation, Bull found his life affected. His recreations were not the same. Raleigh, who had founded the circle of The Mermaid Tavern, was in disfavour from the first with James. The shadow of this displeasure loomed over his circle, deepening rapidly into tragedy. The social intercourse of the intellectuals of the new reign changed its character, shifting to the clubs at The Mitre and The Devil Tavern in Fleet Street, where Ben Jonson presided over the Apollo Club.

With Jonson and his circle, indeed, Bull found at first his only relief from the depression which afflicted him. Even then, it was some time before he recovered himself enough to emerge socially again. The shock of Elizabeth's death had scarcely passed before he encountered fresh tragedy which, in all its implications, seemed ominous for his own future.

The new King's temper towards the former favourites of Queen Elizabeth showed itself quickly. It indicated, in its first manifestation, what would be the likely fate of all those who had taken a hand in her policies and incurred the rancour of Spain. Suspicious to the point of mania, James had always looked with disfavour on Raleigh. Without any evidence, he had an obsession that this favoured courtier of Elizabeth had worked against his accession. The moment he succeeded to the throne, Raleigh was stripped of every office and privilege which he had enjoyed. This, however, did not satisfy the King's animosity. Raleigh was one of the few leading figures remaining who had challenged Spain and consistently borne arms against Philip's forces. Though Raleigh had been in Ireland when the Armada arrived, as Vice-Admiral of Devon he had taken an important part in naval work then. He had headed several expeditions against the Spaniards in America, and he had accompanied Howard and Essex in the expedition against Cadiz, being wounded there. His brilliant and haughty figure irritated James; it reflected the glories of a Court which he disliked to think might outshine his own. James determined on his destruction, in spite of the earnest intercession of his own son, Prince Henry.

On November 17th, 1603, within the first year of James' reign, Raleigh was brought to trial for high treason at

Winchester. The Attorney-General, Sir Edward Coke, had been instructed to secure a conviction at all costs, and he worked brutally for that end. His presentation of the prosecution was an epic of innuendo and equivocacy. His attitude throughout was one of hectoring and sheer bullying. When Raleigh demanded the right to speak for himself, Coke overbearingly shouted " Thou shalt not ! " Yet, in spite of every subterfuge, those who attended the trial sympathized with Raleigh's challenge : " Your words cannot condemn me ; my innocency is my defence. Prove one of these things wherewith you have charged me, and I will confess the whole indictment, and that I am the horriblest traitor that ever lived, and worthy to be crucified with a thousand, thousand, torments." Even one of those who most disliked the accused man said : " When the trial began I would have gone a thousand miles to see Raleigh hanged ; before the trial closed I would have gone a thousand miles to save his life." In spite of all, however, James had instructed his sycophantic judges, and Raleigh had been condemned.

The brutality and injustice of the entire proceedings had affected Bull painfully. Raleigh, for him, was one of the glorious figures of Elizabeth's Court, the colleague of Drake, Frobisher, Hawkins and Howard, the high-visioned dreamer of English colonization, who had founded Virginia in honour of the Virgin Queen, the noble chronicler of Grenville's heroic mortal fight on " The Revenge." The more he pondered the matter, the more he felt that Raleigh was being victimized because of his patriotic opposition to Spain. He did not foresee how his view would be justified by events thirteen years later, when Raleigh finally suffered execution because his seamen came into conflict with Spanish colonists. In spite of the dubious clemency of

James, which withheld Raleigh from the block, but condemned him to thirteen years of imprisonment in the Tower, Bull, knowing how his own life had identified him with Spain's defeat, and knowing yet more deeply that his whole spirit revolted against James' servile attitude to Philip, was strongly perturbed. Dimly, probably as yet remotely, he felt the shadows growing in his own life, closing slowly but surely about him. It was not in him to shrink; but, however bravely he carried himself, however much he carried on his work at Court, he was henceforth always conscious of something latent in the atmosphere of this changed world in which he found himself.

In March, 1604, James decided to mark his first anniversary by "his royall Entrye and proceedinge throvgh his honorable Citie of London, together with our soueraigne Ladie Qveene Anne his wief, & the noble Prince Henrie his sonne, solemnized xvth daie of Marche, 1603."

There was already widespread dissatisfaction among many of the great citizens of London that the King delayed this honour, and much discontent was being felt by many nobles and courtiers with that "king-craft" upon which James prided himself, yet which replaced former brilliance by pompous solemnity. Neither Catholics nor Puritans had received the concessions both expected. On all hands it had become plain that the new sovereign's vaunted learning was often remote from practical wisdom. As Bull had sensed, the death of Elizabeth was not only the passing of a great queen; it was the end of a great era.

In spite of his self-importance and his megalomaniac belief in the Divine Right of Kings, the innate cowardice of James, which was already seeking to placate Spain at whatever cost to the pride and power of England which Elizabeth's ministers and sea-captains had built up, shrank from coming to open conflict with his people. Here, also, he sought to mollify. Hence, notwithstanding his dislike of expenditure, the King made ready to impress the citizens of London with his magnificence.

Yet, again, Bull found himself supplied with a new livery, by order of Sir George Howme, "Master of the Greate Warederobe to the high and mightie Prince, our gracious soveraigne Lord James by the Grace of God Kinge of England, Scotland, Fraunce and Ireland." He was apportioned " iij yardes " of crimson cloth, for wear in the great procession of the Royal Household and was summoned to collect it. James left nothing to chance when he expended. On the way to the Royal Wardrobe at Blackfriars, he and Giles encountered other royal servants, whose attendants bore their material in parcels. Just on the threshold they met the actor, Richard Burbidge, accompanied by his dramatist, Master William Shakespeare, whose servant was carrying their combined allotment of " skarlet red cloth," in which the newly constituted King's Players were to figure in the pageant. There was some banter that "poets and musicians shoulde profitt greatlie at suche tyme by reason of their knowledge of juste measure," before they waved the actor and dramatist on their way to the latter's home in the Bear Garden at Southwark.

Nevertheless, in spite of such touches of fun and some excitement, the day of the great display depressed Bull. It was ceremonial, not festive. A new rigidity of etiquette was becoming manifest. There were many vexed questions of precedence, hotly debated among the higher Court functionaries, before the day arrived, which soured the savour of the event. To Bull it all seemed to resemble the stage-management of the playhouses he knew so well. It was artificial in its effect. It lacked the old, spontaneous exuberance among those participating, as the acclamations of the crowds in the streets lacked the popular surge of enthusiasm of Elizabeth's time. It was not a national demonstration; it was a show, which elicited applause. He remembered, with a poignant stir, the figure of the dead Queen, as she had ridden gallantly to exhort her troops before the Armada. He renewed, for a brief moment, the clamorous joy of the victory night. He recalled how even the malcontent Parliament had risen to cheer her when, turning the situation with Tudor dexterity, she had thanked her well-beloved subjects for aiding her in righting abuses and enabled her to right grievances. He stood very still and upright, almost like a soldier at attention, as the images of these heroic scenes passed again before his mind's eye. He was recalled to himself by a heavy rumbling of wheels and the clatter of horses hoofs, and the King passed by to take his place in the procession. As he glimpsed James' meagre form huddled into the immense gilded state coach with its florescence of plumes and ribbons, he was reminded of some over-blown, forced and wilting bloom, in the heart of which nestled an insect.

He recalled his premonitions when he rode in the new King's pageant then, though it was some months after Raleigh's conviction. His thought added to the unreality of the occasion. He remembered the glorious procession of brain, bravery and beauty which had moved through Elizabeth's court. He reviewed that other pageant of privateersmen, buccaneers, colonists and explorers, poets, dramatists and musicians—adventurers into new worlds of thought and of material territory. Many of them had gone: Sidney, Essex, Leicester, Marlowe, Spenser, Peele—and now Raleigh. Moving in that living procession, he seemed among phantoms. The pageant of the dead was something more living to him then.

The passing of the old era had awakened him, as yet only partially, to the passing of time and his own days. The new-born consciousness of the past epoch had infused his own youth. The new period upon him was one in which youth vanished. By the curious sensitivity of his nature, Bull and England were again identified. The gloom upon his own spirit was laying its hold upon the country. He rode on in the procession, moving in pomp but the glory had departed. Like the land to which his every impulse was linked, he was afflicted by the sense of unknown approaching disaster.

Appollo and the Mermaid

CHAPTER X

APOLLO AND THE MERMAID

BULL's natural buoyancy soon bore him above his forebodings. At least, he was able to put them aside by diverting his thoughts towards fresh activities. His essential vitality prevented him from sinking into brooding overlong. Nevertheless, the disturbance which his initial impressions of the new reign had created in him persisted as an unrealized under-current in his mind. He was no longer consciously aware of it, but it gradually showed in his work. His music became elaborate and involved as it had never been before. It provided some ground for Burney, in a later period of didactic commonplace and superficiality, to affirm that " he entered deeper into the *arcana* of the art, and pedantry of the times, than most of his contemporaries." The psychological state in which Bull was then, tended to complicate his musical thought and style. To one of Burney's extremely limited executive powers, in an age which seldom penetrated beyond the letter to the spirit of things, it might well appear that he " made the invention of new difficulties of every kind which could impede or dismay a performer his sole study "—though it should be remembered that the garrulous author of " A General History of Music " also considered Johann Sebastian Bach similar to Bull in such preoccupations.

Actually, Bull was using his vast technique involuntarily to escape from emotions or meditations which might depress him unbearably. This rendered it inevitable that he would use sheer craftsmanship at times to produce work which, while formally impressive, was slight in inspiration. It was, however, true to his mood at the time and, taken in relation to such circumstances, as well as in comparison with his other work, it had documentary value and was humanly revealing. It was in close correspondence with his general habits then. He was living restlessly, in a nervously unsettled way. He sought distraction and amusement more than at any time since the years when he was fretting against constraint at Hereford; and there was no longer Blitheman's quiet wisdom to calm him. More than he could realize, he was essentially of the age of Elizabeth and the passing of her era with her life was of more profound significance in his life than any sentiment.

Subconsciously, he sensed the commencement of a fresh phase of change. Hitherto he had welcomed this, since it bore him along on vital currents; but this insidious transformation which England was undergoing was without urge or momentum, an enveloping necromancy which seemed to threaten petrification. Its very intangibility made it seem more ominous. His inability to define it troubled him most. It bred a distemper of spirit afflicting his mind, distorting and exaggerating his outlook to a phantasmal extent at times. His whole universe seemed to be disturbed, seen with his mind's eye. England appeared to have swung out of her orbit. The sunlight which had suffused her spirit had receded. The planets in her new circle lacked luminance and starry brilliance; they moved through chill vapours in morbid pomp. The warmth of enthusiastic imagination had gone from a world where wonders had dwindled. The cold, reflective light of the new epoch was lunar, not solar.

However extravagant such mood, in it Bull was again identified with the period, in its phase of change. In him was working instinctively the spirit which was appearing in the morbid drama of Shakespeare's " Hamlet " and the horrific melodrama of Webster's tragedies. The Elizabethan Era was the zenith of an epoch which had fed its imagination upon marvels : by the time that the Jacobean Era commenced, the store of these was growing exhausted. Deprived of its habitual sustenance, public feeling assuaged its appetite upon artificial products, ideas abnormal, sensational, or phantasmal. Even the least exaggerated, most balanced minds assumed a new mordancy, if not cynicism. The Tudor Age had been one of limitless hope. Its universe, metamorphosized by the discovery of the New World, had appeared infinite. With the Stuart Era came disillusionment and pessimism. The glamour of revelation had vanished and all things on the terrestial globe had become finite.

Beneath the sensationalism of its first reactions, however, it was an epoch of realism. It was characterized by a new critical attitude of mind, a new scientific trend of thought. Lacking precedent marvels, it concentrated on the matter-of-fact. It was sceptical; it scrutinized, analysed and recorded. The sixteenth century had discovered wonders and gathered riches. The seventeenth recorded facts and took stock of its inherited wealth. New dynasty, new century and new trend of ideas marked a fresh chapter in national history.

His initial moods apart, therefore, Bull's occupation with the substance rather than the spirit of music at that time, his careful analysis of form and scrupulous regard for detail, even to a complicated degree, his exploitation of a scientifically exact technique, were all in tune with the times. His mind showed a reaction similar to that which produced the closed-packed, involved yet realistic and analytical style of John Donne in poetry and literature. As it settled, there was a new precision and concentration in his music, even a new terseness of musical statement, with an arbitrary rapidity of modulation which had close affinity to the contemporary work of Bacon, with its swift transitions of thought. There was a tendency in it to exploit scholarship and ransack the stores of erudition identical with that which pervaded the prose of Robert Burton's " Anatomy of Melancholy." In his elaboration of style, also, both where it was ornate and where it was chiselled down, Bull showed the same traits as were apparent in the work of writers such as Sir Thomas Browne. The stylism which characterized the " Religio Medici " was the result of the waning of broader and more spontaneous stimuli and the prevalent tendency to substitute for this an elaborate care for detail and the more exquisite qualities of form.

The changed conditions forced him to seek interest outside his former accustomed surroundings. The Jacobean Court rapidly ceased to be the magnetizing and radiating centre of national life which that of Elizabeth had been. The doctrinaire King James shrank from unorthodox imagination. His superstitious nature confounded seership and sorcery and fled for sanctuary into dull, sterile scholarship. Pedantry and an absurdly pretentious pseudo-philosophy were all that this royal " wisest fool in Christendom " could produce to maintain the brilliant prestige of the preceding period. They were poor substitutes for that pervasive vitality which had taken poetry in the stride of its adventurous passion and active prowess. Little by little the intellectual centre of London shifted from the palace to the taverns and clubs where regular gatherings of artists and thinkers were creating a new type of genial, yet thoughtful, social intercourse. It was in such convivial centres that Bull found the main interest of his life at that time.

This form of intellectual group life grew naturally from the regular meetings at places such as the Mermaid Tavern in Bread Street which had commenced in the latter part of Elizabeth's reign. They were gay gatherings, though all the intellectual brilliance of the times could be encountered there. A jovial freedom characterized them; there was neither snobbery nor scholarly solemnity. Social differences disappeared at them. Nobles and knights mingled on equal terms with playwrights, poets, musicians and actors. The arts interested many of the aristocracy more than anything else. For some the interest of London concentrated not about the Palace, but in the playhouse. Rowland Whyte, writing to Sir Robert Sidney in October, 1599, made the comment that: " My Lord Southampton and Lord Rutland came (come) not to the court, the one doth but very seldom : they pass away the tyme in London merely in going to plaies every day." With Southampton, Shakespeare's friend, to whom " Venus and Adonis " was dedicated, were also other peers, such as Pembroke and Sussex, a good friend of Bull, mingling on familiar terms with literary talents in every field, dramatists, poets, philosophers, essayists and scientists, such as Shakespeare, Jonson, Marlowe, Hugh Holland, Bacon, the madrigalist Morley, the lutenist Dowland and Bull himself. It was a bohemia founded by an aristocrat, Sir Walter Raleigh, whose highest nobility for posterity was to exist in his writings.

At the Mermaid Tavern and other meeting-places, such as the Mitre Tavern in Fleet Street, and the Manor of the

Rose crypt, between Duck's-foot Lane and Merchant Taylors School, Bull found both mental interests and light-hearted amusement. The group had its diversions as well as its serious discussions, wit as much as wisdom, in which Bull, with his own humorous whimsicality, found welcome entertainment. No laugh rang louder than his own on the evenings when Skakespeare in his most inconsequential mood, entered on one of " the wit-combates betwixt him and Ben Jonson . . . like a Spanish greate gallion and an English man-of-war." The two represented the types of mind which differentiated the Elizabethan and Jacobean mentalities. " Master Jonson (like the former) was built far higher in learning, solid but slowe in his performances; Shakespeare with the English man-of-war, lesser in bulke, but lighter in sailing, coulde turn with all tides, tack about and take advantage of all windes, by the quickness of his wit and invention."

The playboy in Bull enjoyed the more frivolous and madcap excursions with which such recreations were interspersed, boisterous nocturnal outings through the town when the light-hearted intellectuals

" At Bread Street's Mermaid havinge din'd, and merry,
Propos'd to goe to Holborn in a wherry."

They came as a relief after the self-conscious solemnity of James' Court. They provided a common interest, strengthening his friendship with Giles, his frequent companion in the convivial company so congenial to the boisterous Worcestershireman. They counteracted Bull's own tendency to moodiness at the time, by renewing the usefulness of his nature and stimulating his sense of humour and whimsical fun.

APOLLO AND THE MERMAID

With the Stuart Era, the centre of such gatherings shifted from the Mermaid Tavern to the Apollo Club, founded at the Devil Tavern in Fleet Street, by Ben Jonson. Here the gatherings were less haphazard. The formal trend of the times replaced the casual meeting-place by the regular club. There were also sound political reasons for the change. The continuation of the Mermaid Tavern fraternity after the indictment of Raleigh, its founder, was unwise, King James' nature made it difficult to foresee where his suspicions might be aroused, however slight or far-fetched the cause. Encouraged by the King's fears, unscrupulous informers lurked everywhere and an open tavern allowed strangers too close a proximity to the bohemian circles, who were not always circumspect in their banter, to be safe.

Bull missed something of the old spontaneity and popular atmosphere in the new club. Where Apollo reigned, the spirit of Dionysos appeared infrequently. Ben Jonson, the leading figure, had an essential dignity, which even his escapades could not lessen. He modelled his work, in poetry and drama alike, upon classical models. He belonged to the learned in literature. His mind accepted the new period with an ease which Bull could not feel. Nevertheless, a close friendship existed between the two, probably founded on Jonson's determined opposition to a latinized style in English, born of kindred feeling to that which had caused Bull's own famous stand at Gresham College. At the time, also, Bull was interested in technique and the polished style of Jonson, his impressive elegies, courtly epistles and polished satires, ran in line with the momentary tendency of his thought. In spite of such academic traits, however, there was a deep sincerity and directness of mind in the poet, which appealed to Bull and had strengthened the friendship existent between them

DR. JOHN BULL

for some years. In many ways, Bull owed it to Jonson that he came to realize the possibilities of the new period. The association also prevented his current preoccupations with technique from degenerating into mere pedantry. In the very weaknesses which detracted from Jonson's genius, he saw the reflection of those which might become dangerous to himself. Above all, in an age of sycophancy and mean motives, such as the Jacobean tended to become, Jonson had a generosity of mind and spirit which, probably more than the obvious nature of his literary talents, caused him to be the outstanding figure in his field. The man behind his mannerisms was essentially likeable. He possessed sensitivity, even in his satire. He had a poetic nature which vivified even the classic platitudes of the day. His remarkable discrimination was the outcome of an inherent fineness of nature which survived the coarseness and brutality which the shock of the new realism aroused in many of his contemporaries. In spite of his polish, Jonson had passion and temperament, to a degree which had almost ended his life in tragedy, through his killing of his fellow-playwright, Marlowe, in a duel. It was during that time of trouble that Bull came to know the true being behind Jonson's outward bearing. He was one of the many who interceded ardently for the poet and one of the first to welcome him when he emerged from his term of imprisonment again.

Since that time, the friendship between the two had been intimate. In spite of his studiousness, Jonson had been a man of action. His life had been adventurous, making the ties which bound him and Bull the more sympathetic through common experience. He was by birth a man of the people that Bull loved. He had been bricklayer, soldier and actor, as well as scholar. He had a masterly craftsmanship, akin to Bull's own in music and, like Bull again, he was uncompromising in his principles. Bull admired the faith and conviction which animated his work, even where he himself saw its fallacies. Jonson bowed to no accepted taste or convention which did not accord with his own ideas. Bull recognized the mood of a spiritual kinsman in the challenging phrase with which Jonson ended one of his plays : " By God, 'tis good, and if you like it, you may."

The association proved publicly important to Bull. The profound scholarship of Jonson impressed King James, less for its profundity than its polish. He created an official position for the poet. A national masterpiece of masonry, Westminster Abbey, was to be the last resting-place of the ex-bricklayer, when he died as Poet Laureate. At Court, even then, Jonson was combining his poetic gifts and theatrical experience in entertainments which transcended the prevalent dry pedantry and pompous pretension in new forms of historic promise. The masques which he created, in spite of their classical formality and the overpowering ponderousness to which they were developed by his successor, Sir William Devanant, were the greatest stimulus to artistic imagination of the Jacobean period. They encouraged music to an extent beyond that of the Elizabethan drama even; for they brought about a new combination of the arts by bringing in dancing and choral singing. They were, indeed, the forerunners of both ballet and opera and therefore held the deepest possible interest for Bull. Although he was now most generally referred to as " the kinges Docktor of Musicke," he still had close touch with Court entertainments and the inspiration of the masque is palpable in the number of graciously formal dances which he commenced to write as soon as Jonson inaugurated his productions. Many of these must have been designed for masque entertainments; for Bull's official position as Court musician was reinforced by Jonson's marked preference for his music. Indeed, Jonson must have intended more than an oblique compliment when he wrote " Your Spanish Pavin is the beste daunce," for although that dance-form became popular during James' reign, only one so entitled existed at the time, composed by Bull, whose first printed virginalls piece, published in " Parthenia " in 1610, is in that form. The association between Bull and Jonson was popularly recognized and it provided one of the most brilliant historic scenes recorded of the musician's life.

Meanwhile, apart from his friendship with Jonson, the Apollo Club brought Bull into constant friendly contact with other interesting characters. None of these was more sympathetic to him than a very young fellow-musician, Thomas Ravenscroft, a close friend of Nathanael Giles, by whom Bull was introduced to him. Ravenscroft was much the junior of both, being a student under Bull at Gresham College. The young musician shared Bull's love of folklore and folk-music and they had many traits in common. Their association proved as much a source of inspiration to Bull as to his pupil. Ravenscroft was by nature a musician of the people. His interest lay in popular art. The contact with him provided a healthy counteractive to the temporary depression and obsession with technical devices through which Bull was passing.

Ravenscroft had no patience with the prevalent pedantry. He had a touch of spiritual vagrancy in his nature. His mind moved most happily among the scences of popular life, where the folk-melodies of hills and valleys were born, where traditional dances enlivened rustic revels, where rants and shanties cheered ships' fo'castles, or where streetsongs were whistled or sung and rounds and catches rose from the workshops of busy cities. He was an accomplished musician; the learning and skill shown in his " Brief Discourse," a manual on musical theory and practice, caused Giles to break into some excellent verses " in approbation." Nevertheless, for Ravenscroft, music was at its highest fulfilment when it participated spontaneously in the everyday occupations and amusements of the people.

The pedantry and morbid decadence of much Jacobean thought were alike equally foreign and distasteful to such a nature; but nevertheless, Ravenscroft, by other inclinations, was typical of his time. He represented in music the kind of interest which appeared about then in the " Character," brief, descriptive literary studies on the types of the day, tradesmen, labourers, servants, popular figures of all kinds, essays and chronicles such as those written in Fuller's " Worthies." Such interest expressed the popular taste for realism and fact and it was a healthy reaction to the preciousness and pessimism apparent in the literary scholarship and the poetry and drama of the period.

With such taste, Ravenscroft was a congenial figure in club circles. He had an inexhaustible store of anecdotes and amusing stories of popular life. He had keen observation, which he had used acutely in regard to popular characters and customs. His native wit and a remarkable capacity for mimicry made him one of the most entertaining companions Bull had ever known. He had no self-consciousness when once he was launched on one of his tales of fun. At such times he became a one-man comedy, changing his voice, manner and facial expression amazingly to depict the characters of his narrative, delighting the company by his shrewd touches, his humorous gifts and his antics. He " coulde depicte a whole character in one mouvemente, a lyfetyme in a fewe briefe wordes." His entry into a club immediately drew an eager circle about him, and he could hold his company intent for hours together.

He was not content merely to enjoy and relate his experiences of popular life. Ravenscroft was an ardent collector of folk-melodies, a pioneer centuries ahead in this field. Where others were occupied in working out abstract forms of music, he busied himself wandering here and there, picking up folk-tunes at their source, noting them down with all the peculiarities of local tradition and gathering all possible information that he could regarding the popular ideas, incidents and customs on which they were based. The airs which he so assembled became the rage of clubland and had an immense general popularity in the collections which he published from time to time.

For Bull they were a renewed inspiration. They not only revived his early affection for folk-melody, they extended it to many unfamiliar fields. The first-hand manner in which his friend had acquired them enabled Ravenscroft to show their relationship to popular life in a fascinating way. Their vitality was enhanced by his witty, shrewd, whimsical or sympathetic observations; for Ravenscroft refused to make his hobby as dry-as-dust study. His merry nature delighted in mimicry, even in the setting-forth of the printed title-pages of his published collections, which were delightful parodies of the prevalent pompous style, generally rounded-off by some quip or doggerel couplet which was like one of the unexpected grimaces with which he would round off a comical story. When Bull was oppressed by the ostentatious style or

APOLLO AND THE MERMAID

affected mannerisms of current writers, he found it an amusing relief to glance at the printed volumes which his friend had given him and read

Pammelia

MUSICKES MISCELLANIE: or Mixed Varietie of pleasant Roundelayes and delightful Catches of 3, 4, 5, 6, 7, 8, 9, 10 parts in one. None so ordinary as Musicall, none so Musicall, as not to all very pleasing and acceptable

or, better still,

Melismata.

MUSICALL PHANSIES. Fitting the Court, Citie and Countrey Humours. To 3, 4, and 5 Voyces. To all delightfull, except to the S p i t e f u l l, To none offensive, except to the P e n s i v e.

The effect of his friendship with so volatile a being as Ravenscroft was an antidote to his depression. It also fired his imagination in composition again. From that time he took delight in setting popular airs from his friend's collections, recalling as he did so the jovial evenings at the Apollo Club, where, through the tobacco fumes and the clatter of tankards, the full-throated chorus of voices testified that Ravenscroft's work most certainly was "to all very pleasing and acceptable."

With his lightened mood, Bull threw himself once more into his work at Court. There was a considerable amount to do, although he missed the royal interest which had encouraged him in Elizabeth's reign. James had no interest in the art; but he was a great lover of the drama and a good patron of actors and playwrights. While generally tight-fisted with money, he also liked to impress by the richness of his public functions on occasion. In the masques of Ben Jonson he found a means to gratify both his taste for the theatrical and his delight in the display of material magnificence which was his substitute for spiritual grandeur. In these splendid and ornate Court productions all the royal musical resources were employed, as well as those of the royal actors—the King's Players, the Queen's Revels, the Children of the Revels and the Gentlemen of the Chapel Royal, together, at times, with the choristers of the Chapel and of St. Paul's, now released from the injunction against stage-playing existent for some time previously.

The masques demanded much larger personnel, histrionic and musical, than did the ordinary plays. They were not of the enormous dimensions of the "storiall showes" which preceded Shakespearean drama in early Elizabethan days. Some of those, such as Leicester's entertainment for the Queen in 1575, lasted nineteen days. While dramatic, yet not pageants, they were of considerable duration. They presaged the fashions of the coming generation, when Beaujoyleaulx presented his " Ballet de la Reine " before Louis XIII of France, in a performance lasting from ten at night until five the next morning. They were the legitimate parents of the Restoration " triumphs " of Sir William Davenant.

In the preparations for such events Bull inevitably found himself deeply involved, through his associations with the Chapel Royal. He required all possible assistance from his colleagues, Giles and Morley; and in many such productions other musicians, such as John Dowland, the lutenist, returned from abroad, and Dr. Cooper, or Coperario, as he called himself, combined with Byrd, Tomkins, Hooper and Gibbons, in the musical work.

Fresh friendships formed through such musical occupations. The King's son, Prince Henry, was devoted to music and had the highest regard for Bull, who ultimately became attached to his household. In the royal circle Bull also came into touch with James' young daughter, the Princess Elizabeth, with the events of whose life he was to be associated, and who was herself to play a pathetic rôle in European history, with the coming of the Thirty Years' War. To some degree, these associations, in which he was the warm friend as well as the honoured master, recompensed Bull for the loss of royal sympathy which he had suffered through the death of Elizabeth.

His club associates were not his only intimates. In his own world of music, he renewed old ties and made fresh friendships. A happy reunion came in 1605 when, on June 3rd, " Elway Bevan, by the consent and order of the Right Worshipfull Doctor Monntague, Deane of the Chappell, the Subdeane and Gentlemen then attendinge, was sworne Gentleman of his Majestes Chappell extraordinary."

A younger school of musicians was springing up, many of whom were influenced greatly by Bull's own work. Among these was his own pupil, Ravenscroft, and Giles Farnaby, a Cornishman of whimsical temperament, whose work was largely inspired by the scenes among which he moved, such as his colourful " Poules Wharf." Bull and Farnaby were good companions, as well as master and pupil, and one of their favourite recreations was exploring the streets of London together, where Bull found his own spirit closely reflected in the fantasy and whimsical observations of the young composer of " Farnaby His Humor " and the bizarre and folklike " Giles Farnaby's Dreame."

Through Giles again, he also became acquainted with another young Welshman of congenial character, Thomas Tomkins, now in Giles' old position as organist of Worcester Cathedral, where he had succeeded on the death of Giles' successor, Nathanael Pattrick, whose widow he had married in 1596. The Welsh musician was exuberant in his talent, early showing an amazing skill and prolific productivity. He came to London with his baggage full of gay, humorous madrigals, with light-hearted " fal-lal " refrains which reflected the " hey derry-dando " of his native folk-songs. He had a remarkable gift for picturesque tone-painting, greatly ahead of his time and a technical power as performer which resembled Bull's own. Young though he was, he exercised a certain influence over his elder colleague, since he was already emerging as a pioneer in the development of instrumental ensemble, to which he made some of the earliest contributions with his " Fantasias " for viols and his merry " Worcester Brawls." Already Bull was experiencing that urge towards richer musical media which marked all his later work and which, essentially, showed his dim previsioning of what was to be the orchestra. Unlike Farnaby, Tomkins was interested, not in popular types so much as in the new dramatic forms emerging in the spectacles of Ben Jonson, which he witnessed with Giles and Bull at Court. Bull's own dances delighted him and the two discussed the Masque together. Out of such intercourse came a historic development, when Tomkins emerged with the first explicit British ballet, reflecting his admiration of Ben Jonson in its stately classical title, " Musica Divina."

The unquenchable youth of Bull's mind was refreshed by his contact with these two eager young musicians. It spanned the difference in their respective years and brought him on to a footing where he was able to share their interests and enthusiasms and so move with the times himself. Nothing showed his unassuming, generous nature more than the musical association which grew up between himself, Farnaby and Tomkins. They not only exchanged ideas; they used each other's themes. To Bull, this friendship with the two young men had a warm personal value; but he scarcely realized that, through it, he was impressing his spirit on a coming generation of music and laying the foundations of a future English musical style which was to be developed by Henry Purcell, largely from his study of the young Jacobeans' works.

Meanwhile, a dramatic sensation swept the country. On November 5th, 1605, the Gunpowder Plot to blow up King James and the Parliament, organized by Guy Fawkes and his confederates, was discovered. A wave of indignation and horror passed over England, where many people remembered the painful strain and public danger which the conspiracies of Mary and Mendoza had caused in Elizabeth's reign. The new matter-of-fact world was less able to face such hidden threats than the adventurous Tudor one had been. It was felt on all hands that the frustration of the plot called for national celebration.

The festivities which the national mood produced brought Bull to the forefront of the pageantry of the times. After the National Thanksgiving for the King's deliverance, and that of the people's representatives had taken place, a series of brilliant functions, organized by the burghers of London to demonstrate their civic loyalty, followed fast upon each other.

This demonstration of national feeling gratified James immensely. Obsessed by his theory of the " Divine Right of Kings," he had steadily alienated public sympathy, yet, despite all his pretensions he longed for popularity. As courtiers and civic corporations vied one after another in celebrating his salvation, he was moved to a display of greater generosity than he had ever shown before. Bull already stood in his good graces, on account of his professional prestige and the admiration which James had for all possessed of erudition. This royal favour was augmented by the admiration which Henry, Prince of Wales, had for " the Kinges Docktor of Musicke," which caused him to laud Bull to his father. James was impressed the more because he knew that his son had real musical talent and discrimination, which he respected greatly, since it was beyond his own understanding. Bull himself added the last touch to incline the King towards him. Like all sickly people, James loved to appear in the rôle of athlete and sportsman. He was, indeed, adept enough in his favourite sport of falconry. As a gesture of acknowledgment to the loyal tributes of his courtiers, he organized a brilliant hunt-meet in 1606. For the evening celebrations afterwards Bull prepared the music, the " festal playe," being arranged by Samuel Daniel, Master of the Queen's Revels, featuring " a merrie daunce with althe Children disporting with hobbie-horses intituled ' The kinges huntinge Reuell." The music to which this was danced or mimed was probably that " Kinges Hunting Gigge," by Bull, which has seemed to some since to have so paradoxical a title. In any event, there must have been some particularly gratifying personal touch to cause King James, shortly after, to list Bull's name among those to receive " gold chaines, plates and medales " for their services, on December 31st, 1606.

The climax to the series of festive ceremonies came shortly after, featuring Bull prominently. On December 15th, 1606, he had been admitted to the membership of the powerful Merchant Taylors Company, sponsored by his friend and patron, the Earl of Sussex, to whom he was formally bound apprentice before his full admittance. In July, 1607, the Merchant Taylors Company was granted the privilege of entertaining the King with the Prince of Wales, at the ceremony of installing the Master of the Company. That the event was much more than a corporation function is clear : " why should the Dean, Sub-Dean, Organist, Gentlemen, Master of the Children and the Children have attended in their habits, if only for the purpose of making the Master ? "

It was, in fact, a culmination in the sequence of public festivals. Its magnitude is shown by the fact that the Company expended over £1,000—an enormous sum in the values of the period—on its organization. The best musicians and singers of the day were engaged for the entertainment and the great hall of the Company was decorated with magnificent lavishness. Poets and composers were commissioned to write and compose ceremonial verses and chants and scenic effects were devised along the lines of a pageant.

Bull's association with the Company made it inevitable that he should figure largely in the proceedings ; but his prestige and position in the royal household made this doubly appropriate, and the Company made it abundantly clear that they were aware of the lustre which his presence lent to the occasion. The ceremonial nature of the event was further emphasized by Ben Jonson being commissioned to write verses of a special ode, or hymn, to greet the king, for which Bull was to compose the music, and to supervise the spectacular features. With the Kinges Docktor of Musick and the Poet Laureate as organizers, and the sovereign and the heir to the throne as guests, the function had a truly royal character.

Jonson was immensely concerned in the matter. It was something different from the masques for which he was celebrated; it differed also from the theatre. Yet he felt that it should have drama and pageantry. Giles was brought into the discussions, as Master of the Children and director of the combined choirs of the Chapel Royal and St. Paul's, who were to sing. Conferences took place between the three friends daily. Designs were ordered, revised or rejected. The order of the musical programme was drawn up, amended a dozen times before its final form.

At last all seemed in order. One item alone remained to be completed. This was the ceremonial hymn to Jonson's words for which Bull had to compose the music. The Poet Laureate, knowing the King's delight in displays of scholarship and himself being drawn to the Roman ritual, had written his poem in Latin. Bull had set it in the manner in which he treated church chants. The composition did not satisfy Jonson, however; he wanted something at once impressive and yet capable of being caught up easily by the entire concourse as well as the trained singers. Bull recognized that his work was too elaborate for this and recommenced. His new effort was also unsatisfactory, as were three more attempts. At last, in exasperation, he started to hunt out such themes as he had noted down, but not developed, to see if any would prove suitable and satisfy his friend, since time was growing short.

In his search he came upon the still unpublished manuscript of the hymn which he had written for the victory over the Armada. Without intending if for the occasion in view, he sat down at his virginals and commenced to play through the air. Jonson's attention was arrested immediately. The tune appealed to him. He had only been a boy of fifteen when the Armada was defeated, and was unlikely to recall the tune after so long, during which, with the casualness of the times concerning such matters, the music had lain unused. Bull, himself, gave little attention to publication. His first instrumental work to be printed did not appear until four years later, in " Parthenia," and music-printing, excepting for hymns, psalms and anthems, which would be in regular religious use, or madrigals, rounds and lute-songs likely to make popular appeal and fit into the domestic repertory, was not prolific in 1588. It is extremely probable that he, with his tendency to live in the moment intensely, had not given much further thought to the hymn since he laid it aside. He found it worthy as he played it once more. Jonson found it exactly what he wanted for the coming celebration; but Bull was reluctant to have it put to such use. He had written it in the flush of the Armada triumph, and it had been largely inspired by the dead queen. Memories came back to him as he played it over. He contrasted Elizabeth's heroic figure with that of the sickly, nerve-ridden James. It seemed a sacrilege, whatever the air's intrinsic merits, to use what had been conceived in honour of the great sovereign to gratify her mediocre successor.

Jonson was nevertheless determined. With very little discrepancy, which he had already commenced to amend as he listened, the tune fitted his words excellently. He urged Bull to agree and Giles, who remembered the effect of the hymn on its first performance, added the weight of his opinion to his arguments. In the end Bull, realizing the force of what they said, knowing that it was imperative for him to stand well with the King and having nothing better in mind, consented, provided that Jonson would agree to use one of the other tunes as a preludial chant, to English words. Giles gave him no time to revise his decision. He took the music away immediately for the choral parts to be copied out.

The magnificence of the Merchant Taylors banquet exceeded all expectations. It provided an epic scene in the midst of which Bull, " in a citizen's gown, cappe and hood," was once again in a setting which made him both a type of the times and a figure of future history.

Stowe painted the picture colourfully in words, relating how James dined in a separate apartment opening on to the great hall, " in which chamber was placed a very rich paier of Organs, whereupon Mr. John Bull, Doctor of Musique and a Brother of this company, did play all the dynner time and Mr. Nathanael Gyles master of the children of the kynges Chappell, together with diuers singing men and children of the said Chappell, did sing melodious songs at the said dynner."

The spectacle in the great hall had all the fantastic pomp of the pageantry of the period, ornate and extravagant.

" The musique consisted of 12 lutes, equally divided, 6 and 6 in a windowe on either side the hall, and in the ayre betweene them were a gallant shippe triumphant, wherein were three rayre menne like saylors, being eminent for voyce and skill, who in their severall songs were assisted and seconded by the cunning lutenist."

The " vast company invited " was not only distinguished by courtly brilliance ; a galaxy of artistic talent was present also, including William Byrd and Dr. Coperario, music by both of whom was performed, in addition to the items when Bull " played moste excellent melodie upon a small payre of Organes " and the chants which he had set, by " rayre Ben Jonson."

The success of the banquet was sensational. The King was entranced and could not praise it sufficiently. Not even in his own elaborate Court entertainments had anything equalled the effect of the three picked " singers from poules," Thomas Luke, John Allen and John Richards, as their songs soared in the air on high, or the moving beauty of the massed choirs of the Chapel and " the choir of poules" led by the talented Master of the Children and accompanied by the King's Master of Musick.

The gratification of the Merchant Taylors Company knew no bounds. Their recognition of the illustrious part played by Bull was ceremoniously recorded in their Records:

" Dr.Bull was admitted into the Lyvery of the Worshipfull the Merchant Tailor Company, and the Lyvery hoodes put upon his shoulders but not sworne ; this fauor was done him for havinge composed the Musique which was performed at their Hall by the Gentlemen and Children of the Kinges Chappell when his Maiesty King James the first, Prince Henry and many Honourable Persons dined there on Thursdaie July 16. 1607."

Giles shared in their expression of appreciation :

" The company are contented to showe this fauor unto them for their paynes when the kinge and prince dyned at our hall and their love and kindnes in bestowinge the musique which was performed by them, their associates and children in the kinges chamber gratis, whereas the musicians in the greate hall exacted unreasonable somes of the company for the same. The company therefore meane that the calling of Mr. Doctor Bull and Mr. Nathanael Gyles into the lyvery shall not by any burden or charge unto them further than shall stand with their own lykinge."

So, in almost legendary fashion, awakening the affections of the worthy burgesses, John Bull entered into the heart of that London City which had so long fascinated him and evoked his enthusiasm and love. In the true phantasy of the period, he had come from the haunts of the Mermaid, his song echoing from a soaring galleon, to enter in triumph into the ordered magnificence of the temple of the votaries of Apollo.

Moste Sweete and Fayre

CHAPTER XI

MOSTE SWEETE AND FAYRE

DRAMA dogged Bull all his days. The only thing safely to be expected of him was the unexpected. In 1607, with a blaze of topical celebrity about him and public acclamation ringing in his ears, he made an abrupt exit from the scene of one of the greatest acts of his life. He resigned from Gresham College, on December 20th.

Rumour was busy; but his reason was not far to seek. It was set forth in staid, matter-of-fact terms in the Records of no less eminent and respectable a personage than my Lord Bishop of London. John Bull had made application, on December 22nd, for a licence to marry, at Christ Church, " Elizabeth Walter, of the Strand, maiden, aged about twentie-foure, daughter of —— Walter, citizen of London, deceased."

Bull was in love. Maybe it was not his first passion. Earlier episodes were almost inevitable. He was forty-five and no hermit by nature. Virile and imaginative, with his sensitive alertness, he could not have remained wholly impervious to feminine charms. He moved in high circles in a romantic age, when poets were welcome in palaces and monarchs made favourites of musicians. He possessed the "five wits" demanded of " Graunde Amour "— " comon wit, imagination, fantasie, estimation (judgment) and memorie "—defined by Hawes in 1554. His mind and manners, his figure and fame, alike contributed to invest him with glamour, even in the galaxy around Gloriana.

It was an age of passion, even in its most precious poetry. Those who used the language of Sidney's " Arcadia " in their amours were none the less men of action, the heroes of the Armada and New World adventures. It was a golden age in all its aspects. The radiance of new-found riches was reflected in the gallantry of spirit by which their possession was achieved. Such dual luminance gilded the imagery of Elizabethan speech, often making it appear fantastic and artificial. Nevertheless, this extravagance expressed the exuberance of the era, which inspired alike its daring enterprise and its dreams of visionary empires, El Dorado and Hy-Brazil.

Its ardour, however, ran hand-in-hand with elaborate artifice. Sensuous alertness had been aroused by the dawn of an epoch of revelation. It grew as wonder attained its noontide. In a world of marvels its intensity seemed to demand exaggeration, however excessive.

The adulation exacted by Elizabeth emphasized such euphuism. Her vanity was always strong. She desired to be revered as queen ; but she also thirsted for admiration as woman. Within five years of her accession to the throne she went so far as to cause her minister, Cecil, to draft a proclamation to determine that only the presentation of her admittedly considerable charms of which she approved should be permitted publicly. The document was characteristically drastic :

" Forasmuch as thrugh the naturall desire that all sortes of subiectes and people, both noble and meane, haue to procure the portraicte and picture of the Queenes Maiestie, greate nomber of Paynters, and some Printers and grauers, haue alredy, and doe dayly, attempt toe make in diuers maners portraictures of hir Maiestie in payntinge, grauinge and pryntinge, wherein is euidentlie shewn that hytherto none hath sufficiently expressed the naturall representation of hir Maiesties person, fauor or grace, but for the moste part haue also erred therein, as thereof dayly complaintes are made amongst hir Maiesties louinge subiectes in so much that for redresse hereof hir Maiestie hath lately bene so instantly and so importunately sued unto by the Lords of hir Consell and others of hir nobilitie, in respecte of the greate disorder herein used, not onely to be content that some speciall coninge paynter might bee permitted by accesse to hir Maiestie to take the naturall representation of hir Maiestie, whereof she hath bene allwise of hir owne righte disposition uerie unwillynge, but also to prohibit all maner of other persons to drawe; paynt, graue or pourtrayet hir Maiesties personage or uisage for a tyme, untill by some perfect patron and example the same may bee by others followed."

It was put into effect ruthlessly enough. As Sir Walter Raleigh noted, " by the Queenes owne commandment all pictures by unskillfull and comon paynters were knocked to pieces and cast intoe the fyre." The painters fortunate enough to please Elizabeth—and unfortunate enough to have to meet her whims, had no easy task. Zucharo gained her favour by painting her in regal splendour, holding a rainbow in her hand, with the motto " Hon sine sole eris " on the picture. The painting of herself with her father, sister and brother, by Lucas de Heere, she was content to bestow on Walsingham with the message :

" The Queene to Walsingham this Tablet sent,
    Mark of her people and her owne contente " ;

but Nicholas Hilliard, though he loyally affirmed that

"her Maties curious Demaunde hath greatlie bettered my iudgement besides diuers other like questions in Art by her most excellent Matie," found her exacting. She would sit in no place where shadows might accentuate any harshness in her feature, " and therefore chosse her place to sit in for that purposse in the open ally of a goodly garden where no tree was neare, nor anye shadowe at all, saue that as the heauen is lighter then the earthe, soe must that littel shadowe that was from the earthe."

With such self-consciousness concerning the impression which her portrayal made on the general public, her vanity among Court favourites was extreme. She had to remain sovereign, however, even while gratifying her senses with the homage paid to her as woman. Flattery exceeded itself if it became too openly familiar. Subtler suggestion could be conveyed and accepted if couched in symbolism.

A cult of amorous hyperbole therefore developed at Court. This affected its feminine society in general as well as the Queen. In spite of her jealousy, Elizabeth could not banish all other women from her circle; nor was she foolish or modest enough to choose to surround herself with ill-favoured ladies. Many of those about her were beautiful, and her maids of honour were a "lively and interesting body of young ladies." They were also susceptible and "somewhat free in givinge," and ran precarious courses. Elizabeth Throckmorton fell into disgrace through her intrigue and marriage with Sir Walter Raleigh; Mary Fitton, whom some of future generations were to imagine as "the dark lady of the sonnets" in spite of her blondeness, brought about the banishment of William Herbert, Earl of Pembroke, from Court owing to her presenting him with an illegitimate child; while Anne Vavasour, initially gentlewoman of the bedchamber to the

Queen and maid-of-honour in 1590, having married John Finch, left him to keep house for Sir Henry Lee, and in 1618 was haled before the High Commissioners' Court for having two husbands living, being "partially pardoned" in 1622.

In an age of such excitement and glamour infatuations and intrigues were inevitable. Subterfuge was necessary, however, since the Queen's jealousy made open attachments unsafe, even where these were such as normally could be declared. This was equally true for the sincere and the superficial, and it encouraged flirtation and amorous liaisons—the more so by reason of the very mixed nature of Court society. Poets, dramatists, musicians and soldiers of fortune soared to high places in the royal favour, and at Court the most interesting and extraordinary characters of the day congregated. Personality was to the fore in the period and, however aristocratic the Court ladies might be, they were women for whom those of their own cast, in such a time, might not always be the most attractive. Therefore the reason for concealment and subterfuge was increased. They had not only to beware the Queen's rancour; they had also to avoid offending the prejudices of the times, which were not sufficiently far from feudalism to tolerate liaisons between the aristocracy and plebians. The resultant atmosphere of intrigue, enfolded in flowery manners and turns of speech, did anything but discourage such affairs. The allurement was enhanced because of the watch and constraint which the Queen endeavoured to set upon her ladies. In an age dominated by the spirit of adventure they could not but feel impelled to follow it in the field most immediately open to them. They risked the Queen's displeasure, or worse penalties; but they had the zest of flouting her secretly if fortunate enough not to be discovered.

Bull's touch with domestic circles outside the Court was slight, whereas in the Palace he was a regular member of the circles about the Queen where the Court beauties gathered. He was an attractive figure and could not avoid the prevalent atmosphere, however much he strove not to damage his position or lose the Queen's affection. Any attachment, however, he had to keep hidden from public light; and while this might provide him with interest and excitement in his hot youth, the forthrightness of his nature and his sensitivity could not but make it distasteful to him ultimately; for it is clear from all records and from the evidence of his expression in his work, that such attachments did not exceed a light kind.

The moment came, however, when passion assumed a more serious form for him. He was probably the more susceptible to it because of the moods of isolation and spiritual loneliness which had come upon him since the accession of James I. He no longer had the presence of a jealous queen to constrain him. Most of all, maybe for the first time in his courtly life, he encountered simplicity, yet in his own circle. A new vision of what love might mean to him opened up before him, accentuated by his sense of the passing of time. He had witnessed the domestic happiness of his friend Giles. He had lived alone overlong. Even given the experience of stolen ardours the morning came coldly, and after amorous companionship his bachelor quarters seemed the more solitary. The growing artificiality of the period emphasized his discontent. John Bull, courtier, celebrity, adventurer, wit and club companion, wanted to settle down.

Had he been an opportunist, his mood might have coincided with ambition. In his position, enhanced by his success at the time, he might have aspired to a successful marriage. Had he been less sensitive, some liaison might have developed into such tie as would have brought disaster. His own feeling and his fortune favoured him. Just as his friendship with Ravenscroft renewed for him the feeling for simplicity in the people's songs the woman appeared.

She was not arresting beside many more brilliant beauties. She was a little thing, quiet and retiring. He first became aware of her in a circle where many luminaries shone when invited to play for the Marchioness of Winchester. He did not see her at first. It was a social function, and he was there to entertain and be entertained. As he played, however, he felt, as he had felt once before on meeting Bevin, the intentness of a regard while he played. Looking up, he had met her eyes, straight-gazing, quiet, fixed on him from the corner where she sat, very still and upright, in the background. Her eyes did not flicker as they met his. She neither smiled nor frowned. Just for a brief moment their gaze held each other. Then she lowered her eyes; but there was neither coquetry nor primness as she did so. A transient thing; but in that moment Dr. John Bull, the King's Master and Doctor of Music, the Professor of Music at Gresham College and " the greatest musician of his time," suddenly felt dissatisfied with everything. His unrest expressed itself in the outburst of virtuosity with which he responded to the pleas of the assembly for another piece; but this time the level dark eyes did not raise. She sat simply, obviously listening, but giving no sign. Piqued, Bull followed his display immediately by taking the theme of a folk-melody which he had been going through with Ravenscroft a few days before, playing a set of quiet variations upon it. He played quietly, the feeling of the music coming in marked contrast to his previous display. The company listened with growing attention; it was so unlike his usual social playing; it had a new feeling in it. Bull kept his eyes upon the small, quiet figure in the corner. He was determined that she should look up again.

By accident or because she felt the insistence of his gaze her eyes met his again. He smiled at her, quietly. There was a faint touch of surprise in her expression as she caught his; then, as he underlined the refrain of his air, " What Care You ? " she smiled softly in response, then looked down again.

Bull brought his piece to a swift conclusion. He excused himself from the virginalls and went over to Giles. He was determined to know who the small creature in the corner was. His curiosity was gratified. She was the new maid-of-honour to the marchioness. He would not be satisfied until he had met her, and at last the amused Giles engineered it that the duchess introduced her. Bull felt strangely stirred as he looked down at her. She barely reached his shoulder; but as she stood upright after sweeping her deep curtsey her eyes met his again without any of the conventional pretences. Their level seriousness and directness robbed the intentness of her expression alike of any suggestion of boldness or of the slight touch of impudence which might otherwise have gone with her small nose and her round-chinned, small oval face. She looked so as they spoke briefly together, Bull anxious to say something that might stride across formality, but finding himself strangely at a loss. He did learn, however, that, contrary to usual opinion, his simpler music had appealed to her most, though she was quick to explain that this was probably because she could not claim the musical talent to understand his more intricate playing. Listening, he found, quite idiotically, that it scarcely mattered what she said. He only wanted her to speak and to look at him. It was as though they both understood that it was not their words but some current of thought between them that counted.

Their conversation was brief, for the marchioness was not prepared for her maid-in-waiting to monopolize the distinguished guest's attention. Bull tried to ignore the first call, but its insistent repetition could not be disregarded. He bowed with full ceremony as she swept her curtsey again; but he felt the most insane desire to bend forward and kiss the small round head in its heart-shaped cap as it bent before him—indeed, to pick up the small figure and bear it away in his arms, like any schoolboy, he neither knew nor cared where, just so that it might be somewhere without others around.

Dr. Bull was zealous in paying his respects to the marchioness for some time after that. He was always in attendance at Court when she attended receptions. Still he came to no further intimacy beyond a few more formal phrases with her maid-in-waiting, a renewed acquaintance with her level gaze and quiet voice.

Giles had greeted his first interest in the marchioness' maid-in-waiting with some humour; but the genial Worcester musician's wife saw deeper. Without making her aim apparent, she gradually elicited from Bull how deep his interest lay. They had been good friends for years, and her husband's affection for Bull added to her own warm feeling for him. She decided to try to help him.

How she contrived it Bull never knew, even if he had freedom of mind enough at the time to wonder; but one evening, when he had been invited by Giles for some music, he found the small object of his interest there also, chaperoned by another lady of the marchioness' entourage with her husband.

After some music Mistress Giles asked her guest to sing. The young woman was slightly embarrassed in view of the celebrated musicians present, and said so, also pleading that she had no air by her. Mistress Giles protested that she should sing any air which they might have by them, quoting from a current playhouse success, Myddleton's "Blunt, Master Constable": "Observe it shall be your first and finest praise to sing the notes of every new fashion at first sight." Bull seized his chance. Seating himself at the virginals, he commenced to play again the folk-song "What Care You?" Mistress Walter was obliged to confess that she knew that air, and the delighted Bull had the joy of accompanying her. Her voice was small and untrained enough, but it had the same simplicity in singing that her glance expressed and a sweet quality. As she ended on the refrain "What Care You?" Bull immediately suggested that he could play the right sequence to her song, and commenced immediately his setting of another folk-song, "Why Ask You?" As the significance of the tune became apparent to her, Mistress Walter gave him the satisfaction of a slightly heightened colour and for the first time her eyes fell before his glance.

When she departed with her companions, Bull excused himself to Mistress Giles, who met his quite confused explanations with an admirable seriousness, though her merry eyes twinkled slightly more than usual. Bull accompanied the others to their apartments in the Strand, inventing an entirely fictitious errand to go their way. He was humming to himself as he rode back, and when he arrived back in his rooms at Gresham College he seated himself at his writing-table and commenced working at some music. The dawn was not far off before he had it completed to his liking. He sat back and hummed it over to himself. Then, satisfied, he picked up his quill again and inscribed the title at the top of the page:

" Moste Sweete and Fayre."

He was impatient for morning, when he could dispatch the music. Had he not been obliged to take his musical work he would have ridden to the Strand with it himself. No sooner had the messenger left with it, however, than he began to feel that he had presumed, that he had made a fool of himself, that he had been insane to send it. The whole day his pupils and colleagues found him inexplicably testy and absent-minded. He tried to invent some excuse to himself for his calling upon the marchioness, but could conceive of none.

Fortune favoured him a few days later, however. On calling to present flowers and his respects, he was ushered into an antechamber. In the next apartment he heard the sounds of a virginals and, listening, recognized his own piece. He knew very well who was playing and determined not to allow his chance to slip. Going to the door, he peered in and saw that Elizabeth Walter was alone. Slipping in softly behind her, he was even more delighted to see that she was playing his air by heart.

As he listened she stumbled, her memory failing her. She gave an annoyed little exclamation, then, slipping her hand into her bodice, drew out a sheet of music-paper, which she unfolded and laid on the virginals before her. It was Bull's piece. He stepped forward, eagerly telling her how pleased he was that she found his music interesting. She was slightly embarrassed at having been overheard; but he was already too far established in her thoughts for her to feel annoyed. A little nervously, she complied with his request that she should try it again; but just as she was about to start he took up the music gently and held it between both his hands. She looked at him in surprise, then asked him his reason. Bull decided that it was his moment. He told her that he held the music so close because it had lain so near to her heart. He told her his envy of the inanimate piece of music-paper. In the end, unable to play with words any more under the direct gaze of her dark eyes, he told her of his love.

So it came about that, when the Right Honourable the Marchioness of Winchester graciously appeared to receive Dr. Bull and thank him for his offering, she found a petitioner for a gift. She was taken by surprise; but she was gratified by the reflected lustre which her maid-in-waiting's marriage would bring to her and signified that she would herself attend the wedding.

Bull's decision had not been taken without due consideration. He knew very well that the loss of his Gresham College post meant a curtailing of means which he could ill afford. He knew, however, that if he did not take his decision he would lose infinitely more so far as his personal life went. His mind was set at ease after he had discussed the matter with Elizabeth. She was quite prepared to share his life in any event, even though she knew that the King's Treasury was irregular in paying the Court servants and that Gresham College was Bull's surest source of income.

Bull was not to suffer for following his heart as severely as he had anticipated. As he was gathering his belongings together prior to giving up his quarters at Gresham College, he received a summons to attend the Prince of Wales. He left instructions regarding his effects with Thomas Byrd and the College porter and set out for Whitehall.

Prince Henry greeted him with even more than his usual cordiality. With his characteristic thoughtfulness, he put his idea forward as though asking a favour. He had heard of Bull's impending marriage and that he was leaving Gresham College. He wished to know how Bull viewed the proposition of becoming his Household Musician-in-Ordinary. It was all that Bull required to complete his happiness. Prince Henry offered him £40 a year, the same sum as that which he received as organist of the Chapel Royal, in which post he could continue while officiating for the Prince of Wales. Gresham College had meant £50 yearly to him; so, while he still faced a loss, the Prince's generous thought diminished considerably the amount by which he had feared to have his means curtailed.

Of Bull's wedding no record survived. It could not have been otherwise than interesting. His circle of personal friends included Ben Jonson, Shakespeare and Hugh Holland among the best-known poets and dramatists. Apart from the Marchioness of Winchester and her circle, Bull had long had good friends and patrons in the Pembroke family, and the Earl of Pembroke was a close friend of the Earl of Southampton, whose love of the arts was renowned. Above all, with the Prince of Wales as his immediate patron and the eminence of his office as the King's Organist of the Chapel, the attendance of many Court officials was inevitable, while Gresham College had also its tribute to pay. Nor were Giles, Bevin and Morley likely to allow the event to pass without sharing in speeding their friend's happiness, while Bull's friend and patron, the Earl of Sussex, with Ravenscroft and others of the Apollo Club, assuredly attended.

Elizabeth and Bull, however, were not concerned with grandeur. Quiet, thoughtful and admiring his work, she was happy to have her own home with him. He, full of tenderness for her and with something of wonder at the thing which had befallen him, learned a new serenity. The next years passed in a happy uneventfulness, excepting for the fact that Bull worked with renewed energy under the influence of his new joy. The touch of dryness which had crept into his work occasionally vanished. There was a blitheness in his " Leaping Galliard," and many song-variations followed " Moste Sweete and Fayre," probably to provide Bull with the pleasure of hearing Elizabeth sing them.

In such intimate happiness the outer world seems to have become remote for him for some time. He made no notable public appearances; with his relinquishment of his Gresham professorship his public lectures had ceased. Beyond his duties at the Chapel Royal and the Court functions connected with his service to Prince Henry, he was little seen. Instead of evenings at the Apollo Club, Giles, Ravenscroft, Tomkins, Farnaby, and at times his other promising young pupil, Benjamin Cosyn, gathered for musical hours at the Bull apartments. Another welcome visitor was John Dowland, whose exquisite talents inspired poets in his own time,

> " whose heauenly touch
> Upon the Lute doth ravishe humaine sense,"

who had returned from some years in the royal service in Denmark and was then living in Fetter Lane, close to where Dr. Pepusch was later to preserve Bull's own fame in the intimate recitals given by himself and his wife.

Bull's work in the Prince of Wales's household varied, while it emphasized his domestic interests. In the Prince's family circle he had contact with the other children of the

King. It was there that he guided the first musical talents of the little Princess Elizabeth, who early developed a keen affection for the gay and whimsical Musician-in-Ordinary to her brother, the more so since Bull's happiness brought all his brighter moods to the fore. She was as yet only a child; but she was a fascinating little creature, already showing promise of the charms which were to cause Ben Jonson to extoll her as

" That moste princely maid, whose form mighte call
The worlde to warre, and make it hazarde all
Its valor for her beautie,"

and her outward attractions were enhanced by her happy nature. Young as she was, being barely eleven, she showed talent in music and delighted in it, as in all that she regarded as recreation.

Her younger brother, Charles, later the ill-fated successor to James I, was too young to take more than a very elementary part in musical matters, and only occasionally left his mother to visit his brother's apartments. He was, however, a delicate, rather sickly child, whose weakness early developed his sensitivity. Music fascinated him even while he was too young to take part in it, and he early showed the leanings which eventually made him a talented player on the viol de gamboys, and even a composer of some quite creditable pieces for his favourite instrument.

Bull established himself in both children's affections. He was in a peculiarly happy state to understand them. A wonder had come to his own home. With a comical air of surprise, that always showed itself on approaching its cause, Bull had become a father. His pride and delight in his infant son was touching. He found it amazing to gaze on the small bundle of life slumbering in its cot. With an infinite and ludicrous care, he would occasionally venture to lift it and hold it uneasily in his arms, and once the small fingers had closed around his own John Bull would have frozen alive before he would have stirred to disturb the child. He sang it quaint little tunes, delighted to believe that it showed an interest when he played the virginals, and would sit silently for long spaces watching his wife tend it. He was most happy when it fell to sleep contentedly in his arms, and so rocking it he conceived one of his most gentle pieces, the lullaby for virginals, " Bull's Goodnighte."

Prince Henry encouraged his private work, being sufficiently a musician himself to comprehend that it was as a composer that Bull would achieve lasting fame. If his musician's inspiration flagged he would devise some scheme, some entertainment or family occasion, to stimulate him. Bull recommenced composing more of the delightful dances which he had relinquished when Queen Elizabeth died. He had no reason to regret his resignation from Gresham College so far as his opportunities for creative work went. His patron was not exacting, and he found him generous and ungrudging in providing whatever he required for his musical work, the Prince's household accounts on at least one occasion recording the disbursement of the very high sum of £35, paid to " Jo. Bull " " for sundry sortes of musicke bookes."

It was a short-lived idyll. Its sweetness added to its poignancy in retrospect, though it shed a nimbus around Bull's memories ever afterwards. While his little son was still an infant, Elizabeth died. A chill in a second stillborn childbirth produced its complications. Stricken and agonized, he sat by her bed, praying inwardly in vain hope, while he schooled his features to smile bravely at her. All her small sweetness was accentuated as she lay before him, her features etherealized in her growing weakness. The more her strange, unearthly beauty grew upon him, the more did Bull's heart quiver under the bitter realization that his brief happiness was passing from him.

He was by her to the end. In the dark room, in which the candles had guttered and gone out unnoticed in the black bitterness of his grief, they found him kneeling by her bed, his head upon the small cold hand that had led him into such unforgettable realms of wonder and gladness. The nurse called Mistress Giles, who had been devoted in her care of her husband's friend and his wife during those unhappy days. Together they succeeded in rousing Bull from his stupor. He had by then little consciousness of what had happened. The storm of his grief had spent him. Pathetically, as he staggered to his feet, he put his fingers to his lips as though to warn them against disturbing his dead wife, and then, slowly and heavily, he allowed them to lead him out of the room.

It was weeks before the utmost efforts of his friends could arouse any normal interest in him. Finally it was Mistress Giles who addressed herself to the task. She brought him his surviving first-born, and, though he at first seemed to be wholly alien to his former affection for it, when she at last laid it in his arms his hard mood of dry constriction broke. He held the little boy close to him and then, after a brief moment to master his emotion, commenced softly to hum his " Goodnighte " to him.

Mistress Giles left him so. When she returned somewhat later, he had laid the child in its cot and was seated at his table smiling down at it wistfully. Mistress Giles perceived that music paper was on the table before him, however. She made no comment and went away. John

Bull, for his child's sake, was coming back to the world which had seemed to have lost all interest for him.

Little by little his life resumed much of its normal course. Little by little, as the boy grew, he found fresh interest and joy in his small son. Eagerly he waited for the child's first responses to his music. Many of the simpler pieces which he wrote about that time traced to his desire to attract its attention.

Nevertheless the old gaiety was absent from his music. It had a new tenderness, a new wistfulness. His grief for his wife was too deep for him to voice it musically. There was no trace in his work of the loss he had sustained, beyond its slightly saddened quality, its new touch of pathos. John Bull's happiness was buried in his heart, and even his love of his small son had not the power to resurrect it or revive its voice in his music.

Closing Cadence

CHAPTER XII

CLOSING CADENCE

GRADUALLY Bull's life resumed its normal course. His friends, at first somewhat rebuffed, managed to revive his interests. On all sides sympathy was manifest. To his fellow-musicians, it was a calamity that he had withdrawn so much from public life.

In 1611, however, his name was before the public again, That year, together with Orlando Gibbons and William Byrd, his works appeared in the first printed collection of virginals music, " Parthenia : or the Maydenhead of the First Musick that ever was printed to the Virginals," published by William Hole, of London.

Poets as well as musicians combined to celebrate the occasion. The printed volume was prefaced by sonnets in praise of the composers, by George Chapman and Hugh Holland, whose sonnets in praise of Shakespeare were much in vogue at the time. Holland's contribution to " Parthenia " included the famous lines :

> " Loe, where doth pace in order
> A brauer Bull, then did Europa cary;
> Nay, let all Europe showe me such another,"

which, whatever the merits of the poem otherwise, carried something of Bull's figure in their measure and imagery.

Meanwhile, in spite of this gleam of returning success, the clouds which Bull's mind had presaged for years were gathering. His misanthropy after his wife's death had seriously affected his standing with the King, who, whatever the troubles of others, always demanded that he should stand first in their thoughts and attention. Other influences were also at work. James was scheming fresh political moves. Ever since his conclusion of peace with Spain, which had aroused a deep resentment throughout England, he had been sedulous in cultivating the good graces of the new King there, Philip III. Now, as his son Charles emerged into adolescence, he began to dream of an Anglo-Spanish alliance, through his marriage to Philip's daughter.

Against this there was strong opposition in England. Continually in spite of the King's drastic laws and penalties, the deep-seated animosity between the two nations broke out in sporadic encounters. James determined to extirpate the last traces of those who had supported anti-Spanish feeling under Elizabeth. Raleigh, languishing for years in the Tower, with unrepealed sentence of death hanging over his head, was to be sacrificed to James' desire to placate Spain but a few years later, in 1618.

Bull's withdrawal had distracted James' attention from him. The King had little time for those who were not constantly dancing attendance on him. Now, when he commenced to review all those who might be unsympathetic to his political projects, the memory of Bull's prominent part in the Armada celebrations recurred to his mind. He had no grounds to suspect any disaffection; but reason and justice played little part in his prejudices. Less and less the name of Bull figured in Court celebrations. More and more the figure of Dr. Coperario, whose Italianate mannerisms and name appealed to the pedantic king, appeared.

Nevertheless, the sense of growing shadow was lightened by a happy event for Bull. The young Princess Elizabeth

CLOSING CADENCE

was now seventeen, and her far-famed charms were bringing eminent suitors for her hand. The choice of her father lit on the young Elecor-Prince Palatine of the Rhineland, Frederick. His visit to England was arranged and the moment the two young people encountered each other it was a case of love at first sight.

Many at Court did not view the match favourably, although the young German prince, a pronounced Calvinist, was a prominent leader of the Protestant party in Germany, with which those suspicious of Spain and Austria desired to see England allied. Nevertheless, to his credit, James refused to override his daughter's obvious desires. The young prince was accorded every mark of honour and within a few weeks of his arrival, the betrothal was announced, with the wedding to follow speedily.

Prince Henry was delighted at his sister's happiness, and shared in entertaining her future husband royally. The young princess, already full of the bravery of spirit with which she was to face life at great odds and fend off the hardest strokes of misfortune, made the most of her heyday of happiness and gaiety. Both she and her husband had a keen love of music and drama, and the festive celebrations included a gala season of plays at Court, no less than thirteen of Shakespeare's plays being given in close succession at Court for their entertainment. Princess Elizabeth, with that loyalty and steadfastness which were to make her exemplary in an age not highly distinguished for these qualities, did not forget her old friend and teacher, Bull. Her affection for her father's organist had persisted and she had developed very creditable musical gifts, being remarkably proficient with the virginals and lute and in " sweete singinge and cleere, albeit of no greate voyce."

The music for her wedding was placed in Bull's charge,

and he responded eagerly with the composition of a special anthem, " God the Father, God the Son," " made newe for that purpose by Doctor John Bull." She was gracious to her favourite musician throughout the ceremonies, and his hopes for her ran as high as her own, sharing Sir Henry Wotton's sentiments :

> " So, when my mistress shall be seen
> In form and beauty of her mind,
> By virtue first, then choice, a Queen,
> Tell me, if she were not designed
> Th' eclipse and glorie of her kinde ? "

Later he was to encounter her in adversity, when ill-fortune had lighted upon both. Then he was to realize that, however his hopes and hers had waned before unhappy circumstance, she was still the brave spirit which radiated, gay and careless, in the brilliance of her happy weeks of betrothal and at her nuptials.

This happy time was but a passing gleam, however; the clouds were gathering ever more closely about Bull's fortunes. Right on the heels of the festivities, a heavy blow fell upon him. In November, 1613, his friend and patron, Henry, Prince of Wales, died suddenly.

With Richard, Earl of Dorset, he might well have exclaimed : " Our rising sun is set ; it scarcelie shone and with him all our glorie lies buried." Bull was deprived of his best friend and with this personal loss came material deprivation. With the death of the Prince he lost his position as Musician-in-Ordinary to the Household, thus having to face the loss of a full half of his income.

Difficulties crowded upon him. The Household Treasury of James was never notable for punctuality in settling its accounts and wherever the stingy King could withhold payment as long as possible he did so, and his officials curried favour with him by a similar dilatoriness.

Bull's position grew desperate and he was driven to extreme measures, at whatever cost to his pride. He could see only one way to safeguard the immediate future of his young son; that was to have his own name changed to that of his child by letters patent, so that all monies due to him might be paid to his son, in event of anything happening to himself.

He found one friendly advocate in Sir Christopher Parkins, or Perkins, the King's Master of Requests and Dean of Carlisle. The King, on having the matter brought to his attention, refused to make any decision until it had been considered by Sir Julio Cæsar, deputy Master of Requests.

Bull could have found no kindlier listener to a petition than Cæsar. As Master of Requests under Queen Elizabeth, this son of a naturalized Italian had become so famous for his kindheartedness and generosity that a friend who borrowed his coach complained that the importunities of the crowd of beggars who followed it had cost him more than it would have done had he bought a new coach for the occasion. His career had been one of devoted self-sacrifice, and an outstanding example of Elizabeth's meanness towards her best servants. Although Elizabeth did not scruple to accept from him " a gowne of cloth of silver, richly embroydered, a blacke networke mantel, with pure golde, a taffeta hat, whyte with severall flowers, and a jewell sett therein with silver and diamonds " together with an entertainment costing him some £700 when she visited him as Judge of the Admiralty on her way to Nonesuch in 1598, he yet had to complain that his predecessors " had every three yeares somewhat " yet he " after nine yeares service, received in fee, pension or recompense to the value of one pennie nothinge," but was rather some £4,000 out of pocket.

To such a hearer Bull did not make vain appeal; but the wheels of officialdom moved slowly, if they were actually set in motion at all. In desperation, Bull wrote to Sir Michael Hicks, secretary to the Earl of Salisbury, Lord of the Treasury. The letter was painful to write and painful for posterity to read:

> " To his honorable and singular
>   good frinde Sr Michaell Hicks
>   these

" S^r. I haue bin many times to haue spoken with you, to desire your fauor to my L(ord) and Mr. Chauncelor. Sir, my humble sute is, that it would please my L(ord) and Mr. Cha(ncellor) to graunte me theire fauors to chainge my name in my letters patents, and to (put) in my childes, leauinge out my owne. It is but forty pounds by yeare for my service heretofore, the mater is not greate, yet it wilbe some reliefe for my poore childe, hauinge nothing ells to leaue it. The kinge hath bin moued by Sir Chri. Perkins, who hath order from the kinge to speake with Sir Julio Cæsar. I humbly thank Sir Julio Cæsar. I haue bin with him and (he) hath promised me his fauor; but one worde of yours will spreade it, and make me and my poore child everlastingly bound to you. I humbly desire you, speak in this my humble sute with all the expedition you may, and so with my humble duty remembered I take leaue.

> " Yours euer to commande
>   " J. Bull."

That the matter had been brought up considerably earlier and had become intolerably urgent with Prince

Henry's death, is clear when the endorsement of April 20th is considered on the document.

Bull was not alone in the neglect which he suffered. John Dowland, the most celebrated lutenist of his day, was obliged to go abroad for appreciation and the means to make a livelihood, as his own words, in the preface to his "Pilgrim's Solace on 1612 show:

> 'I haue bene long obscured from your sighte, because I received a kingly entertainement in a foraine climate, which could not attaine to any (though never so meane) place at home.'"

Elizabeth, in spite of her meanness, at least accorded the poets, dramatists and musicians of her day recognition, however long they had to wait for remuneration. James, equally tight-fisted, excepting for his spasmodic bursts of extravagant lavishness, withheld position and office from some of the best talents of his day. The drama fared better with him than music; indeed, it was not to him, but to his musical son, Henry, Prince of Wales, that the musicians of the day owed such encouragement as they received. Otherwise they were thrown upon the casual patronage of the wealthier nobles, the Earls of Pembroke, Surrey, Southampton, Rutland and Dorset. The painters fared better in royal favour and that of nobles whose powers were virtually princely, such as the Duke of Buckingham.

In spite of all, nothing occurred and Bull was driven to a last desperate step. Creditors were pressing him from all sides, and it may well have been, that, in view of later steps against him by James, the crafty monarch considered that imprisonment for debt might relieve him of the necessity for instituting steps which he would have to make some pretence of justifying, if he found it necessary to include

Bull in those whom he desired to penalize to gain the good graces of Spain.

Bull, however, had the wisdom not to wait for such eventuality. On all sides the position for Elizabeth's old favourites was assuming ominous aspects. His private difficulties clinched the matter. The King obviously had little regard for his position or prestige, and still less for him personally. His last remaining royal patron was dead and Princess Elizabeth had left for Germany with her new husband.

He took nobody into his confidence. The matter was too risky. The Cheque Book of the Chapel Royal records what eventually happened:

" John Bull, doctor of Musicke, went beyond the seas without licence and was admitted into the Archdukes service and entered into paie there about Michaelmas and Peter Hopkins a Base from Poules was sworne in his place the 27. of December followinge : his wages from Michaelmas unto the daie of the swearinge of the said Peter Hopkins was disposed of by the Deanne of his Maiesties sayd Chappell."

John Bull had burnt his bridges. The England which he loved so well would know him no more. He had gone into exile.

His reception at Brussels provided some solace for the pain of his departure. The Archduke received him with every token of honour and favour, and he was immediately enrolled among the organists of the archducal Chapel Royal, where among his colleagues—Géry de Gersem, Jan Zacharias, Pierre Cornet and Vincento Guani—he found his own fellow-countryman and staunch admirer, Peter Philips.

CLOSING CADENCE

Four years of calm passed in Brussels, while stormclouds gathered in Europe. At first Bull's peace was disturbed by the malice of James. Scarcely was he installed in the Archduke's Chapel before charges were preferred against him, with a demand for his extradition.

James was not content to accuse his ex-organist of the crime of taking unlicenced leave. He sought to blacken Bull's character to the utmost. To what extent the indictment went was made clear when the English Ambassador at Brussels wrote to his sovereign on the 30th of May, 1614:

"Moste excellent and worthie Soueraigne, findinge, after longe attendance by reason of the Archdukes indisposition, that he was nowe so much amended as he gaue access to some ministers of other princes, I procured audience of him on Monday was sennighte, and accordinge to your Maiesties commandment sent me by Sir Thomas Lake, after I had used some congratulations unto him, in your Maiesties name for the recouery of his healthe—which he seemed to take in uerie goode parte, I tolde him, that I had charge from your Maiestie to acquaint him that your Maiestie upon knowledge of his receiuinge Dr. Bull your Maiesties organiste and sworne seruant into his chappel, without your Maiesties permission or consent, or so much as speakinge thereof to me, that am resydinge here, for your Maiesties affairs: that your Maiestie did justly finde it strange as you were his friend and ally, and had neuer used the like proceedinge either towardes him or any other foraign prince, addinge that the like course was not practysed among priuate persons, much less among these of greater place and dignity, and I tolde him plainly that it was notorious to all the worlde, that the sayd Bull did not leaue your Maiesties seruice for any wrong done unto him or for matter of religion, under which fained pretext he now sought to wrong the reputation of your Maiesties justice, but did in that dishonest manner steale out of England through the guilte of a corrupte conscience, to escape the punishment, which notoriously he had deserued, and was designed to haue been inflicted on him by the hande of justice for his incontinence, fornication, adultery, and other grieuous crimes."

Sir William Trumbull was a zealous and not over-scrupulous servant of his king; but his accusations did not carry much weight with the Archduke, to whom Bull's reputation and person were well known for many years. He refused to act as King James' policeman, and Bull retained his favour and his office at the chapel.

Apart from the friendship of the gentle Blitheman during his life, Bull was too well-known and liked for such slander to carry much weight. The greatest refutation of Trumbull's libels was found in his life in Belgium and the honour accorded him there.

In 1617 Rumold Waelrent, organist of the famous Cathedral of Notre Dame in Antwerp died. The post was one of the most eminent in Europe; but there was no hesitation. By the unanimous vote of the Chapter John Bull was appointed.

More even than Brussels, Antwerp was the centre of the life of the Flemish realm. For long it had been the actual capital. The Archduke held his Court there and its social life was brilliant. There Bull, in his new post, encountered notable figures.

Foremost among these was the Flemish painter, Peter Paul Rubens. Like Bull, the Flemish artist was also dual in his interests, combining artistic activities with political ones. There was much to draw them together. Rubens had a humour akin to that of Bull, shown in the famous anecdote of him while ambassador at the Court of Charles I of England. There he was discovered by an English courtier painting, who remarked that the Ambassador amused himself with painting, to which Rubens drily replied that, on the contrary, the painter occasionally amused himself with diplomacy.

At Rubens' home the brilliant intellectual and artistic society of Antwerp congregated. The painter lived in princely fashion. His home was palatial, with its great colonnades, magnificent halls and the huge studio where he worked with his pupils, many of them the most noted painters of Flanders. To Bull, unfamiliar with Italy, the magnificence of the Italian architecture which the painter had copied from his memories of visits there, was astounding. The vastness of its sweep, with its imposing stairways and the great frescoes of Perseus and Andromeda, the procession of Silenus and the Judgment of Paris painted on its outer walls, overwhelmed him with their grandiose and fantastic extravagance. They were not to his personal taste, much as he admired their mastery; but in them he recognized the broad sweep of mind in Rubens which was akin to his own.

It was the city itself, however, which most attracted him. The more he became familiar with it, the more he felt that the boast of the citizens was scarcely exaggerated. "The whole world is a ring, in which Antwerp is the diamond." The teeming port, not open to the vagaries of the ocean, as were Amsterdam and Rotterdam, but sheltered fifty miles up the Scheldt, was a constant source of interest to him, with his deep-seated love of maritime traffic. Almost every nation was represented in the

DR. JOHN BULL

shipping that crowded its two thousand foot width of river. Its cargoes were fascinating. Antwerp was the chief money-market of the world and noted for its diamond-cutters and jewellers. Its shops absorbed his attention for hours together, when he had time to wander the city. In them, wistfully, he recalled his first boyish vision of London Town.

He was welcome and frequently in request at the Steen, the archducal palace commanding the city, and in his brilliant reception there he found solace for the neglect of his last days in his native land. Nevertheless, his heart ached often for England. He was of its soil and his deep patriotism made his exile bitter to him, in spite of its brilliance.

He spent much time wandering in solitary moods through the city. The ornate mansion of Rubens and the rich houses of the nobles and wealthy burghers interested him less than the old buildings of the city, the richly decorated town hall, where the folk-spirit persisted in the ornaments and paintings, even those by contemporary artists. The old walls of the city were his frequent promenade, as were the banks of the river, on which Rubens' gardens bordered. Most solace of all he found, however, in the cathedral where his own organ was. There was the atmosphere of ancient days about it, which had grown up since its first stones were laid in 1352; but he felt also in the midst of growth in it; for it was not until 1616 that it was completed. With all the beauty of its lofty tower, rising sheerly from the ancient guild-houses surrounding the Place of Notre Dame; with all the magnificence of its interior, with its great Rubens paintings, the Assumption, the Elevation of the Cross and the Descent from the Cross, and the spacious calm of its broad, lofty aisles, he yet found

CLOSING CADENCE

its greatest impression in the scaffolding which stood in bizarre silhouette against the sky around the parts where the builders were still busy, when he returned to his apartments in the Cathedral Place by the south side, on moonlit nights, or viewed them as he left the house on sunny mornings. In them he saw the continuity of art, the persistent growth of a creative dream through the centuries, and in so visioning them he found comfort for the disaster which had overtaken his own life, realizing that in his work that life would continue immortally.

His closest friendship was with Peter Philips, whose trend of musical thought lay close to his own. Philips was deeply interested in keyboard music, in which Bull excelled, and had the deepest reverence for his English colleague. Continually the two paid each other visits to and from Brussels and Antwerp. From this association Philips benefited enormously, as he frankly allowed. In it he probably conceived his idea of working out the great contrapuntal vocal works as pieces for organ or virginals, which were the first known musical arrangements and the forerunners of the choral preludes of Buxtehude and Bach.

Bull's friendship with Sweelinck continued, heightened by similar visits to Amsterdam from time to time. Sweelinck thought ever more highly of Bull and in his famous work on composition he was careful to include a fugue of Bull as an example of mastery. Bull's own affection for Sweelinck was shown in the homage which he expressed in the magnificent Fantasia on a theme by the Dutch musician when Sweelinck died in 1621.

His life was not luxurious; but he lived in comfort and was more and more venerated as the years passed by. His house in the Place Verte was a centre for those who loved music and cared to enjoy it intimately. Nor were all his interests centred in his immediate circle. The life of the people, in Flanders as ever elsewhere, was a constant source of interest and delight to him. He caught up the countryside refrains on his promenades along the canals and fields; he attended the Kermesse and the village festivals, and watched the people's dances. He listened to their choruses and the strong simplicity of their hymns and from all these he derived fresh inspiration.

It was a productive period. He sought to forget sorrow in his creative work. His feeling for the Flemish folk resulted successively in his delightful " Boerendans," and in the joyous madrigal, " Den Lustelijken Mey," from which his lively virginals piece was developed. The simple faith of the people found expression in his lovely chorale, " Ein Kindeken ist uns geboren."

His work showed that his virile nature was still capable of humour, as in the pieces written for the Archduke's entertainments, such as " Het nieu Bergamasco."

Meanwhile, inwardly, his nature was deepening daily. The " Pavane sinfonia " showed how his creative thought was progressing towards that richer impression which caused one of the most thoughtful musicians and musical writers of three centuries later, Sir Hubert Parry, to write: " His instinct in the direction of brilliant effects was so abnormal that he anticipated some of the devices of modern pianoforte music." The Fantasia on Sweelinck's fugue was another instance of the growth of his broader style.

A touch of the intimacy which recurs in his music came with a pathetic event. Elizabeth, the gay young Princess at whose wedding he had played, had fallen on evil days. Crowned Queen of Bohemia at Prague in 1618, when her youthful ambition had persuaded her young husband to accept the throne, she had won all affections by her charm and gained the popular title of " The Queen of Hearts." Unfortunately, the politics of the day were not ruled by affection or much human feeling of any kind. Her bright visions of a gay court had been scattered into dust. Her reign endured barely a season, and then the lovely young " Winter Queen " found herself an exile in Holland, while her husband continued his fight against Austria.

The thought of the young girl, whom he had known in all the fresh flush of her youth and hope, being, like himself, an exile, stirred Bull deeply. He could not present himself to her, to express his feelings : the young " Winter Queen " was at the Court of the Protestant Prince of Orange and, although the Archduke held as much aloof from the unhappy conflict in Central Europe as was possible, his domains were under the Habsburg Empire, which was now in full strife with the German Protestant powers. With his mind full of the matter, Bull turned to his music to find expression. The delicate " Courante de la Reine," a chivalrous gesture to Elizabeth Stuart's short-lived reign, was the result, a salutation to the royalty which he beheld in her always, but of which fortune had deprived her.

It was the last echo of his former life. Henceforth his days passed in his new environment. It was as though, with some consciousness of symbolism his salutation to Elizabeth of Bohemia had been his leave-taking of all that his native land had meant to him.

There were no more adventures in the material world to be recorded of him ; but, in spirit, he was exploring new regions. The years, in their passing, were ticked off by brief, matter-of-fact entries in the Cathedral Chapter Act Book—" 12 livres d'Artois," as payment, at fixed intervals.

He was not unhappy. It was not in his character to sentimentalize himself or seek refuge in pathos. The essential simplicity of his nature, never given to small egotism, together with the calm kindliness of the country which had taken him to its heart, were not such as made his state tragic, in fact or fancy. Even the passing of his beloved friend, Sweelinck, did not darken his days. The "Fantasia" which he composed as a memorial was not so much a lament as an exaltation of the large spirit of the Dutch musician, soaring with something of his "sweep of wings," not brooding. As his life lengthened to its evening, it took on the quiet of a gentle dusk, in which the vista merged into broad stretches of soft twilight.

In that quietude serenity grew, with such calm acceptance of life that it had no sadness. One by one, the confusing images of his experience slipped into their place in that kindly twilight of remembrance in which all harsher outlines were softened and blended into broad pattern. From afar, the recollected scenes of England took on a nimbus of tenderness, colouring his musical imagination as he wrote his " Kingston " and the gentle folk-song setting, " Bonny Well, Robin." It was the mood of happy remembrance rather than of melancholy resignation, which spoke in them.

To the end, his vital nature persisted. He was not one who could be content with retrospect. The living world around him was too interesting for him to grow isolated from it. His years and his achievements were gradually rendering him venerable and those about him regarded him with reverence; but he assumed no solemnity. He still shared in the moods of the folk about him. " Het niew Bergamasco " (" The New Bergamasque ") came with a genial flash of the old merriment, attuned to the popular humour of the clowning dance.

In the place of public interests, he found private ones.

CLOSING CADENCE

His touch with those about him became closer, preventing monotony. The old courtly grace had not deserted him; it had simply taken on a new dignity, though its fantasy remained. He could still turn a cavalierly compliment, though with an added graciousness of diction, as in his " Galliard : Madamoyselle Charlotte de la Haye "; and in his friendships were many inspirations. He took pleasure in using the themes of his friends for variations or fantasias, as in the " Fantasia op de fugue van Mr. Jan Litterje," or as musical compliments, as in the " Fantasia op de fugue van La Guanina." In his public life similar traits showed. There was a stately gesture in the music " Door Dr. Bull gemacht, ter Eeren van Goduart van Kappell."

In the growing breadth of his consciousness, he identified place and people. His affection alike for the folk and the city which had afforded him refuge and taken him to its heart was recorded in his music, delicately pointed by the title of his virginals piece, " Het Juweel " (" The Jewel "), painting at once the atmosphere of Antwerp and his own feeling for " the diamond in the ring of the world."

As the glow of his late afternoon took on the deeper hue of sunset, the rich, yet calm surety of his mind broadened. His work was imbued with a fresh mood of serene faith. It suffused with splendour his " In Nomine " one of the most beautiful works ever written for the organ." It inspired the broad fresco of his double setting of " Telluris Urgens Conditor." Having explored wide tracts of new musical territory during his earlier life, with an intrepidity which left them still original after centuries, he, like the returned wanderer, now set about rounding-off his musical edifice with the riches which he had accumulated. In the Modes he had material for the further development of architectonic tradition and he utilized it superbly, in the " Prelude and Fantasia on the 8th

Mode" and the similar work on the 5th Mode, music which provided a noble culmination for the period which, historically, he epitomized and which ended in him.

His mind, however, was still that of the pioneer. His " Pavane Sinfonia " showed its trend at the very close of his life. Sweelinck had conceived the Suite; Bull, with something of prophecy, here envisaged the greater symphonic mould in which his legitimate successors, Buxtehude and Bach, would move towards Haydn, Mozart and Beethoven.

It was a fitting sunset to a life which had known its eager gleam of dawn, its pulsating glow of high noontide. It was a radiant culmination, splendid in its spiritual triumph; for all these works came in swift succession the last year, a swelling cadence bringing his song to a close.

The serene assuredness of faith in him found its epitome in his " Alma Redemptoris." Its significant title indicated his new vision. It is impossible to avoid the feeling that here Bull not only expressed a mood of deep religious conviction, but also a transcendental exaltation of that other Alma, his country, which had always been his ideal, seen in its spiritual power, rather than its material pomp.

Philips, visiting him from Brussels, was extraordinarily moved by this music, and could not forbear from exclaiming that, while Bull was England's greatest grace, his exile was England's greatest disgrace. Bull, his hands still on the organ-keys, turned to reprove him gently: beside the fame of England his own was insignificant. Philips took in the calm features, the silvered hair caught by the evening light through the windows, the serene devotion of his friend's words and expression. Linking these to the music, he affirmed that Bull was beyond country and time, a spirit of immortal glory. Very quietly came the answer,

CLOSING CADENCE

the aged musician's eyes fixed on some vista of his mind,—in God's infinity of stars, his glory was a small thing.

The words make a fitting epitaph. Ill-requited for his devotion, wronged, exiled and ignored in the land to which his undeviating love and thought had been given, he was still John Bull of England, great in his humility, humble in the grandeur of his achievement. He had transcended bitterness; he had not fallen into the small egotism with which lesser natures would have solaced a smaller pride. Past the illusory appearances of his day, he saw the glory which was to be, and which was not only England, but the evolving world. He was serene and contented in having played his man's part among men; but he saw mankind in an eternal scheme in which he was a human mite, great only by his part in the whole.

Factual or legendary, such a speech attributed to him shows the impress of his thought at the time on those who knew him. It came then as his final confession of faith. In March, 1628, John Bull died. He was buried in the cathedral where he had rounded-off his life-work in the city where he had learned the intimate values of human intercourse more closely than anywhere. On the quiet current of his faith, he, who had weathered storms, passed serenely to his last haven. His resting-place was symbol of the sanctuary he had found, in life and in his suffered spirit.

Seen in its material aspect, his end was undramatic; spiritually, it was triumphant. It was the fitting closing cadence to a life which had resolved its discords. In God's infinity of stars, a small thing, maybe; but in the round of human existence and effort, something touched with grandeur and glory.

BIBLIOGRAPHY

Musical

ARKWRIGHT. " Catalogue of Music in the Library of Christ Church, Oxford."
ATKINS. " The Early Occupants of the Office of Organist and Master of the Choristers of Worcester Cathedral."
I ARRETT. " English Glee and Madrigal Writers."
BEVIN. " A Briefe and Short Introduction of the Art of Musicke." 1631.
BOEHME. " Geschichte des Tanzes."
BONAVENTURA. " Storia e literatura del Pianoforte."
BOYCE. " Cathedral Music." 1760.
BRIDGE. " Twelve Good Musicians " (John Bull in this). " The Past and the Future."
BROOKE. " Old English Psalmody."
BUCK. " The Influence of the Organ in History."
BULL. Works by Dr. John Bull. (See Appendix D.)
BURNEY. " A General History of Music." 1776–1789.

" Cambridge Modern History."
CHAPPELL. " Popular Music of the Olden Time." " Musicke's Handmaid." 1678.
CHURCH. " An Introduction to Psalmody." 1723.
CLARK, R. " An Account of the National Anthem." 1822. " Never Before Published." 1837. " To the Lovers of Research." 1841.
CLARK, MASON. " Bibliographical Dictionary of Fiddlers."
CLOSSON. " Chansons populaires en Belgique." Collections of old Belgian Harpsichord Music. (Durand, Paris.)
COMBARIEU. " Histoire de la Musique." " La Musique, ses lois, son évolution." " Le Chant Choral."
CROWEST. " Dictionary of British Musicians."
CURZON. " Musiciens du temps passé."

BIBLIOGRAPHY

DAVEY. "History of Music."
"Dictionary of National Biography" (Musical articles in).
DICKINSON. "The Growth and Development of Music."
DOWLAND. "Pilgrims Solace." 1612.
DUPONT. "École de Piano."

"Early English Musical Magazine," No. 3, 1891.
EDMONDSTOUNE-DUNCAN. "Carol." "Minstrelsy."
EITNER. "Quellenlexicon der Musiker und Musikgelehrter."
"Bibliography of Musical Compositions, XVI and XVII Centuries."
EINSTEIN. "Geschichte der Musik."
ELSON. "Shakespeare Music." "Universal Encyclopædia of Music."

FELLOWES. "Elizabethan String Music." "English Madrigal Composers."
FÉTIS. "Biographie univérselle des Musiciens."
FULLER-MAITLAND. "The Consort of Music." "The Fitz-William Virginal Book" (with Barclay Squire).

GALPIN. "Old English Instruments of Music."
GASPERINI. "Storia della Musica." "Dell'arte di interpretare la scrittura della musica nel cinquecento." "Storia della semiografia musicale."
GLAREANUS. "Dodekachordon." 1547. (Ed. H. Lovit.)
GLYN. "Elizabethan Virginal Music and Its Composers."
GODDARD. "The Rise and Development of Opera."
GREW. "Polymetric Edition of XVI Century Vocal Music."
GROVE's "Dictionary of Music."

HABERL. "Bausteine für Musikgeschichte." "Magister Choralis." "Jahrbuch."
HAWKINS. "A History of the Science and Practice of Music." 1776.
HENRY, LEIGH. "The Story of Music." "Music: Its Growth in Form and Significance."

KREBS. "Die Frauen in der Musik."

BIBLIOGRAPHY

LEICHTENTRITT. "Geschichte der Motett." "Deutsche Hausmusik von vier Jahrhunderts."
"Lute, The," No. 30, 1883-99.

MORLEY. "A Plaine and Easie Introduction to Practicall Musicke." 1597.

NAGEL. "Geschichte der Musik in England." "Annalen."
NAUMANN. "Geschichte der Musik." (Addenda on English Music by Grove.)
NORTH. "Memoirs of Musick." (Ed. Rimbault, 1846.)

PARRY. Notes on John Bull, in "Oxford Dictionary of Music."
PARRY, Sir H. "Oxford History of Music" (Polyphonic Period).
"Parthenia" (Bull's works in). 1611. Edited by Margaret Glyn, 1931.
PAUER. "Old English Composers."
PULVER. "Biographical Dictionary of Old English Music." "Dictionary of Old English Music."

QUITTARD. "Un musicién en France au XVIIiéme Siècle."

RAVENSCROFT. "A Briefe Discourse of the true (but neglected) use of Charact'ring the Degrees by their Perfection, Imperfection, and Diminution in Measurable Musicke," etc. 1614. "Pammelia: Musickes Miscellanie." 1618. "Deuteromelia." 1609. "Melismata: Musicall Phantasies." 1611. "Whole Booke of Psalms." 1621.
RIEMANN. "Musik Lexicon." "Tänze des 16. Jahrhunderts."
RIMBAULT. "Old Cheque Book of the Chapel Royal." 1872.
RITTER. "Woman as a Musician." "Student's History of Music."

SANDYS. "History of the Violin & other instruments played on with the bow."
SCHLESINGER. "Bibliography of Musical Instruments."
SCHURE. "Histoire du Drame Musical."
SEIFFERT. "Geschichte der Klaviermusik."
SMITH. "Musica Antica." 1655.
SQUIRE, BARCLAY. "Cataloque of old printed music in the

BIBLIOGRAPHY

British Museum." Articles in " Dictionary of National Biography. " Articles in Grove's " Dictionary of Music."

TABOURET. " Orchésographie." 1586.

VAN DEN BORREN. " Les Origines de la musique de Clavier en Angleterre." " Les Musiciéns belges en Angleterre au temps de la Renaissance."
VAN DUYSE. " De melodie van het nederlandsche lied."
VAN ELEWYCK. " Discurs sur la musique religieuse en Belgique."
VAN MALDEGHEM. " Trésor Musical."
VAN DER STRAETEN. " La musique dans les pays bas avant le XIXième siécle." " Voltaire comme musicién."

WARMAN. " The Organ : A Comprehensive Treatise on its structure, capacities, history, etc."
WEST. " Cathedral Musicians."

GENERAL

AITKEN. " Memoirs of the Court of Elizabeth."
ALLEN. " Anne Cecil, Elizabeth and Oxford."
ARKWRIGHT (Ed. by). " Fortune by Land and Sea."
ARBER. " Register of Stationers' Hall."

BURGON. " Life and Times of Sir Thomas Gresham."
BURCKHARDT. " Renaissance."

CUNNINGHAM. Extracts from the " Accounts of the Revels at Court."

DURUY. " Short History of France."

Ellesmere Papers (Ed. Collier).

FRUIN. " Het Karakter van het Nederlandsche volk."

GREEN. " Calendar of State Papers, Reign of James I."

Hamilton Papers (Ed. J. Bain).
Harleian MSS (British Museum).
HUNTER. " New Illustrations of Shakespeare."

MSS. in the Ashmolean Museum, Oxford.
MACAULAY. " History of England."

BIBLIOGRAPHY

NORTH. " English Bells."
READ, CONYERS. " Sir Francis Walsingham."
RIMBAULT. " Old Cheque Book of the Chapel Royal."
RHYS. " Minor Elizabethan Drama."

SCHOTEL. " Oude seden en gebrusken en Nederland."
SYMONS, J. A. " Renaissance."

TREVELYAN. " History of England."

VON RAIMER. " Geschichte des XVI u. XVII Jahrhunderts."

WALTER. " Church Bells of England."
WARD. " Lives of the Professors of Gresham College." 1740.

ANTIQUE (Literary and Historical)

ALDRYDGE. " Liber Niger; or Records of the Order of the Garter." 1534–38.
AYLOFFE. " Archaelogia." " Calendars and Ancient Charters." 1774.
BARNES. " Devil's Charter." 1607.
BARNFIELD. " Minerva Britanna." 1626.
BARRET. " Alveanie: or Quadruple Dictionary." 1580. " Practicke of Moderne Warre." 1578.
BASSOMPIERRE. " Journal de ma vie." 1579–1640.
BATMAN. Additions to " Liber Niger Domus Regis." 1579. " De proprietatibus rerum." 1582.
BECKETT. " Table Talk; or musique for a banquet of wine." 1620.
BROWNE. " A true and faithfull relation." 1621.
BURTON. " Anatomy of Melancholy." 1621.

CAMDEN. " Britannia," etc. 1586. " Annales." 1615–17.
CHAPMAN. " Alphonsus—Emperor of Germany." 1621. " Certain Trauailles of an uncertain Journey." 1653.
CHAPPUYS. " Histoire." 1606.
CHETTLE. " Englandes Mourninge Garmente." 1603.
CHURCHYARDE. " Dreame " (Collection " Chippes "). 1578.
COGAN. " Haven of health." 1593.

BIBLIOGRAPHY

CORYAT. " Crudities." 1611.
CROMPTON. " Mansion of Magnanimitie." 1599.
" Compleat Gamester." 1680.

DAVIES. " Orchestra." 1607. " Nosce Teipsum." 1622.
D'AUBIGNÉ. " Memoires." " Histoire universelle." 1550–1601.
DEKKER. " Belman of London." 1608. " English Villanies." 1632. " The Gul's Horn Booke." 1602.
DOWLAND. " Pilgrims Solace." 1612.
DRAYTON. " Polyolbion." 1612.
D'EWES. Collection of " Records of Parliament." (Harleian MSS., British Museum).
DU PERRON. " Ambassades." 1590–1618.

EDEN. " Historie of trauayle." 1577.
ELLIS. " Briefe itenery of trauells," etc. 1597.
FAITHORNE. Map of London, 1658. (Bibliothèque nationale, Paris.)
FALCONER. " Marine Dictionary." 1612.
FLORIO. " Italian and English Dictionary." 1692.
FULLER. " History of the Worthies of England." 1662.
FYNES MORISON. " The Itenery of his trauales," etc. 1589. (Publ. London, 1617.)
T. F. " A Letter sent from sea." 1589.

GRAVELLE. " Politiques royales." 1596.
GROTIUS. " Annales et historiæ de rebus Belgicis." 1557.

HACKLUYT. " Voyages." 1589. " Virginia richly Valued." 1609.
HAPTON. " Concordancy of Yeares." 1615.
Harleian MSS. (British Museum).
HAWES. " Graunde Amour." 1554.
HEYWOOD. " Epigrams." 1598.
" Historia Histrionica." (Ed. Wright.) 1699.
HOLINSHED. " Chronicles." 1587.
HUMBLE. The Theatre of the Empire of Greate Britannie." 1578.

KEMP. " Return from Parnassus." 1606.

BIBLIOGRAPHY

LELAND. "Collected Appendices." (Ed. 1770.)
LITTLETON. "Latin-English Lexicon." 1675.

MAINWARING. "Seaman's Dictionary." 1670.
"Military Art of Trayninge." 1622.
MASSINGER. "A Gorgeous Gallery of Gallant Inventions." 1578.

NORTH. "Memoirs of Musick." (Pub. Rimbault, 1846.)

PHILIPS. "A briefe Chronicle," etc. 1622.
PARKINSON. "A Garden of all sorts of Pleasant Flowers." 1629.
"Polimanteia." 1595.

RAVENSCROFT. "A briefe Discourse," etc. 1614.
REED. "Glossary to the praise of Yorkshire ale." 1697.
RICH. "Farewell to Militarie Profession." "Souldiers Wishe to Britons Welfare." 1604.
RIMBAULT. "Old Cheque Book of the Chapel Royal."

SAVIOLO. "Of Honor and Honorable Quarrels." 1594.
SCOT. "A Tablebooke for a Prince." 1621.
SEGAR. "The Book of Honor and Arms." 1590.
SMITH. "Musica Antica." 1655.
STOWE. "Survey of London." 1598. "Annals; or a Chronicle of England" (con. by Howe). 1631.
STRUTT. "Sports and Pastimes" ("Glig-Gamena Angel-Dead"). 1801. "Regal and Ecclesiastical Antiquities of the reign of Elizabeth." 1773.
STRYPE. "Annals of Queen Elizabeth." (Ed. 1708-9.)
STYWARD. "Pathway to Martial Discipline." 1581.

TABOURET. "Orchésographie." 1586.

VILLEROY. "Memoires d'État." 1574-94.

WARD. "Lives of the Professors of Gresham College." 1740.
WEEVER. "Epigrams." 1599.
WOOD. "Fasti Oxonienses." 1691. "Athenæ Oxonienses." 1691.

APPENDIX A

Bull and the Authorship of the National Anthem

Bull's authorship of the National Anthem has been a source of contention for years. Even to-day there are many who cast doubts upon it. Yet the evidence on all hands, if fully considered, seems conclusive.

The existence of work, under the title " God Save the King : Variations," in the list of his compositions, is indisputable. It is set forth, not only in Wood's " Lives of the Professors of Gresham College," but also exists in the works preserved by Pepusch, filling pages 53–66 of Bull's collected MS. works. That Bull composed a work so entitled has never been disputed, and the counter-claims to the authorship of the National Anthem, as we know it, have been extremely vague and strongly contested. He was indisputably the first to compose an air entitled " God Save the King."

One source of confusion has been the title. This led Richard Clark astray in his otherwise very soundly advanced arguments in Bull's favour. His assumption was that, being known as " God Save the King," the work had always been so entitled. As the only king on the English throne during Bull's lifetime was James I, he naturally concluded, on the basis of his assumption, that the anthem had been composed for that monarch, and the memorable scene in which Bull figured at the Merchant Taylors' banquet in 1607—at which James I was present and at which Bull's anthem, to Latin words by Ben Jonson, was sung, to celebrate the King's salvation from the Gunpowder Plot—led Clark further astray.

Such error, however, affects only the time of Bull's composition of the work. The most considerable authorities, such as Fetis, freely allow that Clark established his argument for Bull's authorship.

APPENDIX A

The examination of that argument, sound though many of its conclusions are, nevertheless shows that the work pre-dated the discovery of Fawkes' plot. Clark himself admits that the theme was one which Bull probably used earlier, and in the somewhat spiteful comments of Bull's successor, Peter Hopkins, we learn that, though it featured effectively at the Merchant Taylors' function, "the ayre was in no wyse mayd new, beinge but a parte of that mayd in the reigne of the late queenes Maiestie for the greate victorie."

The example of the first form which it assumed, as put forward by Clark, also seems to substantiate this. To that example is attached the date, 1555. At that time, however, Bull was not yet born, though the example given bears his name.

It might be, indeed, as Clark suggests, that Bull, with his familiarity with folk-song, adapted a folk-tune already known; but the whole nature of his work, as preserved, is original and can by no stretch of the imagination be regarded as a folk-melody transcription. Hence, even if such theme were adapted and developed by him, the resultant work is of such character as to give him full right of authorship. The circumstances under which it was performed and accepted as his work also substantiate this.

The example given by Clark, however, is one printed by him two centuries after Bull's lifetime and admittedly transcribed by Clark himself from earlier sources.

It is obvious that if the air were a folk-song, however well known at the time, it would, in the state of musical research prevalent during Bull's lifetime, not be dated, since many original compositions remain undated and folk-melody was then utterly unexplored from the angle of bibliography.

On the other hand, it is clear that the manuscript from which Clark obtained his example bore a date; and it is very important to remember that his source was a manuscript of the Elizabethan Era, written in the caligraphy of the time, with every possibility of the embellishments and flourishes then in fashion.

Anyone familiar with such manuscript writings will admit that the writing of the figures 5 and 8 was very close, and the decorative trend of the times, while it might leave the initial figures clear, would tend to exaggerate the final ones.

APPENDIX A

So seen, and allowing for Clark's own errors of transcription, the date on the initial example—the part of the air alone—which he cites, would read 1588. That year was the year of the victory over the Spanish Armada.

The evidence, however, is not only circumstantial. There is more positive testimony to the writing of Bull's anthem having coincided with England's great triumph.

That the air performed at the banquet given for James I was not a new work was, as has been seen, affirmed in Bull's own lifetime; and in that affirmation is the positive statement that the air then used was one previously written, in the reign of Elizabeth, for the great victory.

Further evidence is also found in records of Bull's own time, and at a date previous to the accession of James I.

It is clear that none other than Bull could have been meant when a writer in 1591, dealing with a minor naval engagement, wrote : " Bee it no mater so greate withal her Maiesties organiste to hymne it, as hath bin made for the deliuerance by Gods grace from the grrate Armada, yet doth it make braue showe and worthie of Songe."

It is true that, at the time of the Armada, Bull had not yet succeeded to the organ of the Chapel Royal. Blitheman, however, was at no time notable for compositions for special functions, and the list of his works is extremely brief. In none extant is there any claim to a work of the character of the National Anthem ; nor has any claim ever been advanced for his authorship of " God Save the Queen."

By 1591 Bull, for the public, would be " her Maiesties organiste," the more so since his appointment that year would still be fresh in the popular mind. The passage, therefore, seems clearly to establish that not only was a hymn composed for the Armada victory sufficiently familiar to the general public to justify such reference to it, but also that it was known to have been composed by the Queen's organist, who, when the passage was written, was Bull.

Clark bases much of his argument on the admitted fact that, previous to the reign of the king in which he wrote, the anthem had been known as " God Save great James, our King." His initial contention was against the arguments previously advanced

APPENDIX A

that this anthem, so entitled, had been written for the Chapel of James II; and, according to the judgment of Fétis and many other authorities, he clearly proves the impossibility of this having been the case.

The claim of Clark's day, other than this, seems to have been that of the son of Henry Carey, and here Clark is on very sound ground indeed. At no time in his life did Carey advance any claim to authorship; and his son only put such claim forward with a view to obtaining a pension for himself in view of this " Royal service " which he alleged his father had rendered. His petition was not granted.

It is clear, however, that at the time when Clark wrote, the words of the National Anthem had already been adapted from " God Save great James our King " to " God Save our Gracious King," and an even earlier adaptation must clearly have taken place.

It is therefore significant when we read of the Elizabethan populace " makinge greate shoutinge and singinge, with God Save our Virgin Queene," words which, by metrical measurement, fit precisely to the National Anthem as we sing it to-day. This significance becomes deeper when we find, not only that the words of the National Anthem fit Bull's " God Save the King," but also that the air now nationally used exists, almost without discrepancy, in his MS. works, on page 98, an air reprinted by Sir George Smart as the original of the National Anthem, with the title, " God Save the Queen."

A most remarkable feature of the whole question is the popular attitude to Bull subsequent to the Armada. No other musician of his time—and, indeed, few of later times—was ever accorded such public reverence in act and speech as he was.

Comparatively obscure up to the time of the Armada, he leapt into prominence immediately afterwards. The great universities vied in honouring him, and he was appointed to the highest positions in his profession which existed.

Such fame was not confined to his own country. In his own lifetime, as records show, his name became synonymous abroad with his country.

It is true that tours on the Continent established his unrivalled prestige as a performer, and that he received the most astounding

APPENDIX A

honours, with munificent offers of payment and position, to tempt him to accept employment in foreign countries.

His works were evidently known widely also, even in times when the dissemination of music was slow. Others equally well known, however, were not so singled out for foreign recognition as he was. His name unquestionably had a unique significance far outside the boundaries of his native land.

Even though England at the time was so musically famous, it is more than improbable that a musician's name would be adopted as a national synonym abroad unless circumstances other than purely musical achievement had singled him out for notice.

Assuredly nothing but his association with the Queen under extraordinary conditions would have caused him to be generally known as " Her Maiesties Master " and the " Queen's Organiste " in so emphatic a manner as he was. Others holding precisely the same positions as those which he occupied were variously referred to as Master of the Chapel and Organiste of the Chappell, but never so explicitly linked with a sovereign regarded as symbolic as was Bull, or in such especial manner. For there is no denying that his public achievements were regarded as of national significance, and that his figure was one of national fame to an extent far beyond the field of music.

For that national aspect of Bull's personality to impress itself on the mind of countries abroad some distinct association with an outstanding event in contemporary English history seems necessary. No event of Elizabeth's time can compare in importance with the victory over the Armada. With it the whole European status of England underwent metamorphosis. At a bound she became the leading maritime Power, the hitherto dominant position of Spain brought low before her.

That Bull's name emerges coincidentally with this triumph as a nickname for the Englishman abroad, as well as that of a famous musician, could not be without significance.

The man was identified with his nation's glory. With the Armada celebrations he gave us not only our National Anthem; he became for all time, and no matter how changed by the passing of years and the transformations of national thought, the original of that John Bull of England which is the national figure throughout the world.

APPENDIX B

Documents relating to Bull

Birthplace. Anthony à Wood, "Athenæ Oxonienses" and "Fasti," 1691. Wellow Parish Register. Wood, Bodleian MSS.

Education, Chapel Royal. Wood, "Athenæ Oxonienses," "Fasti." Records of the Chapel Royal (Cheque Book).

Hereford Cathedral. "Fasti Herefordenses." Act Book of the College of Vicars of Hereford Cathedral.

Gentleman, Chapel Royal. Cheque Book of the Chapel Royal.

Bull's Salary as Organist, Chapel Royal. Cottonian MSS. Tib. B. III, fol. 248. ("Fees granted to sundry persons in the severall offices and places.") Cheque Book, Chapel Royal.

Petition of Bull for lease of £30, presented to Queen Elizabeth. Salisbury MSS. at Hatfield.

Academic Degrees. Wood, "Fasti."

Bull and Phelps (Attack at Tewkesbury). Cheque Book of the Chapel Royal.

Queen Elizabeth's Letter to the Lord Mayor of London and Aldermen, recommending Bull for Gresham professorship. State Papers, Eliz. Dom. Ser., cclx, 113, Docquet.

Lease to Robert Holland, "in consideration of the service of John Bull, organist of the Chappell." State Papers, Eliz. Dom., Ser. cclxii, 91.

Title Page, "Oration of Maister Iohn Bull," etc. Harl. MSS. 5936, British Museum. Stationers' Register, Arber.

Books from John Bull's Library. Library, Cambridge University. Volume, "Discantus Cantiones," listed by Ward.

Journey Abroad. Wood, "Fasti Oxonienses."

Incidents Abroad, etc. Idem.

Bull and Mourning Livery. Lord Chamberlain's Records.

Liveries for Entry of James I into London. Accompte of the Master of the Greate Warederobe to James I.

APPENDIX C

Gifts of James to Bull. State Papers, James (Lord Chamberlain's Records).
Marriage Licence. Episcopal Records, London.
Bull and Prince Henry. Household Accounts, Prince of Wales, 1610; entries *re* payments to Bull for music books. Idem; list of household musicians, headed by Bull's name, salary £40 p.a.
Letter of Bull to Sir Michael Hicks. Add. MSS., British Museum, 6194.
Departure of Bull from England. Cheque Book of the Chapel Royal.
Bull in Flanders. Records of Chapel Royal, Brussels; Act Books of the Cathedral of Notre Dame, Antwerp (payments of 12 livres d'Artois to Bull, 1617, 1619, 1622, 1623).
Trumbull's Letter to James I re Bull. British Museum Add. MSS. 6194.

APPENDIX C

BULL'S ASSOCIATES

ELWAY BEVIN.—Welsh composer, *circa* 1570–1640. Seiffert: " Ein Komponist aus Welsh " (" Geschichte der Klaviermusik "). Organist of Bristol Cathedral, 1589–1637; expelled on score of being Catholic (*vide* Wood).

1631, published first printed manual on Canon: " A Briefe and Short Introduction of the Art of Musicke, to teach how to make Discant of All Proportions that are in vse uery necessary for all suche as are desirous to attaine to knowledge in the Art; and may by Practice, if they can sing, soone be able to compose three, foure and fiue parts. And also to compose All Sorts of Canons that are usuall, by these directions of two or three parts in one, upon the Plain-Songe." Composed " Ye Sis Services for the Kinges Royall Chappell."

APPENDIX C

The work was dedicated to the Bishop of Gloucester, "unto whom," Bevin states, he has "beene much bounde for many fauors." The book is prefixed by a set of verses by Thomas Palmer, of Bristol.

Cheque Book of the Chapel Royal, June 3, 1605: "Memorandum that the third day of June, Anno 1605, Elway Beuan, by the consent and order of the Right Worshipfull Doctor Mountague, Deane of the Chappell, the Subdeane and Gentlemen then attendinge, was sworne Gentleman of his Maiesties Chappell extraordinary, who, at the takinge of his oth, did uoluntarily binde himselfe thereby not to seeke by any meanes direct or indirect, as by frendes or otherwise, to be admitted into an ordinary place and pay in his Highnes sayd Chappell, untill he shall be called and approued fitt for the same by the Deane, the Subdeane and the maior part of the Gentlemen then beinge. And for testimony thereof the sayd Elway Beuan hath hereunto subscribed his name the day and yeare aboue written in the presence of many of the Gentlemen then assembled. Elway Beuin."

Studied under Thomas Tallis in London.

Described as "a verie olde man" on visitation of Laud to Bristol, 1634.

WILLIAM BLITHEMAN.—Apparently entered into office at the Chapel Royal after the death of Richard Edwardes, Master of the Children. Before that was apparently Master of the Choristers of Christ Church, 1564. Bishop Tanner states: "Blitheman belonged to Christ Church quire; seems to have been master of the choristers there." There is some slight doubt concerning this reference, as Tanner refers, not to William, but John Blitheman; no other Blitheman is known in the musical or royal household records of the times. "Died much lamented, 1591" (Wood).

Composed a small number of musicianly virginals and organ works and some church choral music.

The inscription on Blitheman's memorial tablet in the Church of St. Nicholas Olave, "an engraven plate by the north wall of the chancel," ran :

APPENDIX C

" Here Blitheman lies, a worthy wighte
　　Who feared God aboue ;
A friend to all a foe to none
　　Whom rich and poore did loue.
Of princes Chappell gentleman
　　Unto his dyinge daye
Whom all took greate delighte to heare
　　Him on the Organs playe ;
Whose passinge Skill in Musickes art
　　A Scholar left behinde
John Bull by name his Masters ueine
　　Expressinge in eache kinde.
But nothinge here continues long
　　Nor restinge Place can haue :
His Soule departed hence to Heauen
　　His Body here in Graue."

WILLIAM BYRD.—Born Lincoln, 1538; died Slondon, Essex, 1623. Pupil of Thomas Tallis and his associate until the latter's death in 1585. Held a patent of monopoly conjointly with Tallis for printing and selling music in England, granted 1574 for 21 years. Was organist of Lincoln Cathedral, 1563–72. Sworn a Gentleman of the Chapel Royal 1569. Published the first collection of printed madrigals, " Musica Transalpina," 1588. Wrote many motets, madrigals and organ and virginals pieces, together with Fantasias for viols.

BENJAMIN COSYN.—Pupil of Bull. Compiled collection of pieces known as " Benjamin Cosyn's Virginall Booke," now in Royal Library at Buckingham Palace. Was organist at Dulwich College between 1622 and 1624. Organist, Charterhouse, 1626 to date of his death, 1643.

WILLIAM DAMEN.—Flemish musician and publisher. Born at Liège. Came to England 1661 (*vide* G. E. P. Arkwright, Ashmolean Records). Court musician to Queen Elizabeth. Published first printed Psalter, 1579, in which was included Bull's anthem, " Attende unto my Teares," in the collection of Sir William Leighton, " Teares : or the Lamentacion of a Sorrowefull Soule."

APPENDIX C

GILES FARNABY.—*Circa* 1568. Mus. Bac. Oxon., 1592. Published "Canzonets to Foure Voyces, with a Song of eight parts. Compiled by Giles Farnaby, Bachilar of Musicke, London." Noted for his whimsical virginals pieces, which closely resembled Bull's style, "Farnaby's Dreame," "His Reste," "His Humor," "Pawles Wharf," etc. Was a Cornishman, of a Truro family.

NATHANAEL GILES.—*Circa* 1560–1633. His memorial tablet, Windsor, St. George's Chapel, bears the statement that he died aged 75, which would make the date of his birth 1558. A great deal of the information given there is erroneous, however, both as affects Giles and his wife. Evidence elsewhere seems to establish 1560 as the correct date.

West, in his "Cathedral Organists," states that Giles was nominated a clerk of St. George's Chapel, Windsor, on October 1st, 1595.

According to Sir Ivor Atkins ("Occupants of the office of Organist, etc., at Worcester Cathedral"), Giles became Organist and Master of the Children at Worcester Cathedral in 1581, leaving the post to become Master of the Children of the Chapel Royal, in succession to William Hunnis, in 1585.

"It seems clear that he was descended from a family belonging to Worcestershire and that he was born in that county" (Pulver, "Biographical Dictionary of Old English Music").

Vide Fuller-Maitland, "Grove's Dictionary of Music" and "Dictionary of National Biography."

His father was organist of St. Paul's Church, London.

HUGH HOLLAND.—Welsh poet and writer. Became Fellow of Trinity College, Cambridge. Spent some years at Oxford "for the sake of the public library" there. Made a pilgrimage to Jerusalem, "to do his devotions to the holy sepulchre." Wrote a well-known obituary poem on William Shakespeare, with whom and Ben Jonson he was long associated. Wrote the introductory sonnet on John Bull in "Parthenia," 1611. Also wrote an obituary poem on James I, entitled "A Cypres Garland For the Sacred Forehead of our late soueraigne

APPENDIX C

King James." Died in the city of Westminster, 1633. *Vide* Wood, "Athenia Oxonienses"; also Fuller's "Worthies," where he is mentioned as "No bad English, but a most excellent Latine poet."

BEN JONSON.—Poet and dramatist. *Circa* 1573–1637. Poet Laureate under James I, at stipend of £200 per annum. Was originally a bricklayer; became a soldier, then an actor. Noted for production of masques for Queen Elizabeth and James I. Most famous comedy, "Every Man in His Humor." Associate of Shakespeare and member of famous Mermaid Tavern circle. Founded Apollo Club at Devil Tavern, Fleet Street, in reign of James I. Underwent imprisonment for killing Christopher Marlowe in a duel in 1593. Was later imprisoned for his libels on the Scots under James, but was restored to favour. Buried in Poets' Corner of Westminster Abbey.

THOMAS MORLEY.—*Circa* 1557–1604. Famous madrigal composer. Wrote "A Plaine and Easie Introduction to Practicall Musicke," 1597. Was organist at St. Paul's Church, 1591–92. Sworn Gentleman of the Chapel Royal, 1592; continued in such position until 1604.

THOMAS RAVENSCROFT.—Born 1592. Died 1635. Chorister at St. Paul's Cathedral under Edward Piers. Student at the Gresham College lectures of Dr. John Bull. Became closely associated with his master, who used many of the folk-melodies which he collected as themes for virginals pieces. Admitted Bachelor of Music at Cambridge University 1607, in which year he published his first collection of folk-tunes, "Pammelia: Musicke's Miscellanie," by which he became the pioneer of British folk-music collecting. Published his "Brief Discourse, etc.," a notable treatise on music, in 1611. In 1621 he contributed a memorable work to ecclesiastical music, the "Whole Booke of Psalms, with the Hymnes Evangellicall and Songs Spiritual," in four parts, a collection of religious tunes popularly sung in England, Scotland, Wales, Germany, Italy, France and the Netherlands, in one volume. This was the forerunner of works such as Hymns, Ancient and Modern. Ravenscroft contributed 48 settings

APPENDIX C

himself, taking works by leading contemporary composers for the rest. In this work he set the example, for the first time, of naming hymn-tunes after the towns and localities with which they were associated by derivation and folk-tradition.

JAN PIETERSZOON SWEELINCK.—Dutch composer and famous organist, 1562–1621. Of a Deventer family. His father, " Mr. Pieter," was organist of the Old Church, Amsterdam, to which Jan Pieterszoon succeeded on his death, holding the post from 1577. Translated the " Institutioni harmoniche " of Zarlino while studying in Italy previous to 1577. Close friend of Bull, who used one of his themes—a fugue—as the basis for a memorial fantasia when Sweelinck died. Sweelinck cited a theme of Bull in his work on composition.

THOMAS TOMKINS.—Welsh composer, of Cornish family from Lostwithiel. Born at St. David's, Pembrokeshire, 1575; son of precentor of the cathedral there. Pupil of William Byrd. Became organist of Worcester Cathedral in 1596, on death of Nathanael Pattrick, whose widow he married. In 1613 an organ was built at Worcester Cathedral to his specification at unusual expense; 1615 was an organist of the Chapel Royal " to attend in rote "; 1621 sworn as Gentleman and one of the organists of the Chapel Royal; 1625, 40 shillings paid for " composinge many songes against the coronation of King Charles." Was appointed " composer for the voices and wind instruments " by the Bishop of Bath and Wells. His " Musica Deo Sacra et Ecclesiastica Anglicana " (1638), " to the use of Cathedrals and other Churches of England, especially the Chappell Royall of King Charles the First," consisted of ninety-five anthems and five whole services. His " Songes of 3, 4, 5 and 6 Parts " (1622) sold out the first edition in twelve months. Wrote one of the first choral ballets, " Musica Divina." Died at Martin Hussingtrees, Worcestershire, 1656. Was a prolific composer, especially notable for his virtuoso style in virginals and organ music. Wrote pieces on themes by Bull, who reciprocated by using his themes in turn.

APPENDIX C

SIR FRANCIS WALSINGHAM.—1530-90. Sat for Banbury in Parliament 1558-59. Re-elected, 1562-63, preferring to sit for Lyme Regis, seat which he held at same time. During reign of Mary and Philip went into voluntary exile. Speaking French and Italian well, studied foreign political methods while abroad. Returned to England on accession of Elizabeth. Attracted attention of Lord Treasurer Cecil. Commenced unofficial organization of English Government's secret service, 1569. Sent by Cecil, with Sir Henry Norris, to negotiate marriage between Elizabeth and Henri, duc d'Anjou, brother of Charles IX, at French Court, 1570. Massacre of St. Bartholomew's Eve frustrated hopes of Anglo-French alliance. Gave sanctuary to Sir Philip Sidney during massacre. Sidney married his daughter Frances. Returned to England, 1573. Appointed Secretary of State jointly with Sir Thomas Smith, December 20th, 1573, retaining post until his death. Shared main responsibility of government with Lord Treasurer Burghley, being virtually Minister for Foreign Affairs. Devoted his private fortune to maintaining secret service. December 1st, 1577, knighted at Windsor Castle. April 22nd, 1578, constituted chancellor of Order of the Garter. Same year sent to Low Countries to support policy opposed to his own. 1580, consolidated his position through making ally of Royal favourite, the Earl of Leicester. 1583, persuaded Elizabeth to buy neutrality of Scottish king (afterwards James I of England), by payment of a pension. Latter part of his life impoverished through having to meet debts of Sidney, who was killed Zutphen, having gone security for him. Gained no profit whatsoever from his office.

THOMAS WARROCK (or WARRICK).—*Circa* 1570. Belonged to a well-connected Cumberland family. His son, Sir Phillip Warrock, became Secretary of State. Succeeded Bull as organist of Hereford Cathedral in 1585. The Old Cheque Book of the Chapel Royal provides an interesting sidelight on his later career, after his resignation from Hereford : " 29. March, 1630 : Mr. Thomas Warrick receaved a check for his whole paye for the moneth of March becawse he presumed to playe verses on the organe at service tyme, beinge formerly inhibited by the Deanne from doinge the same, by reason of his insufficiency for that solemn service."

APPENDIX D

WORKS BY BULL : MAJOR COLLECTIONS, PRINTED EDITIONS, ETC.

Printed
" Parthenia " : first printed collection of virginals music, 1611. Engraved by Hole, London. Pieces by Bull, Byrd and Gibbons.
" Attende unto my Teares " : anthem, in " Teares : or Lamentacions of a Sorrowefull Soule." Collection by Sir William Leighton. Printed by William Damen, 1579.
" Laudes Vespertinæ B. Marie Virginis." Published by Phalese, Antwerp, 1629. (Contains hymns to Flemish words and madrigal, " Den lustelijcken Mey.")
West. Old English Organ Music. (Two pieces.)
" John Bull " : two volumes of virginals works. Transcribed for piano by Margaret Glyn. (Stainer and Bell, London.)
" John Bull." M. Glyn. (Joseph Williams.)
" Parthenia." Transcribed for piano by Margaret Glyn. (Idem.)
" The Kings Hunting Gigge." Arranged for piano by H. Craxton. (Anglo-French Music Co.)
" Musica Antiqua." Collection edited by John Stafford Smith, London, Preston, 1655.
" Cathedral Music." Collection by William Boyce, 1760. (Contains an anthem by Bull, " O Lord my God.")
" École de Piano." Edited by Dupont. (Breitkopf u. Härtel.) (Virginals pieces by Bull, transcribed for piano.)
"Old English Composers." Collection by Emil Pauer. (Augener.)
" Fifteen pieces by Bull." Transcribed for piano by Eitner. (Breitkopf u. Härtel.)
Anthem : " O Lord my God." (Curwen.)
" The King's Hunt." Transcribed for orchestra by Sir Granville Bantock. (in " Old English Suite." Novello, London.)

APPENDIX D

Anthem : " Frail man, despise the treasures of this life." (Choral Handbook.)
" An Elizabethan Itinerary." (Pieces by Bull from various lands, arranged for orchestra.) Leigh Henry. (Composers' Corporation.) (In the press.)
" John Bull." The Man in his Music. Suite for orchestra, transcribed from Bull's works by Leigh Henry. (Idem.)
Pieces by Bull. Arranged for piano by Sir Granville Bantock. (Novello.)
Dickenson : " King's Hunt." Arranged for piano. (H. W. Gray & Co.)

Collections

The FitzWilliam Virginal Book. Cambridge Library. (Publ. Breitkopf und Härtel, 1899, 2 volumes.)
Benjamin Cosyn's Virginal Book. King's Library, Buckingham Palace.
William Foster's Virginal Book. (Idem.)
Barnard's Collection, 1641. Royal College of Music. (Two anthems.)
Queen Elizabeth's Virginal Book. Buckingham Palace.
Collection in British Museum, once belonging to Dr. Pepusch, and later to Queen Caroline. Add. MSS. 23623.

Note.—A detailed list of Bull's complete keyboard compositions, giving all collections, titles and library reference numbers, is contained in Margaret Glyn's excellent and insighted " Elizabethan Virginal Music and its Composers."

Collection of Canons, written in geometrical figures. (Bull's cypher method.) Buckingham Palace. (Eitner, " Ein Heft Rätsel-Canons in Buckingham-Palast.")
Five-part Motett. Transcribed by Dr. Burney (*q.v.*).
MSS. Hofbibliothek, Vienna (Ms17771).
MSS. Christ Church, Oxford. Four anthems to 2–5 Voyces.
MSS. virginals and organ pieces, etc. Paris, Bibl. Nat. 18548.
MSS. virginals and organ pieces, etc. New York ; Drexell 5612.
A prayer and plain chant, with organ obbligato. London, 1843. Royal College of Music.
MSS. An anthem. Ely Cathedral.

APPENDIX E

Claims to the Authorship of the National Anthem

Thomas Arne (1710–78).—A version of the air "God Save the King," as sung to-day, was harmonized and arranged for voices and orchestra by Dr. Thomas Arne, the friend of Haendel, for a performance at Drury Lane Theatre, London, 1745. Sir George Smart published this arrangement in the triplicate version by Bull, Purcell and Arne reprinted in "The Lute." The period of Arne and Haendel was considerably in advance of the date when Haydn is alleged to have composed "Heil Dir im Siegerkranz."

John Blow (1648–1708).—No evidence supports the legend that Dr. John Blow composed the air, "God Save great James, Our King," for the Chapel of James II. Blow was organist of Westminster Abbey, 1669–80, during a time when Purcell used the air without acknowledging it to him.

John Bull (1562–1628).—Dr. Pepusch appears to have possessed Bull's manuscript of "God Save the King," on the evidence of Dr. Burney and Dr. Wood. He also owned the manuscript folios in which the Variations so named are preserved (pp. 53–66). The theme of these fits the words popularly sung exactly; but the air only partially accords with that recognized to-day. On page 98 of Bull's manuscript works, however, the air sung to-day appears with little variation, though without the title.

Richard Clark (1780–1856), a member of the Chapel Royal, traced the composition of "God Save the King" to the reign of James I, identifying it with the hymn sung as "God Save Great James Our King" at the Merchant Taylors banquet to James I and Henry, Prince of Wales, after the discovery of the Gunpowder Plot, in 1607. The idea that the air had first been entitled "God Save Great James Our King" arose through Dr. Burney's assertion that "Old Mrs. Arne, the mother of Dr. Arne, assured me at the time

APPENDIX E

(of the performance of her son's arrangement, 1745) (the lady who sang it at Drury Lane bore her out) that " God Save Great James Our King " was written and sung for King James in 1688, when the Prince of Orange (William III) was hovering over the coast, and she remembered hearing it sung in the streets." As the air had been used by Purcell in the reign of Charles II, it was clear that the King James mentioned could not have been James II, who succeeded Charles II. The Variations in Bull's manuscript works conclusively show that he was the first to compose an air named " God Save the King." The popular development of his air, on page 98 of his manuscript works, as the National Anthem which we now know most probably arose from traditional perpetuation of that air, as the one which he composed for the Armada victory, with the title " God Save Our Virgin Queen," as contemporary evidence shows. Bull was disinclined to give that air a title dedicating it to James I; hence he wrote the air of his later Variations as " God Save the King." It is the Elizabethan version, however, which Sir George Smart, an eminent authority on Elizabethan music and the editor of Gibbons' works, published as " God Save the Queen," restoring the original title almost exactly. That air is the one which is our National Anthem to-day, with scarcely any deviation. Therefore, as the first known composer of an air entitled " God Save the King," and as the composer of the actual Anthem tune as now sung, Bull appears to have indisputable claim to title and theme. Various claims have been put forward to the authorship of the words, notably by the Rev. W. H. Henslowe (" God Save Victoria," 1859) and, by Clark, for Ben Jonson (" God Save Great James, Our King," 1607). It is clear, on contemporary evidence, however, that " God Save our Virgin Queen " was sung for the victory over the Armada, Bull being directly referred to at the time as " Organiste of hir Maiesties Chappell," as its composer. Henslowe's claim is confuted by the existence of Arne's arrangement of the air sung still, to the words " God Save Great George, Our King," which, on the evidence of Burney and Clark, was simply a variant on " God Save Great James, Our King."

APPENDIX E

The admitted original refrain, " God Save Us All," points to the anthem having been composed first for the Armada, a peril threatening the entire nation much more than the Gunpowder Plot, which affected the King and Parliament only, or than the Rebellion of 1745, for the suppression of which Arne arranged his version, at a time when a great proportion of the country was Jacobite and opposed to the Hanoverian king. Finally, while Clark cited a version of the air dated 1555, Pepusch gave the date of the original air as 1588, the year of the Armada. It is clear that Clark erred, since Bull was not yet born in 1555 ; it is probable that he confused the flourishes of the caligraphy of Elizabethan days, when the numerals 5 and 8 closely resembled one another. The judgments of Burney and Clark alike, as affecting Bull's scripts, must be taken with reservations, as neither was highly efficient in deciphering old manuscripts, Burney being certainly lacking in the technique to play Bull's music, on his own evidence. Clark's arguments disposing of the claims of Arne, Carey and Purcell to the authorship of " God Save the King " are, however, accepted by authorities such as Fétis, who states, in his " Biographie univérselle des musicièns " : " Dans un édit intéressant intitule ' An Account of the National Anthem : entitled " God Save the King," ' M. Richard Clarke à prouvé (p. 67 et suiv.) que cet air célèbre à été composé par John Bull à l'occasion de la Conspiration des poudres, 1607," further affirming : " Au reste il résulte des réchêrches de M. Clark que toutes les traditions qui ont attribué l'air dont il s'agit à Haendel, à Smith, son élève et ami, à Henri Carey (v. son nom) et même à Lully, sont sans fondement." (Idem.)

HENRY CAREY (1696-1743).—A claim was put forward by this composer's son, George Carey, with a view to securing a pension for himself. No official notice was taken of this, nor was any pension granted.

During the lifetime of Carey the composer himself advanced no claim whatsoever. He died two years before the date on which his son claimed that the air was composed, 1745-46.

APPENDIX E

In this connection it is worthy of note that, as Richard Clark pointed out, Carey himself was ignorant of the air and that the attribution of the authorship of " God Save the King " to John Bull had been advanced by Dr. John Ward three years before Carey's death, in " The Lives of the Professors of Gresham College," 1740, without evoking any protest from Carey.

Much earlier, John Bull's variations on " God Save the King " were listed by Dr. Christopher Pepusch in his catalogue of Bull's works, the manuscripts of which were admittedly in his possession, many of them later being included in the collection which came into the possession of Queen Caroline and are now among the Additional Manuscripts in the British Museum. From these manuscript works of John Bull, Dr. Pepusch and his wife, a talented clavecin player, performed Bull's works regularly, both of them being enthusiasts for his music, in which they awakened a great interest through their musical evenings in Fetter Lane, London, at a time when Pepusch was at the height of his popularity as the composer of the music, based on English popular airs, for Gay's famous " Beggars' Opera."

JOSEF HAYDN (1732–1809).—For some time it was alleged that the Austrian-Czech composer was the author of the melody of " God Save the King." The melody of the Austrian hymn, " Heil Dir im Siegerkranz," is, in point of fact, identical with that of " God Save the King." It is a moot point, however, as to whether or no Haydn himself ever laid claim to the original creation of this tune. In many cases he employed known themes for his works, especially under the pressure of the demands made upon him by his patron, Prince Esterhazy, who for seasons together expected him to turn out a symphony daily, to be played after the evening meal, Haydn having to combine with his musical duties service as a scullion. In any event, Haydn did not lend his name to the Austrian hymn until after his visits to London to appear at the Solomon concerts. He spent some time in England and even visited Wales, whence

APPENDIX E

he took back with him several well-known folk-tunes, which he used in later clavichord works, etc., in many cases without acknowledging their source. Such appropriation was common enough at the time and even earlier. Among the Elizabethans it has been difficult to sort out the authorship of various pieces. Titles were often given without the names of the composers in the various virginals collections, and the whole set became popularly known by the name of the musician responsible for their collation. Haendel was a notable appropriator of other musicians' themes, as others of his day used his. Even in Purcell are to be found themes taken from the earlier works of John Jenkins, the pioneer of the " consort of viols," to which Purcell's work owed much in many ways. It is therefore extremely probable that Haydn either took the theme of " God Save the King," which, on other authority was already known in England, among the other British themes which he carried back to Austria, or that he reproduced it subconsciously, after having mentally registered it through hearing it sung in England. Assuredly, had Viennese musicians regarded Haydn as the composer, Ludwig van Beethoven would have emphasized the fact when he set " God Save the King " in celebration of Wellington's victory over Napoleon at Vittoria, 1813, whereas he congratulated the English on possessing such a fine air, which he had previously arranged for solo and chorus, violin and pianoforte, nine years earlier.

HENRY PURCELL (1658–95).—The alleged authorship by Purcell of the melody " for the Chapel of James II " has been fairly thoroughly disposed of by Richard Clark, who has pointed out that Purcell had already used the fragment on which the authorship has been attributed to him in one of the sonatas which he composed for the twenty-four violins of the King, Charles II, whose reign preceded that of James II. (See Appendix: Clark.)

www.ingramcontent.com/pod-product-compliance
Lightning Source LLC
Chambersburg PA
CBHW051645040426
42446CB00009B/992